FIVE MEN OF FRANKFORT

THE STORY OF THE ROTHSCHILDS

MARCUS ELI RAVAGE

UE

Facsimile Edition.

Marcus Eli Ravage. *Five Men of Frankfort*
First published in 1929.

ISBN: 978-2-925611-29-5
Printed in the USA.

www.ultimatumeditions.com

FIVE MEN *of* FRANKFORT

The Story of the Rothschilds

By MARCUS ELI RAVAGE

Author of "An American in the Making"

With Five Portraits by

KARL S. WOERNER

NEW YORK

LINCOLN MAC VEAGH · THE DIAL PRESS

LONGMANS, GREEN & COMPANY

TORONTO

1929

K
W
NATHAN
VON ROTHSCHILD

PORTRAITS

By

KARL S. WOERNER

TABLE OF CONTENTS

FIVE MEN OF FRANKFORT

CHAPTER I

JEW MEYER, CURIO DEALER

ON a spring day in the year 1764 a young man was seen going up the narrow, cobble-stoned Jews'-Street of Frankfort-on-the-Main. Tradesmen and market women paused in their bargaining to glance at him, but did not recognize him. Tall and spare, with marked Semitic features, a short, pointed black beard, and a rabbinical stoop in the shoulders, he was clearly a son of the Ghetto. A certain good-humored look around the eyes and mouth suggested something familiar about him, and from the unhesitating manner in which he walked straight on before him he seemed to be at home in the teeming street. He had entered by the south end, the one nearest the center of town, and was proceeding steadily northward in the direction of the Bornheimer Gate, which was the poorer section of the *Judengasse*. Not far from the gate he turned right, halted before a house which had a sign with a crudely painted saucepan on it, and disappeared into the yard. Then only, the curious who had been watching him from their doorways remembered. Why, it was Meyer, "the little Bauer," the son of Amschel and Schoenche, the unfortunate couple who had died within a few months of each other now more than eight years ago, leaving five young children homeless, parentless and with barely enough means for their rearing.

The young man's unheralded turning up reminded the neighbors of the sad episode. Meyer must now be just about twenty. When his father passed away in the High Holiday season of '55 the boy, then a little over eleven, was at school in the Yeshivah of Fuerth near Nuremberg. Poor Amschel had been ambitious for his bright first-born son, and had sent him up to the Talmudical college to make a learned man of him, perhaps even a rabbi. The boy was taking hold finely when the sudden death of first one parent and then the other had forced him, child though he still was, to go out into the world to earn his bread. His two older sisters and his two younger brothers scattered among friends and kin, in Frankfort and out. Meyer was taken in by relatives in Hanover, who secured employment for him in the great Jewish mercantile and banking house of Oppenheim in that city. In Hanover he had remained all these eight years, while the two smaller boys, Moses and Kalmann, after a meager schooling in the Jewish communal school of Frankfort and an apprenticeship in a Judengasse shop, had gone back to the ancestral home, the back-yard house at the sign of the Saucepan, to set up in trade for themselves. And now their elder brother was evidently coming back to join them. Their sympathetic neighbors wished them well. It entered no one's head that this quiet return of an unknown Jewish youth to his native street was the prelude to the most spectacular chapter in the financial history of Europe.

II

Among the boys of the Ghetto before he went to Fuerth Meyer had been nicknamed "das Baeuerchen." Now he was a grown man with a beard and a shop of his own, his former playmates dropped the diminutive ending and Meyer, like his father and his grandfathers for generations came to be known as Bauer. He had no notion why his people were called that way. The word meant "peasant," and generally those who were tagged with it were ambulant traders who bought and sold among the village folk. But his father and also his grandfather had kept shops in the Judengasse and both had been money changers in a small way. Some remoter ancestor, then, had been the man with the pack. In any event "Bauer" was obviously a trade by-name, just as "Rothschild," the other designation of the family, must have come from the house with the red sign down the street. As legal names neither had any standing. Jews were not allowed the privilege and managed somehow to get on without it.

As a boy Meyer had sometimes gone with his mother to the old Jewish cemetery during the month of Elul to pay homage to the dead, and while his parent knelt and prayed at the graves he amused himself with spelling out the Hebrew names on the tombstones. A bright youngster with a taste for such things, it had not taken him long to reconstruct the family descent. At first the absence of a uniform name had stumped him a little, but the Jewish practice of giving the name of the dead man's father was helpful. Seven generations, stretching back some two hundred years, he had thus contrived to identify. Then the thread broke off, or possibly his remoter forebears had laid their bones elsewhere. The earliest of his fathers was one Elchanan, who had died in 1546. In those far-off days the family must have been much more important and prosperous than it was now; for Isak, the son of Elchanan, had built the big house with the red sign in the more fashionable southerly end of the Judengasse. But fortune did not smile on the family for long. Two generations later there was a marked decline. Isak's grandson Naftali Hirz had sold, or lost, the ancestral home, and had been obliged to move to the humble quarters in the rear of the Saucepan, where his descendants had continued ever since. Things dropped still another peg with Kalmann, in the next generation; it was he who was the first "Bauer;" and though there had been some slight upward movement since, the family had never again lifted itself to the level of old Isak.

On the whole, the Bauer-Rothschilds had been successful people. If none of them had ever amassed great wealth, neither had they quite sunk to poverty. Through all the ups and downs of two centuries they had remained independent merchants of the middle grade. Many of their neighbors, it was true, had soared away beyond them in riches and importance, but then equally as many had fallen below them. They had kept an even, if modest, tenor throughout. No scion of the Saucepan or of the Red Sign had even become a leader in the Ghetto, or intermarried with its first families, or got a foothold in the princely courts of the region; but on the other hand, none had ever fallen back into the classes that worked with their hands. Neither scholars nor rabbis nor great merchants distinguished the family. Plain, pious, substantial tradesmen, without influence or pretensions, sometimes more prosperous, sometimes less—thus they had begun and thus they seemed destined to continue. Their fortunes were perhaps as low now as they had ever been. The sudden death of poor Amschel, before he had reached his full powers or provided for his dependents, had left his estate in chaos. It was for his sons to restore it to order.

III

Meyer's younger brothers, Moses and Kalmann, had been apprenticed to a second-hand dealer, and naturally when they launched out for themselves they followed the trade they knew best. They were already established when Meyer came back. He took on the business with a sinking of the heart. This was not at all what he had looked forward to. A litter of retired garments and superannuated household goods, dust and disorder, noisy bargaining with the poorest and humblest of the Ghetto, he had neither taste nor training for such commerce. For eight years he had longed and prayed to be home again, to be independent, and to see his own flesh and blood. Here they were, those little brothers whom he had idealized from far away, grimy, disheveled, rough men, rummaging in junk, vociferous in the jargon of the Ghetto. The scene shocked him. What a climb-down this was even from his father's shop, as he remembered it! To be sure, the money-changing on which his parent used to pride himself so had been more decorative than real. But the shop at least was trim and clean, with its neat cloth-shelves, its pleasant odor of tea and tobacco and wine, its solid custom. Unreasonably he had expected to find things the way he had left them, as if nothing had happened since he went away.

Indeed, his homesick imagination had played tricks on him and had led him to expect much more. In the English-owned city of Hanover Jews were so much freer, business was so much less hobbled, that he had almost forgot what the Frankfort Judengasse looked like, and had come to fancy it in Hanoverian colors. The House of Oppenheim, though his own functions in it were lowly enough, was a great export and banking firm. It occupied a dignified building. Its personnel, down to the humblest clerk, were decently dressed and well-groomed. Its business was for the most part with merchants, German and English and Dutch. Very little merchandise was actually handled on the premises; nearly all the trading was done with pen and paper. Yet he had thrown up that paradise and had come back here, because Frankfort was accounted the greater center, almost the leading commercial city of the Continent. He was horribly disillusioned.

It was some time before he could adjust himself and see a way of coöperating with his brothers. No team had ever been recruited out of material so ill-assorted. Their schooling, their ideas of business, their training, their very speech, were poles apart. He had come home with a vague idea of setting up an Oppenheim's of his own in Frankfort. That firm had also started with three brothers and had come up from small beginnings. But now he took stock of his resources and was profoundly discouraged. How was he even to make a start without capital or credit or connections and, what was worst, with such hopelessly crude assistance? When he came right down to it, moreover, his own knowledge and experience were distressingly limited. He made himself no illusions on that score. Held down by his Hanover employers, he had barely got a smattering of the more vital phases of the business. He knew all but nothing of banking or the commission trade. His eight years of service had only taught him how complex the affairs of a great concern were, how involved was their technique, how vast were their capital and credit requirements. Of the general conduct of the house he had not even got a glimpse. Only toward the end he had been allowed to stand at what might be called a responsible counter, and then it had been the rare coin department, the most negligible of the firm's specialties. It had no more real bearing on his ambition than a beard and earlocks had on the rabbinate. What he had dreamed of was that his brothers would second him with at least as much training as he had. But alas! These raw old clo' men, with the speech, the manners, and the outward refinements of junk dealers!

IV

He went to work patiently to make the best of a bad situation. It was no good complaining. His brothers were not to blame: they were what circumstances had made them. Happily they and he were young men, and with energy and persistence the bad turn that fortune had played them might yet be repaired. For the moment common sense as well as necessity dictated but one course: to go along with their simple resources, work hard, not force things and keep an eye on the future. Moses and Kalmann had, after all, done the sensible thing when they had gone into a business that they knew. Meyer decided to do like them. He understood rare coins and allied trinkets—medals, curios, old jewelry, and a little of antiques generally. Very well, he would start with that. When all was said, the two trades—his brothers' and his—were not so very far apart really. Curios and antiques were in fact nothing but a sort of gilded junk. There was not much more than a step from one to the other; he would groom his brothers to bridge it. At present they bought up the contents of Ghetto homes; they must gradually take to going out into the city and do the same with burghers' villas and the mansions of the gentry. Men who could appraise pine tables and earthenware dishes would learn readily enough to judge mahogany cabinets and feather-beds. No doubt, the city clientele would find Moses and Kalmann a bit unpresentable. Well then, he, Meyer, would do the talking, not only for the pictures and heirlooms and fine pieces but for the entire collections; the younger men would be coming along merely as his experts for the plainer things.

The plan, on being tried out, worked better than Meyer had hoped. The two trades dovetailed admirably. Householders in town who wished to sell out preferred to dispose of their goods to a single buyer; and the richer class of Ghetto dwellers, hearing that the rear-shop at the Saucepan dealt in high-grade stuff, soon crowded out the humbler custom. Meyer's presentiments, also, that the noble purchasers of his rare coins and medals would mix badly with his brothers' clients, proved groundless. For as experience showed, gentlemen rarely went bargain-hunting in the shops; they expected the dealer to keep them informed thru bulletins and to bring his wares to their homes.

The brothers thus found themselves running two separate businesses. Moses and Kalmann still operated a

Judengasse shop, except that the quality of both goods and custom were greatly improved. Meyer, however, was seldom about. His velvet-lined case filled with quaint jewels, old gold and silver medals, rare coins and kindred objects, he spent the better part of his time on the stage coaches between Frankfort and near-by places, following up inquiries elicited by his catalogues. The Saucepan shop with its living quarters in the back served him merely as a base and an address. A small display near the entrance, alone informed callers that the firm had interests of a nobler sort. Traveling about, too, enabled Meyer to keep abreast of sales, not only of the genteel and costly objects for his own trade but of the mundaner ones for his brothers as well. And as the younger men by degrees acquired an understanding of coins and curios, Meyer likewise learned to judge and evaluate house-contents, so that in time he became the exclusive buyer, while his brothers gave their whole attention to the inside trade.

Twice a year Frankfort had a great fair, which brought together merchants and holiday makers, Gentile as well as Jewish, from all parts of the empire. All these strangers had money to spend, and most of them had drafts or currency to exchange. For though nominally one country, Germany was at this time a riot of independent kingdoms, dukedoms, principalities, so-called free cities and every other species of petty state, vaguely held together by a common language and tradition, theoretically united under the decayed Holy Roman Empire (which was neither Holy nor Roman nor an empire) and in fact chronically at war with one another. The political confusion expressed itself in a tangle of frontiers, restrictions on travel and trade, and a chaos of monetary units. Each princeling possessed, and most of them exercised, the right to coin his own money, which his neighbor felt free to, and usually did, declare unacceptable. Thalers of half a dozen different weights and values, as many kinds of florins, ducats, carolins and what not circulated in their respective and very narrow domains; and a merchant or a traveler going half-a-day's journey from home must convert his money into the legal tender of the "foreign" land in which he had arrived before he could have his lunch. In this state of things nearly every tradesman was a money-changer on the side. The larger the business, the bigger the "Wechselstube." Virtually all the bankers of the period began as merchants in goods, developing the two businesses simultaneously, and rarely divorcing the one from the other till half a century or more later.

The Frankfort fairs and the currency chaos and German disunity were not lost on Meyer. A smattering of finance he had brought with him from Hanover, capital was accumulating in his till, and customers from out of town were being turned away by his brothers at the shop for lack of local cash. So he hung out a "Wechselstube" shingle and initiated his partners in the mysteries of exchange and note discounting. Sooner than he had hoped on the day of his return home, the business began taking on the aspect of his late father's establishment. In the curio shop back of the Saucepan was laid the first stone of the banking house of Rothschild.

V

On taking their first annual inventory Moses and Kalmann discovered, what they had long suspected, that their elder brother's combination was pretty largely decorative. The firm was kept going and thriving, not by the art and the antiquities, but by the lowly traffic with the inhabitants of the Ghetto. They did not complain; they were aware of the value of prestige; but they did submit the question to Meyer whether this commodity might not come a little too high. All told their balance sheet showed a net profit of some five thousand florins (about two thousand dollars) for the year, of which four-fifths had been yielded by the shop and no small fraction of the remainder by exchange operations. Considering that Meyer knew as much now as his brothers about the main business, and that the "Wechselstube" was his creation, would it not be at once more profitable and less laborious if he were to give up most of his traveling and devote his energies to the shop and the bank? What with his ability as a buyer, the connections he had established in the country around and the expansion of the exchange department, the business could easily double its earnings next year. Why not let the genteel trade go hang?

But Meyer was looking to the future, and there were aspects of the rare coin and medal business which his young partners overlooked. It was not merely immediate prestige he was thinking of; he was investing in a career for the years to come. Thus far he had made barely more than a start; the clientele he had gained was among the minor gentry only. But things were coming along nicely, and it would not be long before he planted a foot in the châteaus and palaces of the sovereign princes themselves. Within fifty miles of Frankfort lay half a dozen reigning courts, and each little monarch whiled away his boredom by collecting one thing or another. There was Hanau, just a stone's throw away, and Cassel and Darmstadt and Weimar, and a number of others. He was even now sending them his catalogues; on some of them he had already called in person; at Hanau he was in touch with a courtier or two; soon the doors were bound to open. And then,—ah, then affairs would turn a corner and no mistake.

For selling curios to princes was no more than an entering wedge. Certainly no one got rich by selling anything to the highnesses. Yet every big Jew in the southerly end of the Judengasse, in Hanover and elsewhere had got his start as a court purveyor. For one thing, the Ghetto looked up to the court Jew; it saw in him a superior and cleverer member of the tribe, a man who shone in the reflected glamour of his prince. Moreover, his entrée to the seat of power made him a privileged person. He enjoyed the rights and exemptions almost of a Gentile. Functionaries treated him with deference; he could travel freely, trade without restrictions, marry and give in marriage with little regard to the law which limited Jewish unions to a stated annual number; in short, he was hardly a Jew at all, as far as disabilities went. Not only that; there was money in the high windows. The pettiest of the sovereigns had estates to manage, taxes to farm out, forests and mines and landed properties to exploit. They might not like the Jewish religion, but they had confidence in the Jew's honesty and ability. Nearly all of them had investments abroad, and the dividends on these must be collected and converted into the coin of the realm. When they were in funds they bought luxuries at high prices; and when they were financially embarrassed, they borrowed and paid interest. A Jew with a foot in the right kind of a court had little to worry about.

In June, 1765, little more than a year since his return, it looked indeed as if the opening for which Meyer had been longing had come. A windfall in the shape of a particularly choice collection of old coins fell into his hands; he hurriedly got out a special descriptive catalogue and sent it off to a select list of personages, big nobles and sovereigns to whom he had as yet gained no access. To his boundless delight he got replies from the Duke of Weimar (the celebrated patron of the poet Goethe), from the wealthy and powerful Prince Thurn und Taxis, the postal magnate residing at Frankfort, and from a General Estorff, a former client of his department in Hanover but now in the entourage of the little court at Hanau. Meyer attached especial value to this latter inquiry; he hoped that Estorff was writing not in his own behalf but in that of his master, the reigning count of the tiny dominion. A connection at that little court was, for any number of reasons, about the most desirable thing he could think of. For one thing, and by no means an unimportant one in those days of stage-coach travel, Hanau was the nearest sovereign capital to Frankfort. The young count, moreover, was a rare specimen of the genus princeling. Wealthy in his own right, thrifty, and with a head for business, he had a goodly sum invested in English government stock (his mother being a daughter of King George II) the interest on which came to him every quarter and afforded a profitable operation for some lucky money-changer. Lastly, he was the son and heir of the aging Landgrave Frederick of Hesse-Cassel, and would one of these days govern that very considerable principality as well as possess the immense fortune his father was said to have amassed.

So Meyer packed his case with the finest specimens out

of his newly-acquired collection and journeyed hopefully to Hanau, and the young Count William noted a few days later in his books: "To Jew Mayer, for medals, 38 florins, 30 kreutzers." Not as big a transaction as Meyer had looked forward to—in fact, the profit would barely pay his stage fare—but a beginning all the same. And highness must have been pleased, for he sent out word that the dealer was to call again; which Meyer did without waiting to be asked twice. Later endeavors, however, were rewarded with similarly meager purchases. William's business head was functioning much too efficiently for comfort; it knew precisely what it wanted, appraised values with the closeness of a Judengasse tradesman, and rarely let itself go. But Meyer was a man of patience, and bided his time. Presently his oft-repeated petitions to be given a chance at the English dividend-drafts were granted. His hopes whispered in Estorff's ear, he dropped a hint to one or two other courtiers whom he got to know—highness himself being invisible, of course—about his ambitions. Nothing happened; four years passed, and beyond an occasional sale and now and then a small English draft, nothing whatever happened. The gentlemen at court were friendly; they found "Jew Mayer" a likable if slightly ineffectual tradesman. But there were more hard-hitting Jews after the business, and Meyer had better not be discouraged.

VI

One rich prize he did carry off from his court dealings. The moment he got his foot inside he began begging for a bit of a title. In eighteenth-century Germany men did not modestly sit about for honors to come to them; they pulled strings, and at need asked for them outright. What was the good of being a court-Jew, however diminutive the highness and insignificant the services, unless one's friends, neighbors and competitors could be made to see the distinction on one's shop sign, catalogues and the like? Glory aside, moreover, having one's palace connections bodied forth in some visible form was equivalent to a permanent passport and spared one annoyance at the hands of frontier guards and officials. Meyer, therefore, sought the aid of the friendly courtiers at Hanau, at Weimar, at all the courts where he made a sale, and on being told that a direct application to the sovereign lord was required by etiquette, he sat down and flourished off a letter to his noble patrons. It ran thus:

> "It has been my particular and high good fortune to serve your lofty princely Serenity at various times and to your most gracious satisfaction. I stand ready to exert all my energies and my entire fortune to serve your lofty princely Serenity whenever in future it shall please you to command me. An especially powerful incentive to this end would be given me if your lofty princely Serenity were to distinguish me with an appointment as one of your Highness's Court Factors. I am making bold to beg for this with the more confidence in the assurance that by so doing I am not giving any trouble; while for my part such distinction would lift up my commercial standing and be of help to me in so many other ways that I feel sure thereby to make my way and fortune here in the city of Frankfort."

It was a form letter, and went broadcast to wherever it was likely to do good. Meyer rather believed and hoped that, with his reputation for munificence, it would be the Duke of Weimar that would grant his wish. Hanau might be richer in prospects and more conveniently located, but Weimar was a bigger palace and its badge would carry more weight. But the Duke's eye noted the faulty grammar and the little Jewish touches that all Meyer's efforts could not prevent from creeping into the German, and did not reply; while the business-minded young monarch at Hanau considered that, as Meyer had naïvely blurted out, a humble title was a rather inexpensive way of buying the good will of a tradesman who might be grateful enough to shave down the note discount rate and the prices of medals in future deals. In any event, William graciously complied; and on the first day of autumn 1769, the Judengasse beheld a new sign hanging over the house at the Saucepan bearing the arms of Hesse-Hanau and underneath, in gilt letters, the German equivalent of "By Appointment." And Meyer invested in a wig and pig-tail, donned a three-cornered hat and pinned a lace-jabot under his coat-front.

It was not precisely a title of nobility, but the effect of it—on Meyer, on his brothers and on the community—was tremendous. The young men themselves saw in the portentous event so sure an earnest of greater things to come that they at once began negotiations for purchasing a fraction of the building in which their home and business was housed, and two months later actually acquired a modest quarter-share. Neighbors, friends and business associates were profoundly impressed, and came around to offer congratulations and assurances of future success. The Judengasse match-makers saw the light, and became active. Fathers (and especially mothers) with marriageable daughters, not all of them in the northerly half of the street either, took notice. Not only Meyer but his brothers also shone in the blinding halo. Matrimonial offers of an incredibly flattering nature were brought to Moses and even to the youthful Kalmann, to say nothing of their distinguished elder brother. Wolf, son of Salomon, known by the by-name Schnapper, a solid merchant with a thriving shop near the southerly gate, thinking better of Meyer's long-standing attentions to his pretty seventeen-year-old Guetele, consented to the betrothal, and the wedding was celebrated before the summer was over. Shortly after it was the turn of Moses. The good people of the Ghetto stepped along. It was not every day young men of the street became recognized court purveyors. Whatever their past, the Rothschild-Bauer boys had a future. It was as well to snap them up before they got too big.

VII

Meyer led his bride back to the bachelor quarters behind the shop, and there Guetele kept house for her husband and her rapidly increasing family for sixteen years. Within the year their first child was born, a girl who according to the pious Jewish custom was named Schoenche after Meyer's mother (presently to be changed to Jeanette). Then followed in quick succession three sons—Amschel (the future Anselm) so named in memory of Meyer's father, Salomon (the later head and founder of the Vienna banking house) and Nathan, the genius of the family and the architect of its greatness—and two more daughters, Belche (Isabella) and Breinliche (Babette). Not till Kalmann's death, in 1782, when Meyer was left in sole possession of the shop and its adjoining living quarters—Moses having withdrawn at the time of his marriage—did the young Rothschild have enough space to breathe in. It was not only that Meyer's affairs failed to keep pace with the growth of his progeny; the housing shortage in the rigidly circumscribed Jews'-Street was chronic. For ten years, by which time the family had increased to a half dozen, they must prepare meals and consume them, work and sleep and receive guests in those three rooms (counting the shop) which constituted the ground floor of the Saucepan rear-house; and after that all that Meyer could contrive to add was but a further eighth-share. Unless a family died out or emigrated (and that did not happen often) there was no leg-room to be had. Every inch of building ground in the Ghetto had been occupied a hundred years before Meyer was born.

But Meyer's affairs had begun to stagnate. The splendid promise of the year before his marriage remained unfulfilled. For nearly nine years the firm's income continued stationary, without Meyer's share rising above twenty-four hundred florins (less than a thousand dollars) annually. The shop held its own; the exchange counter spurted forward a bit; the coin and curio business declined decidedly. Was it Moses's defection and Kalmann's death that had sapped the concern's vitality? Doubtless Meyer was hampered for lack of his brothers' competent and reliable assistance. He had neither the energy nor the interest in the shop of his juniors. Still, the stagnation had set in before the separation. It seemed as if the firm had gone as far as it could, that it was running on as satisfactorily as it did on sheer momentum but would never make any further progress.

For Meyer's first choice of a calling was the right one. At heart a scholar, he had chanced to fall in with a business that tallied with his gift for learning. Rare coins, medals, heirlooms, curious jewels and antiques interested him quite apart from their commercial possibilities. He loved and fondled them, studied their histories and vicissitudes and could talk about them so interestingly that buyers were moved to share his enthusiasm. But he lacked utterly the instinct for gain, the cupidity, the pugnacity and the flair of the salesman. A mild, kindly, rather shy man, he took No for an answer too readily, was prone to be upset by rebuffs, hated competition and ran away from a fight. He would have made an admirable rabbi, and had he but had the connections he would have been a successful court Jew. Intelligence, honesty, administrative gifts, willingness to work, and the humility demanded by princes, he possessed in ample measure. Where he fell short was in the initial driving power. The humdrum trade he had inherited from his brothers wearied him. He drifted away from it gradually, and by the time his eldest boy had grown up the place back of the Saucepan had taken on the aspect it had borne away back in the days when Meyer was himself a child. The used articles had gone entirely. In their place had come wine and coffee, tea and tobacco, cloth and ready-made garments. The Wechselstube flourished, and although the sign with the arms of Hanau still hung outside, Meyer rarely went voyaging with his velvet-lined case.

Guetele was not unhappy at the change. A warm-hearted, cheerful, affectionate young Jewish woman of the old school, she took great pride in the scholarly tastes and attainments of her husband. She loved having him near her, particularly in the long winter evenings after the shop was closed and the children were asleep. Then Meyer would take down a tome of the Talmud, and while he hummed the sacred words she would sit beside him knitting or mending. Why strive and pursue after vain ambitions? They were better off than most people in the Judengasse. Meyer had started with empty hands, and here he was the owner of a thriving establishment—not certainly a bigwig in the Ghetto, but a substantial and respected merchant of the middle rank. Their children were bright and good and strong, a credit to their parents. What had they to worry about?

And then before their seventh child was born, the miracle happened: a family did move out of the Judengasse and Meyer bought an entire house for almost twelve thousand florins. It stood on the edge of the street, too, not in a court, about half way between the two gates. Four stories, a spacious shop, an enormous cellar under all, and ample elbow room, they were as comfortable as princes. In this house "At the Green Sign" (zum gruenen Schild) four more children were born to the couple, and though Guetele lived to see her sons richer than kings and the possessors of palaces in Frankfort itself and in several of the capitals of Europe she and Meyer spent here the remainder of their days.

There were times during these quiet idyllic years when Meyer, recalling the ambitions of his young manhood, grew restless and discontented. Slowly middle age was creeping up on him; his boys were growing up in the crude, untutored environment of the Judengasse. What were they going to turn into? Plain, humdrum tradesmen like himself, without even the meager schooling he had received away back in Fuerth. Frankfort, or at least the Jewish part of it, was all business, and he had not the means to remove them to some purer, loftier, more thoughtful atmosphere: there were too many of them.

Enough Hebrew for piety, a bit of commercial calculating, hardly enough German to write a respectable letter—it was all the *Talmud Torah* of the Ghetto had to offer. How far would they ever get with such an equipment? And what had become of his young dream to be the father of scholars? His efforts to supplement their teachers' instruction seemed to fall on stony ground. The boys had no taste for learning. Keen and alert at the exchange counter, their attention drooped over a page of Rashi, and a finespun casuistical argument from the Talmud put them to sleep. It was almost too late: the Frankfort Ghetto air had got into their bones.

At such times Meyer would shake himself out of his lethargy, fill his medal case after his family had retired for the night, and arising with the sun hop on the stage-coach and go haunting the palace gates of his neglected clients. It made him feel young and fiery again, to sniff the air of courts, to spread out his rare coins and curios, and discourse learnedly on the origin, the previous ownership and the strange destinies connected with each piece. He felt transported to a higher plane, to the world he belonged in. Now and then he would make a sale, and for a moment he would feel an inner excitement and resolve to throw up his cosy, stifling shop altogether and be on his travels once more. But he would return home wearier and more resigned than he had started. He had his escapade, had taken a draught of the stimulant he craved. But alas! there was no sustenance in it, and he was the father of ten children. To live and rear a family on the beloved trinkets was unthinkable; the great courtly business to which they were to open the way was a forlorn hope; it was useless.

The one prince from whom he once expected everything he had now cut from his itinerary altogether. Young William of Hanau was much too shrewd and trying a personage to do business with for Meyer's gentle temper. What vistas had not he opened up, away back in '69, when he so readily granted the title others had refused! But almost immediately disappointment had followed. For that sly serenity meant to be forever rewarded for his munificence. He expected dealers whom he had honored to sell him their goods at a loss, and he was not above having his courtiers say so outright. For the better part of twenty long years, therefore, Meyer had given Hanau a wide berth. And then, in 1785, William had succeeded to his father's throne in the somewhat distant seat at Cassel, and the once hopeful connection seemed broken for good.

And yet, had Meyer had the gift of looking into the future, he might have seen that his early vague intuition about Hanau was well-grounded, and that the young Landgrave was some day to make the fortune of his house. He had no such gift, and it was a long time before he could bring himself to approach the imposing palace on the Wilhemshoehe at Cassel.

CHAPTER II

PORTRAIT OF A PRINCE

NOTHING could have seemed more fantastic and preposterous, say about 1800, than that history would remember Landgrave William IX (later Elector William I) of Hesse-Cassel chiefly for his affairs with "Jew Mayer" and his sons. Meyer was an unknown tradesman of the Frankfort Ghetto, without antecedents or standing or prospects, the humblest petitioner at His Serenity's court; while William was one of the outstanding half-dozen reigning Princes of Germany, a hopeful candidate for the royal crown, and the richest man in Europe. Five centuries had travailed to produce his house, his name and his fortune. His family had been rulers since the middle ages; with him it was about to reach its highest pinnacle; a future, even more brilliant than the past, seemed to await his successors. Save for the imperial house of Hapsburg, there was scarcely a prince in the whole length and breadth of Germany who could venture to compare pedigrees with him. Son of Mary of England, he was a grandson of George II and a first cousin of George III; the king of Denmark was both his uncle and his father-in-law; Gustavus III of Sweden was his brother-in-law, and his son and heir was married to a daughter of Frederick William II of Prussia. To top it all, his enormous wealth, not all of which had come to him by inheritance, had made nearly every sovereign in Europe, from Britain to Russia, his debtor.

Good fortune had begun to attend him in advance of his birth. He was actually a younger son. But an ancient curse which had been pursuing the family for generations had carried off his elder brother in infancy and had assured him the succession. When he was still a child, an estrangement over religion between his father and his grandfather had made him the independent ruler of the principality of Hanau. As the heir of the considerable and strategically placed Landgravate of Hesse-Cassel and of the reputedly vast fortune that went with it, his military talents had been flatteringly noticed by no less a personage than Frederick the Great, and the courtly match-maker of many an ancient and financially embarrassed kingdom had looked hopefully and indulgently toward an alliance with him. His choice had fallen upon the princess royal of Denmark. Educated in Copenhagen, whither his grandfather and his unhappy mother had sent him to escape the influence of his Catholic father, he had fallen desperately in love with his youthful cousin Caroline, and had married her before he was twenty-one. And then, in the prime of his youth, his father had died leaving him in possession of his millions, his throne and his unfulfilled ambitions. Shrewd to the point of sharpness, capable, autocratic, thrifty almost to avarice, he early set to work to augment his patrimony. While still Count Regnant of Hanau he had been the first to supply his English cousin with troops to combat the revolting American colonists, a transaction which had netted him several million crowns. By repeating the profitable operation whenever opportunity offered, holding his court down to an austere

Spartan simplicity, and astutely reinvesting his gains in safe British government bonds, he had succeeded in amassing the largest private fortune since the time of the Fuggers. With his money, his military prowess, his family connections and what he mistakenly took to be his political capacity, he was on the point of attaining the goal toward which his predecessors had striven in vain.

But there were contradictions in his nature and cross currents in the age, which were destined to thwart his desires. He came into the world either too late or too soon. If he had been born fifty years before his autocratic conception of the state would have fitted in with the age. In the nineteenth century he would have been a great captain of industry. As it was he swung uneasily between the era just passing and the one struggling to be born, an absolute monarch in an age of revolution and a man of business before commerce had either perfected its instruments or become quite respectable. He looked upon himself as the father of his subjects, and his Hessians were unbelievably loyal to him. He took men away from their homes and kindred, sent them to die in wars in which neither they nor he had any concern, appropriated the price of their blood to his own uses, and then generously compensated their bereft families by reducing their taxes. Yet he had no qualms over the rightness of his conduct and there was no revolution in Cassel or Hanau. He lent money out at interest, like a Jew, to kings and princes, to artisans and tradesmen, but demanded the respect due a monarch, and got it, too. In the age of Voltaire and the Encyclopedia, he was a devout conventional Christian. In the halcyon days of Versailles and Sans-Souci, at the crest of the most profligate period Europe had ever known, he strove to be a self-contained model husband. He failed, and his failure destroyed his self-respect and the bases of his happiness. But worse things were in store for him. The kindling ambition of his career, the hope to wear a royal crown, which was the key to his toilsome, contradictory, pathetic and somewhat preposterous life, was never to be realized, and he died a disappointed man.

II

His marriage was his first misfortune. The moment his stormy courtship was over and he was left alone with his girl-wife, misery seized upon him and it became, as he confided to his diary, "positive torture to play the tender spouse." Poor Caroline was a cold, unmatured child of the North, who was repelled and frightened by her cousin's ardent advances. Seeing his mistake, he tried to woo her with patience and gentleness. It was too late. And then a year after he had brought her in triumph to Hanau, she was taken ill with a dreadful malady. She survived it; but when she arose from her sick-bed, her beauty was gone and she was pock-marked for life. After that for four years William faithfully kept his marriage vows. They had several children together; it was, he felt, his duty to his country, his throne and his line. Through all this time he fought bravely against temptation, but in the end he succumbed. His first liaison—with the pretty young wife of his own Master of the Horse—nearly shattered him, and he recoiled from it in utter dismay. It was not the affront to Caroline, but the sudden collapse of his ideal of himself, that hurt him. He had wanted so much to be a noble example to his subjects! The undignified slinking in the dark, the compromises, the deceptions, humiliated him. He made a clean breast of it to his wife. There were tears, mutual forgivenesses, reconciliations. But presently he slipped again. His susceptible nature craved beauty and affection, and his timid, melancholy, passionless, disfigured wife was unable to give them to him. He had four children with his new concubine—a robustious daughter of the people who had known how to "spread her net" for him. He hated her and himself; she was "common, ignorant and vulgar;" their relations were "loveless and wholly carnal;" and after repeated resolutions and backslidings, he cast her back into the obscurity whence for a period he had raised her up, and nothing more was heard of her.

He believed he was cured, but within the year he was in the toils of a new and violent passion. Rosa Wilhelmina Dorothea Ritter was educated, well-born, clever, and she demanded that her status be recognized without ambiguity. She was offering up her girlhood, her beauty, her future, and she must have something in return. He bought her an estate, he conferred a title of nobility upon her and their eight children, he gave himself wholly to her and neglected Caroline utterly. It was not enough; he must put her right in the eyes of the world. She bobbed up suddenly at an officers' ball, and made her lover acknowledge her publicly. When he did that none too graciously, she insisted on being received at court. He yielded again, and the Princess was outraged. There was open talk of a separation, the palace buzzed with rumors and alarms, a clique formed to champion the affronted wife. By this time, however, William's conscience had adjusted itself and his self-approval returned. He saw himself as no longer a sinner, but as a much-tried unloved husband who had a right to live his life and seek happiness where he could find it. Once and for all his wife must understand that it was she who was to blame for their ship-wrecked love. He came down in shining armor upon her and her defenders, scattered the clique and forced her to accept the situation. Thereupon calm was reëstablished. Caroline must take what satisfaction she could as the official consort and the mother of His Serenity's legitimate issue. And then, just as everything began going smoothly, Frau von Lindenthal (née Rosa Wilhelmina Dorothea Ritter) had the effrontery to cast lustful glances upon a young officer in her lover's employ. William's long-suffering patience snapped. He deprived the ungrateful hussy of her estate, her title and her children, and banished her forever from his sight.

Within a few months came the grand passion of his life. He was by this time a man of forty-four, while Juliane Albertine von Schlotheim was only nineteen. For a space this thought made him hesitate. "I had nothing to offer her but the heart of a married man twice her age;" but his scruples soon vanished when "my love and the dear creature for whom I felt it met in a devotion so tender, so true and so enduring as I had never known before." Enduring it certainly was, and William at least never questioned its depth and sincerity. Insofar as a woman's love could satisfy his restless, ambitious soul, he was happy with her to the end of his life. Toward no one else, surely, was he so generous and so trustful as toward her. He suspected and quarreled with his father, his wife, his son, his ministers, his financial advisers; but the radiant beauty who filled his prime and his old age with joy, who stood by him in his misfortunes and followed him into exile, had his whole heart and his unreserved confidence. Without her asking it, he established their relationship from the outset as a *mariage de conscience;* her own tact and modesty made it easy for the Princess to receive her; and when the first of their nine children was born he settled her in a palace of her own and gave the emperor no peace till she was made a countess.

It has been said that William did not know himself the exact number of his offspring. As a matter of record, there were four by the first *liaison,* eight by the second, and nine by the Countess von Schlotheim, in addition to the three legitimate children of the Princess. Each of his families had its own name and title, and for each he provided as befitted his station. An augmented tax on salt enabled him to meet the extraordinary burden, and gave his subjects the opportunity to share it with him. The daughters born without the law married almost as well as their princely sisters; of the sons many lived to be generals and ministers in the service of numerous German states. The notorious Austrian General Haynau, the suppressor of revolts in Hungary and Italy, who as the "Hyena of Brescia" narrowly escaped mobbing in London, was the most noted of them.

III

Comfort, delight, even ecstasy, his concubines and their prolific progeny gave William. They did not fill his heart. Women were the playthings of life, the rewards and relaxations of a busy man. He would have despised himself as an idler and a fribble if he let them absorb him. He was an ambitious monarch, and he wanted to be king over a greater Hesse than his predecessors had left him. Even his enormous wealth, its administration and expansion, were a secondary concern, a means to the supreme end. His late father had striven to prepare the way for him, alas! in vain, and he must begin at scratch. Before a mere landgrave could touch the regal crown he must secure the Electoral hat. Seven princes, temporal and spiritual, wore that dignity and enjoyed the privilege of choosing an emperor. William was prepared to abase himself before them, to join with them in their wars, even to lend them money, if only they would vote him into their company. For fifteen years he pulled strings and danced attendance on them. He was mistrustful and jealous of the king of Prussia; yet he hung about the court in Berlin, flattered Frederick William II and his successor, took service as a field-marshal in the Prussian army—a step which almost cost him his freedom later on—all to win that monarch's support for his ambition. His ego was lacerated whenever he must play second fiddle; yet, with the same end in view, he busied himself with the military ceremonies at Frankfort when Leopold II came to be crowned there in 1790, and again at the accession of Francis II, entertained the assembled magnificoes at lavish cost, erected a memorial arch in honor of the event, only to be rewarded for his pains with an empty letter of thanks from Imperial Majesty.

The French Revolution came, and three years later the leading German princes met in conclave to free the imprisoned Louis XVI and crush his rebellious subjects. William had no stomach for the enterprise; but if he was to participate, his vanity demanded that he be made commander in chief, and his avarice that the Hessian troops be paid for. He yielded on both points because the king of Prussia and the Emperor agreed to do their part toward winning him the coveted hat. Five years later he allowed Prussia with his eyes open to outmanœuvre him in the secularization and partition of the spiritual princes' dominions, on the same ground. Time and again the exposed position of his country and prudential regard for its interests bade him go over to the side of France, especially after the advent of the Consulate; but he dared not displease the Emperor, lest he endanger his chance for the electorship and the grand goal toward which it was the stepping-stone.

Finally in 1803 he bagged it. And then to his vast disappointment and disgust, it turned out that he had labored and intrigued in vain. One year later Napoleon proclaimed himself the successor of Charlemagne, and the Holy Roman Empire—after existing for a thousand years—was abolished. The new Elector William I of Hesse-Cassel never voted for an emperor at all.

IV

This evil turn from the master of Europe was but an earnest of future incompatibilities. Worse was to come. From the first William was outraged and scandalized by the high-handed doings in France. The Revolution burst rudely upon all his hopes and schemes, violated everything that he cherished and believed in, and encouraged everything that was obnoxious to him. At heart he still thought of himself as an old-fashioned husband and father, and the rebels flouted the sacredness of the family. He dreaded and detested the new abhorrent fashions in theology, in government, in costume and hairdressing. Nor did the monstrous business stop there. In 1792 a French army led by General Custine bombarded Frankfort and in the very shadow of his palace launched a proclamation to his subjects calling upon them to cast off the yoke of "the tyrant, the tiger who sells your blood to fill his purse," and describing his subsidy transactions with England as "this commerce in troops." The abusive phrase caught on and popular discontent rose to a high pitch, so that he was obliged to adopt counter-measures. He commanded the pastors to preach in their churches the virtues of docility and obedience and the holiness of the "good old German traditions" of absolutism. By way of ridiculing the new modes he ordered that the jail population be shorn of their pig-tails and, accoutred in pantaloons and stiff round hats, set to sweeping the streets. And when next year he again sold twelve thousand soldiers to Britain he voluntarily decreed a general reduction in taxes.

Not for a moment did he believe but that the upheaval was a passing mania, engineered by crazy agitators, without roots in history, without social significance and without a future. The advent of the Consulate only confirmed this opinion. Not that he perceived the genius of Napoleon. From first to last he saw in him nothing but a lucky adventurer. But he felt sure that "so despotic a general" could not bring the misled French people to their senses and make them wish their old rulers back. Even the long series of brilliant victories culminating in the proclamation of the empire did not sober him. Geography and the logic of events and the timid hints of his advisers impelled him into an alliance with the new powers, but he could not and would not conquer his aversion for "the usurper" and went on putting his trust in blind Prussia and bankrupt Austria.

By a curious irony Napoleon took up, shortly after his coronation, a favorite scheme of William's for a union among the Rhenish princes. In September 1804 the Emperor came in person to Mayence to preside over the assembled sovereigns. The Elector of Hesse-Cassel was invited to the conclave, but failed to put in an appearance, offering as an excuse a sudden attack of the gout. It was not only that with the Corsican's finger in the pie, the dish had lost its savor for him; he deemed it shrewd diplomacy to keep Napoleon guessing. The Emperor was hinting broadly that he was prepared to reward William for his adherence with Britain's Hanoverian possession as well as with the title of majesty. That was cruelly tempting; but England, on the other hand, was dangling fresh subsidy contracts before his nose. Too bad that he could not be friends with both parties and fulfil all his ambitions at one stroke. The moment he threw in his lot with one camp or the other, he would be obliged to give up for good some of his dreams. Temperamentally he very much disliked making up his mind anyhow. Moreover, coming out openly for France meant breaking with all his friends; it meant probably that the powers in London would confiscate his very large investments there; and it meant almost certainly that he would have to fit out an army and go to war at his own expense.

So, without positively declining either offer, he decided to steer a middle course. Neutrality had its joys as well as its dangers, and it appeared likely to be the most remunerative policy to boot. In the back of his head the notion that Napoleon was a bird of passage had taken firm root. Who knew? Perhaps by the time he had come to a decision the struggle would end and he would gain both worlds. In the meantime it was most agreeable to have the two great coalitions sitting on his doorstep and bidding against each other for his friendship. In the meantime, too, however, Napoleon's scheme for the confederation of the Rhine principalities prospered apace, the two Electors of Bavaria and Wuerttemberg became kings, and both England and the Emperor were becoming ever more irritated with William's dilatory tactics. Still he hesitated. Austria was knocked into the dust, the Napoleonic steam-roller flattened out Prussia, all Europe hurried to fling itself either at the "usurper's" feet or to join the alliance against him; but William still hoped for miracles. The wolf was at the door, and he proceeded to charm him off by tacking signs up around the frontiers of Hesse-Cassel asserting his neutrality. At last both England and France lost patience. London confiscated his investments; and Napoleon, having gobbled up bigger fry, swooped down upon his capital with fire and sword, ordered him taken prisoner as a Prussian field marshal, and occupied the country. By the sheerest piece of luck William managed to escape. For seven long years he wandered in exile, a suppliant at strangers' doors.

With one exception, nothing so auspicious had yet occurred for the future of the Rothschild family.

CHAPTER III

THE BOYS

THE exception was the sudden departure of Nathan, Meyer's third son, for England.

The family had not been long in the house with the Green Sign than Meyer was obliged to take stock of his situation. By and large, the inventory was not encouraging. The purchase of the home had made a deep hole in his capital. His responsibilities were increasing, while his affairs barely held their own. A seventh child had come, an eighth was expected, and space was once more becoming a problem. What with the shop occupying the street floor, the growing family had all it could do to keep up appearances, without so much as thinking of comfort. What he ought to do, what was sorely needed, was to separate residence and business altogether. It was not a question of luxury. Poor, tired Guetele had not a fit place to do her work in. At night, after the children had gone to bed, she must mend and darn in the shop. And that was not all. Schoenche, their eldest, was seventeen, nearly eighteen, and should marry. The match-makers of the *Gasse* were busy with offers; but there was not a proper sitting room in the house to receive either them or the young men they proposed bringing around. What was more, marriage meant a dowry. Where was it to come from?

Finally, there was Amschel, the eldest of the boys. Not

that *he* was a problem exactly. The youngster was alive with energy; and he had brains. Long before he had been confirmed, he had begun turning his hand to things. At first it was helping in the shop; then he took to running out into the market on his own, buying and selling whatever came along, cotton-cloth for the most part. It was good business, too; the difficulty was capital. If he had money or credit, it might really be a big thing. As it was, he could only make commissions, middlemanning for those who had.

But the boy did have brains; or at least he kept his ears open. Out among the tradesfolk he had heard talk: to wit, that the *Poritz*, the Landgrave at Cassel, was handing out English drafts—interest on securities he had there—to various merchants he trusted; some of them were Jews even; and he did not want them cashed right off, for fear of depressing the exchange rate; so he left them with the merchants till Frankfort Fair time, which might be six months off, free of interest. Now this Landgrave, wasn't he the *Poritz* father knew, the man who gave father a title once, twenty years ago, because he had sold him some coins and trinkets? He was, indeed! Well then, it was like this: the free use of capital was one thing; but besides, there were the cloth dealers from Manchester. They had to be paid in drafts on London. Why not pay them with the Landgrave's interest checks, and save the discount both ways?

If only father would take a trip down to Cassel and warm over the old connection!

So Meyer packed his medal case again and hopped on the stage that went from Frankfort to the Hessian capital.

The boy was right: it was an idea. Why hadn't he thought of that himself all those years? It was better than all the court-business he had been angling for and never got. With his past services and his Court-Factorship for prestige, he ought to get a chance easily. And then the dowry for Schoenche and the launching for Amschel and the younger boys!

It did not go quite so fast as all that. His Serenity—without, of course, admitting the tradesman to his presence—did surely enough take the trinkets Meyer brought down for his inspection. The prices were too temptingly low. He even made a shrewd guess why the Jew was so generous, and sent out word that the next time he had checks to cash he would see to it that Meyer was remembered. But that, for the time being, was all. Meyer went back to Frankfort and sat down hopefully to wait. He waited for an entire year, but the court did not remember.

It was risky, but Meyer saw no other choice than to remind Highness of his promise. So he wrote him a letter recalling the services he had rendered back in Hanau, the low discounts he had been content to work for, his punctual payments, and his loyalty and devotion. He was, he declared, again prepared to match the highest bidders, to be grateful for the most modest credit allowance, and to be in all ways His Serenity's most faithful humble servant. After all, he concluded, I am not exactly a stranger to Your Princely Serenity, having these many years enjoyed the distinction of being a Hessian (which sounded better than Hanau) Court-Factor. Upon all these asseverations "the records of the Most-High Princely investment office and state treasury department will not fail to bear me out, and I have no hesitation in referring myself to them."

It seemed, however, that the Landgrave had completely forgotten Meyer's constancy and services. Moreover, the officials at Cassel knew nothing of the affairs in Hanau. Therefore the references (which poor Meyer had given more for their sound than for their substance) were very thoroughly looked up; and it being found that the transactions at the little capital had been few and of the most passing and trifling nature—of English check discountings not a trace could be discovered—the inquiry was extended to Frankfort. From the business community there the reports were equally unimpressive. Among the great firms no such person as Meyer Rothschild was known at all, favorably or unfavorably; the others, while giving him a good character as a reputable and honest tradesman within his sphere, were in no position to state anything definite about his financial standing or responsibility. The only safe guide as to that might be the assessment lists of the Jewish community; which being consulted, showed that Meyer Rothschild was paying taxes upon a fortune of two thousand florins, and that this rating had remained stationary for fifteen years!

The upshot of all this research was that the court, after months and months of further delay, graciously resolved to redeem its promise by authorizing for the petitioner a credit allowance of one thousand pounds sterling—the next time a batch of drafts arrived from London. In the closing months of 1789 checks in the amount of eight hundred pounds actually were turned over to him. It was by that time nearly two years since the hopeful transaction with the medals.

Matters went along at the same snail's pace for over a decade. The following year when Meyer applied to have his credit raised to ten thousand pounds, Highness munificently doubled his previous allowance, making it two thousand at the same time that a Cassel Jew named Feidel David was put down for twenty-five thousand. But Meyer, egged on and abetted by his boys, hung on; so that, little by little, his credit increased. The French Revolution came, and cotton cloth rose into the luxury class; but what with Amschel's device of paying the Manchester dealers direct with the Prince's drafts on London, the firm of Rothschild obtained first choice. The shop grew and prospered. A bombardment of Frankfort by French Revolutionary troops in 1796, doing great damage to the Ghetto street and resulting in the City Council's granting Jews the right of free domicile, had given Guetele and Schoenche their long-desired sitting room. The "Green Sign" had, as it happened, been barely struck; but the shop was now in rented quarters on the centrally located Schnurgasse nevertheless. And (as the surest measure of the family's prosperity) the Jewish community for the first time in nearly a quarter of a century raised Meyer Rothschild's tax-assessment.

II

But the greatest thing was yet to come: Two years later Nathan, the third of the boys, suddenly decided to go to England. It frightened Meyer at the time. He had taken the young man with him to look at the Manchester dealer's samples; and before he knew what was happening, some hot words had been exchanged between the two, the Englishman had snapped his cases shut angrily, and was showing father and son the door. Lord, but this was serious! The family's whole prosperity and future was bound up with the textiles, and the dealer knew it—that, and also that he had the entire Frankfort market in his pockets; no competitor touched the town. The Revolution and the strained relations along the Channel made trade too hazardous for very many merchants to venture over to the Continent; with the consequence that the few who still did come across had things their own way.

But the high-spirited Nathan did not seem disturbed in the slightest.

To the salesman he flung back over his shoulder: "I don't want your shoddy anyhow. I know where to get stuff as well as you do."

Then he reassured his parent: "It is all right. I am going to England tomorrow. I'll send you all the cloth you want." And he kept his word.

That amazing youth of 21 had hardly had time to get his bearings in the alien land and to pick up the most fragmentary smattering of English—in all his forty years of residence he was never to lose his Judengasse accent—than he had begun showing what he was made of. In less than a year he had tripled the little capital he had brought with him. For the present he was confining himself to cotton cloth for export to Frankfort. But he was already looking beyond Manchester to London. There in the world's business and financial capital were opportunities worthy of his talents. His affairs with the Lancashire weavers had progressed far enough to enable him to operate at a distance. But it was useless to go to London without money. The only place he knew of where big money was to be had was the palace at Cassel. His letters, piously addressed to his father but intended chiefly for his brother Salomon, begged for that money. Could they not somehow get nearer to that pig-tailed miser in the court of Hesse, and whisper in his ear? Was there not someone about the treasury who did have his ear? It did not matter in the least what his price was. Buy him at any price, and get the money, and send it to where it will do the most good. The Landgrave will lose nothing and we will become rich, richer than he. It is the opportunity of a lifetime. Get the money, the money . . . Nathan's letters became an insistent clamor, a bombardment.

It made the young men at home feel sick and helpless. Now they realized as never before how very little they had yet accomplished. They were nowhere at court; their credit was insignificant; and they had no friends, none at least of any consequence. The petty discount business they got from time to time was the barest beginning toward what Nathan had in mind; the really big affairs at Cassel they were not allowed to touch, and if they were they had not the experience or the education to carry them out. They were shopkeepers, not bankers. All that they had to recommend them was their energy, their ambition and their native gifts. But what good were these in face of the handicaps they must overcome? Their path to the Landgrave's treasure was barred as by a triple wall, of mistrust, jealousy, prejudice. The Prince was indeed not the man to let sectarian considerations conflict with a good bargain. Still, he was of his time and class. Everything else being equal, he preferred to transact important business with German firms of patrician antecedents. His courtiers more than shared that sentiment. Naturally, the great bankers of Frankfort, like the Bethmann Brothers and Rueppell & Harnier, made the most of their advantage and jealously kept the prejudice at Cassel warm. To complete the encirclement, the Jewish merchants at the Hessian capital looked upon the court business as their special preserve and hounded their foreign coreligionists bitterly, relentlessly.

What were the young Rothschilds to do? Somehow or another, straight-forwardly or by indirection, by fair means or otherwise, the capital which Nathan clamored for must be secured him. Only one possible door was open. It was not the most promising approach, not the most dignified; it was, in fact, a back-door. Oh, well, they were in no position just now to consider dignity. It might, if successful, force them to be unfair to those who opened it for them. So be it; ambitious men could not, at this stage of their progress, afford to be over-scrupulous. It might lead to a fight; there was no choice but to risk it, and arm for it in the meantime.

The plan was as simple as it was ingenious. Those old established German banking firms, though they guarded their connections with the Landgrave jealously, heartily disliked dealing with him; and the Rothschild boys knew it. Cassel was, to begin with, in these days of stage coaches, a long way off. That, however, was a minor item. It was Serenity's business manners that tried the patience of a self-respecting banker. William was arrogant, petty, mistrustful, vacillating, greedy, exacting. One never could be sure with him until he had actually signed a contract, whether a deal was closed or not. He dickered and haggled worse than a Judengasse shopkeeper, and then he stood off loftily and demanded special consideration for his rank and wealth. The smallest transaction necessitated repeated journeys and endless correspondence before Highness's doubts were dispelled and his cupidity appeased. And yet, with all his faults, no banker could afford not to reckon with him: he was one of the richest men in the world.

In these circumstances it was not surprising that Rueppell & Harnier and—after a good deal of persuasion—the Bethmanns gave serious attention to the proposal which the young Rothschilds brought to them. It was briefly this: You are great and important houses. You have your dignity and traditions to consider. The Landgrave is a big buyer of securities, but a trifle difficult. If we may put it that way, it sometimes wearies you so to do business with him that you are on the point of dropping the connection. That would be rather reckless, however; don't you think? Now, we are young men, without any particular antecedents or position to worry about. We are ambitious, we want to make more money, and we shall feel honored to work for such distinguished houses as yours. Well, let us be the buffers between Serenissimus and yourselves. We can handle him. His nonsense won't disturb us; we are used to tough customers. If you will pay us a small broker's commission, we will take the fuss and bother and haggling off your shoulders. In all honesty, we are moved to offer you our services by one consideration of which we have not yet spoken. For a number of years our father and ourselves have been attending to little matters for His Highness—those English drafts, you know. But our coreligionists in Cassel are making trouble for us. If we can go to the palace as your brokers, it will make things a bit easier.

There were one or two other, even more moving, considerations, as will appear directly, which the keen young men omitted to name. Why overplay their hand unnecessarily? The plan was going over as it was. Ruppell & Harnier agreed right off; the Bethmanns seemed impressed. In the two years that followed both houses willingly turned over their court business to them. Again and again the Rothschilds sold the Landgrave parcels of Danish bonds issued by the Frankfort concerns; in one or two instances they were allowed to convert the interest coupons; once at least they arranged a partial Danish amortization for the Bethmanns. Everyone was pleased: Prince William was delighted to have his investments attended to by men to whom he could talk as he liked; the bankers were happy to be relieved of an irritating client while retaining his account; and the brokers were for the first time taking a hand in financial operations on the grand scale. The plan functioned without a hitch; there appeared to be no reason why it should not go on indefinitely. But just then a curious thing happened. Just as the German firms began congratulating themselves on having found a perfect instrument, the very men who had devised it withdrew from the arrangement. The Rothschilds ceased to wait on their patrons in Frankfort, for what cause they did not vouchsafe to explain. Rueppell and the Bethmanns were sorry and mystified, but they were too proud to ask questions. It was by that time the year 1804.

III

The Rothschilds had been as truthful as they had said they were when they named the opposition of the Cassel Jews as their motive for offering to act as the brokers of the two old Frankfort houses. They had merely not told the whole truth. Two further incentives spurred them on. Their ultimate goal was nothing less than to become the chief, if not the sole, bankers of the Landgrave of Hesse (the Elector of Hesse since 1803), so that by having his huge uninvested surplus on deposit they might supply their brother in England with the capital he required. To arrive at that goal they must learn a great deal more of banking than they yet knew, and—even more important—make friends at court. By 1804 both these objectives had been attained and passed. The Bethmann and Rueppell connections had served their purpose. It would have been idle to continue them, yes even risky. In the same year Nathan left Manchester for London.

So long as the Rothschilds remained on the outer fringe where their services were restricted to the trivial business of draft discounting, their opportunities either to make valuable contacts with the men close to the millionaire-prince or to gain anything like a comprehensive view of his affairs were almost nil. The English note transactions were a routine matter; clerks gave out the checks, clerks received the money. Bond-selling, more especially interest and capital collecting, were quite another thing. They came under the head of grand finance; they involved discussion and negotiation with high officials. Moreover, the brokers to some degree reflected the prestige of the great houses in whose name they acted. Thus, without transition, the young sons of Meyer Rothschild suddenly found themselves translated into the innermost circle of the Prince's entourage, but one remove from direct contact with All-Highest himself.

It took Salomon, the diplomatic genius of the family, only a very little time to get the measure of William's men. All in all, he decided, the best choice he could make was Karl Friedrich Buderus. Buderus fulfilled all the requirements. He was still a young man, yet he had gone far and seemed likely to go very much farther still. Son of a schoolmaster, who back in Hanau had been tutor to some of Highness's numerous natural progeny, he had entered the Prince's service as a bookkeeper attached to the tax office of that little principality. He had risen gradually in his master's esteem, so that when the latter became Landgrave of Hesse Buderus was left in charge of the finances at the old capital. In '92 he had been called to Cassel, where his progress had been extraordinarily rapid. He now held the title of a War Councilor and was the Director of two of the state's four treasury departments, one of which—the so-called War Treasury—contained the fabled millions and handled the investments. As nearly as anyone could, Buderus enjoyed his master's confidence and was consulted by him in all the more important financial operations. Quiet, diligent, painstaking, reserved, his clerical exterior gave no hint of the man's real talents. Salomon saw in him a collaborator ideally suited to his purpose,—discreet, competent, dependable, a good soldier who in a scrape would know how to fight his way out, a courtier remarkably free from the sectarian prejudices of his class.

Terms were a detail. The Rothschilds needed protection

in the worst way; Buderus, if anybody, could give it to them; he should have whatever he asked. Of course, Buderus had his price; they all did. That was the standard, recognized method of doing business around courts. The highnesses themselves tacitly encouraged it; it enabled them to keep large staffs at small expense. The courtier, having come to a cordial understanding with one of the firms supplying his master, saw to it that as much trade as possible went to his friends and as little as possible to those of his colleagues. In return for his amiability, the merchants remembered him and his with suitable gifts at certain seasons of the year, and helped him out from time to time with a loan—which neither side, naturally, expected to be repaid—to enable him to meet extraordinary obligations for which Highness's salary scale made no provision. Even princes' younger sons and heirs to thrones themselves, when the parental allowance was not elastic enough, did not disdain mercantile gratuities in exchange for a bit of quiet support—as William of Hesse, recalling the lean years before his accession, was not unaware.

Salomon Rothschild and his brothers diligently cultivated the man Buderus. They found him a friendly soul, once his thin reserve was penetrated; he liked a chat, did not even mind exchanging confidences. Nothing uppish about him. And his conversations about the courtly finances were immensely instructive. They had had no idea until now of the real magnitude of the quarry they were after. The Prince, according to Buderus, was a fabulously wealthy man. His loans and investments were scattered all over Europe, from London to St. Petersburg, from Copenhagen to Vienna. Those stodgy old bankers in Frankfort had barely scratched the surface. If they had been alert and energetic, if they had even halfway availed themselves of their opportunities—of their sheer geographical position, to mention but one—they could by this time have got exclusive control of the business. Why, William's income alone was more than a million thalers a year, most of which, under the frugal economy he maintained, had to be reinvested. Naturally mistrustful and suspicious, he parceled out his affairs to all sorts of people everywhere. There were, for instance, the Van Nottens in Amsterdam, with their branch in London—another petrified ancient house, of splendid traditions and moribund vitality. They handled the Dutch and English business. The Russian loans were attended to by a St. Petersburg concern, the Austrian by a Viennese firm, and similarly all the way through. It was all nonsense; a fortune, like a state, should be administered from a single, central point. He, Buderus, had been urging that policy for years. One sound bank, run by young and capable men, accessibly located for easy supervision, ought to have the entire thing in their hands. They could too, if they would go after it, and had the right kind of backing at court. . . . The hungry Rothschilds' mouths watered at the prospect. God himself had guided their footsteps when they chose this man for their friend.

The loans, now: there were a half dozen profits to be made out of each one, which under the existing system often went to as many separate firms. First of all the business had to be negotiated; a commission was paid for that service. The terms having been agreed upon, and the contracts signed, the funds must be conveyed to the borrower. For this there was a second fee. After a time the interest coupons began falling due. Somebody had to turn them into cash, and naturally he must be compensated. The debtor paid, usually, either in foreign currencies or in notes. Bankers were needed to convert both into legal tender, at a discount, of course. Lastly, the loans themselves matured; which, again, involved deliveries, conversions, exchanges—and commissions. This entire gamut of operations was being performed at the Cassel offices almost daily, through a dozen hands or more. Buderus could see no reason why a single pair could not much more efficiently do all the work, and earn all the commissions.

But, upon being cautiously sounded, Buderus seemed to betray not the slightest interest in seasonal presents or periodic personal loans. That was rather astonishing, as well as deucedly inconvenient. Was it possible that he was that nine-days' wonder, a courtier unsusceptible to bribery? Bah, there was no such animal! One encouraging sign was that the diplomatic conversations were not broken off. Buderus continued friendly and talkative. Sometimes he discussed one thing, sometimes another; the important point was that he kept on chatting. Salomon was of the opinion that there was a sort of direction to these apparently aimless remarks, that Buderus was getting at something; only what that thing was, was not clear. Thus, for instance, Buderus occasionally alluded to the lack of generosity in his master's composition, his parsimony, and the way he underpaid his staff. But when Salomon, sensing an opening, tried to step in with a suggestion about how income might be supplemented, his friend hastily added that he was not thinking of himself, that he was interested merely in the general principle and in the efficiency of the service. As for himself, he had no cause to complain. He was a lucky fellow: he had begun at the bottom, here he was at forty-two Director of two departments, and still rising. . . . Wasn't it perfectly dreadful how, with the disorders in France and the unceasing wars, the cost of living had soared? However, they, his family and himself, were people of simple tastes, who had learned how to restrain their wants. . . . Without being immodest, he was probably the most influential man connected with the Landgrave's financial administration. . . . It was fantastic how many petty houses Serenity insisted on employing. But some day he would see sense, and then the concern that had in the interval gained his confidence would have an account worth talking about.

His family—Buderus was like a Jew in his devotion to his own people. Just as one thought he was coming to the point, he suddenly waved his hand philosophically and wandered off to "more agreeable topics." He never wearied of telling one about his splendid children, his excellent wife, his happy home. And this would lead up to what seemed another small, uncertain opening. The dearest wish of his heart—he would confide—the one thing in life for which he labored and hoped, was that he might assure his children an independent income and a title of nobility . . . Then once, in an undertone, Salomon was sure he caught something to the effect that men of the world should understand. . . . That was enough. Salomon, being a man of the world, understood. He understood, namely, that a friend who had the will and the power to do for him what Buderus would do, merited something better than trivial gratuities. Why, he would not insult him by even suggesting such a thing. Buderus deserved a share in the Rothschild firm's earnings. He should have it, by all means.

Mutual comprehension having been achieved, Buderus

had an idea. There was a man he knew up Altona-way, in Holstein, a banker by name of Lawaetz—Johann Daniel Lawaetz. He was in excellent standing with the Danish finance authorities, had been doing business with them for a great many years. There was even talk of giving him a decoration of some sort. Also, he and the Landgrave were old friends, the Hessian ruler having been educated in Copenhagen and having married a daughter of the Danish king. Suspicious though he was of all the world, William had faith in Lawaetz. Well now, Buderus would approach this splendidly connected man, ask him how he would like to negotiate a Danish loan with the Landgrave's money, on the understanding, of course, that the Cassel end of the transaction be entrusted to the House of Rothschild. He would get a letter off to him forthwith.

IV

Lawaetz was willing. So, after a little dickering and hesitating, was Serenity. The royal Dane was more than willing. The Copenhagen exchequer, chronically at low ebb, was in the year 1804 more than usually dry. A loan was in fact at that moment being negotiated with the Bethmanns, who on the plea of the great money stringency, demanded the exorbitant interest rate of eight per cent; so that Lawaetz, acting for an "enormously rich capitalist in Frankfort who was uncommonly well-disposed toward the Danish court," and offering to take up the entire issue at four and a half per cent, seemed nothing less than a god-send. The Elector of Hesse was delighted not only because the transaction enabled him to dispose at one stroke of the greater part of his then very troublesome surplus, but even more because by the Lawaetz plan the identity of the lender would be kept from his poverty-stricken relatives in Copenhagen. And the Rothschilds, in their turn, were not averse to screening themselves behind their Altona correspondent for reasons of their own. They had a presentiment that the good patrician bankers of Frankfort who had so lately initiated them into the mysteries of state loans might take it in bad part were they to learn that it was their protégés' competition that had caused their own eight-per cent offer to be rejected.

For more than two years, during which no fewer than four loans were arranged between Hesse and Denmark, the ingenious system worked without a hitch. The borrowers themselves did not know from whom the money was coming. Every so often an instalment of the bonds, made out to bearer, was forwarded to Lawaetz. Thereupon he notified Buderus of their arrival and total value. Buderus then sent on the money through one of the Rothschilds, who paid it over to Lawaetz, received the securities and returned with them to Buderus. Not a soul in Frankfort had any inkling of what was happening.

By this time it was early in 1806. In January of that year negotiations for still another loan were in progress. Whether by now the Lawaetz-Buderus-Rothschild consortium had become over-confident, or the Elector William had begun to fear that excessive secrecy might lead to detection, or the Danes had raised some objection, in any event the veil was now for the first time partially lifted. William's part in the proceedings remained as hitherto unrevealed, but Lawaetz did at last mention by name his "enormously rich capitalist" in Frankfort. It so happened that the firm of Bethmann Brothers were these days also offering Denmark a loan of a half a million. They had been smarting under their repulse of two years ago, and were determined to win back their old clients from those mysterious competitors, whoever they were. Who those elusive people might be, had been bothering and puzzling the Bethmanns a good deal. There were circumstances, seemingly unrelated to that Danish defeat, which simply cried to be resolved. There was, for instance, the strange behavior of the Rothschild boys. Three, four, five years ago, they eagerly snapped up the smallest crumb which the great banking houses deigned to toss them. Now they were oddly indifferent, astonishingly busy. One or another of them was continually on the road; their affairs seemed to be prospering hugely, too. They had lately managed to secure a warehouse on the Kurtrierplatz, although Jews were expressly forbidden to take part in the bidding. Very remarkable, again, their father had in 1803 been appointed an *Oberhofagent* to the Hessian court, and the two eldest boys now bore titles of Hessian Pay Office Agents. It was all very, very odd.

Oddest of all was their coldness to the brokerage arrangement which they had themselves so recently pleaded for. The Bethmanns, counting on the Elector William to take up a portion of their forthcoming Danish loan, had had the young Jews approached, only to be put off with shrugs and excuses. It appeared that Rueppell & Harnier had had a similar experience. The Bethmanns had then addressed direct inquiries to the Cassel War Treasury (Karl Friedrich Buderus, Director). Would His Serene Highness be interested in investing a hundred thousand thalers or so in a Royal Danish loan about to be issued? To which the cool reply had been, in effect, that the

Elector of Hesse was not buying any Danish bonds today, thank you.

In the meantime, in Denmark those dark competitors were again busy. Once more they were offering easier terms, as well as a larger sum. Certain men in the royal finance department at Copenhagen were favoring their bid, and the Bethmann offer was again in danger of rejection. Thereupon vigorous measures had become necessary. Who, the Bethmanns demanded to know, were these people who had the effrontery to make offers to His Majesty without coming into the open? Oh, it was an enormously rich capitalist of Frankfort who was uncommonly well-disposed toward the Danish court. What was his name? Why, Rothschild! Or was it Gruenschild? Something like that.

At this the Bethmann agents laughed bitterly and uproariously. Rothschild! Did they say Rothschild? That was a pretty bed-time story. Did His Majesty's servants know who the Rothschilds were? The father was a petty curio peddler of the Frankfort Ghetto. His sons ran a shop, which until very lately had been housed on the street floor of their Judengasse home. Enormously rich capitalist, fiddle-sticks! Why, they were nothing but irresponsible, insignificant fly-by-nights, without capital or credit or connections, as anyone in the city on the Main would testify. Let the Royal Government take warning. It was quite out of the question for these men to market a bond issue of such magnitude. They might, relying upon an investing public which in the present disorder of Europe and Germany had ceased to exist, think they could. But the moment they went out and tried, they would strike the inevitable snag, and then they would simply leave His

Majesty in the lurch. They were that kind of men. Besides, there would really be no other choice for them. The ancient and honorable House of Bethmann, on the other hand, had great resources of its own, upon which it could count with perfect safety. Let Denmark consider ere she plunged!

Denmark, however, took the warning lightly, and closed with Lawaetz-Rothschild-Buderus. How should the Bethmanns know that the combine had in the past two years thoroughly proved its soundness by repeated loans successfully placed? On July 2, 1806, Lawaetz wrote Buderus:

"I am asking Rothschild to inform you that the new Bethmann Danish loan, which seems purposely to have been kept secret from me in Copenhagen is actually a fact. I am told in a letter at the same time that it was not possible to say No to this old Bethmann House, which felt rather humiliated; and I observe that those who are not well-disposed toward our good Rothschild have held out promises that the Bethmann loan would cost less and be more promptly liquidated than Rothschild's. In order to contradict this last to the best of my ability, I shall this very day take up the entire remainder of the loan out of my own resources, and relying upon your coöperation look forward confidently to the final remittances from you. . . . I hope people will finally become convinced that he (Rothschild) is a good man who deserves respect, let envy say against him what it will."

The result of Lawaetz's energetic procedure was that the snag which the Bethmanns had so confidently foreseen was actually encountered by themselves. That summer Prussia lay prostrate under the heel of Napoleon; investors throughout Germany ran to cover; and the surplus of the millionaire Elector of Hesse was, through the good offices of shareholder Buderus, at the disposal of the House of

Rothschild. Regretfully Bethmann Brothers found themselves driven to write to Copenhagen in November that in view of the terrible events of recent date, which no man could have foreseen a few months earlier, and the consequent ruin of the most prosperous German lands, they must ask to be released from their promise and for the return of their initial advance. The ancient, patrician firm did not easily forget the humiliation of this letter nor their erstwhile young brokers who had obliged them to write it.

Next came the turn of Rueppell & Harnier. The lifting of the veil on the Copenhagen mystery had given them an even broader peep at the proceedings behind the scenes than the other banking house had got. The Elector, as it chanced, wanted a portion of the 1806 loan to be paid in old Danish bonds which were due to mature that September. That loan, however, had been issued through Rueppell & Harnier—interestingly enough, it was the very one in which the Rothschilds had for the first time acted as their brokers—and, if it was to be called in, the notice to Copenhagen must go through those bankers' hands. This concern, naturally, had its own friends at court; wherefore, in the course of time, the news was brought to them that the purpose for which Serenity desired those securities was to convert them by way of part payment toward a new loan, which not only was being negotiated by the House of Rothschild but—in order to screen Highness's identity—actually carried the Rothschild name on each bond as the lender!

Rueppell & Harnier were a younger firm than the Bethmanns; that is, they had a great deal more pugnacity and considerably less business. They were, therefore, not going to take a thing like this lying down. For that matter, as will presently be seen, neither did the Bethmanns. Unfortunately for the cause of both houses, there were several important details about the affair of which neither of them had the remotest inkling. They were not aware that in these two and a half years the Rothschilds had put through several loans between Cassel and Copenhagen (via Altona) and had made themselves extremely solid with the royal ministry of finance. They had never as much as heard the name of Lawaetz. Least of all did they know—at this time they did not even suspect—that the real villain of the piece was a gentleman named Karl Friedrich Buderus who, close as any man to the Elector, was even closer yet to the brothers Rothschild.

So, rather amusingly, Rueppel & Harnier opened hostilities by addressing a protest to the very man in Cassel who was the source of all their trouble. They Lordshipped and High-Well-Born-ed him all over the place—in point of fact, the modest schoolmaster's son was not even knighted till some months later—and begged him to consider how impossible it was for them to call in those bonds after the six-months' notice period had passed. But chiefly and bitterly they complained of the humiliating necessity of explaining to the Danish authorities that it was in order to make the Rothschild investment possible that these bonds must now be so irregularly amortized. "The conclusion which the Royal Finance Ministry might draw from this is that it is not the Danish state credit itself but solely the Jewish name of Rothschild which enables Danish state securities to find a market in Hesse; and this is surely so contrary to His Electoral Serenity's Highest intention that we account it a merit on our part to call your Baronial Well-born and High-Well-Born

Excellency's attention hereto" as well as to a counter-proposal of their own.

The plan suggested by Rueppell was, of course, not adopted. But the temper of the letter gave Buderus more than one sleepless night and frightened the Rothschilds greatly. A fight was clearly coming. They were not yet ready to join issue with the most powerful banking houses in Germany. Satisfactory though their progress had been these last two or three years, their position was not yet solidly intrenched enough for such a struggle. How would it end? And in an open break what would that incalculable man on the Hessian throne, the timid, suspicious, vacillating William do about it?

And then, just as things looked their darkest, came Napoleon, the man who was so often to smooth the path unconsciously for the Rothschilds, and saved the day. On the last day of October, 1806, French troops, heedless of the Elector's "no trespassing" signs, crossed the frontiers into Hesse. In the middle of the night of November first Serenissimus hurriedly clambered into his carriage, and fled from Cassel in a panic. His beloved Hesse was not to see him again for seven years. Karl Frederich Buderus, silent partner in the House of Rothschild, was left in all but complete control of the princely finances at home.

By an interesting coincidence, the years of the Elector's exile were also the decisive years in the rise of the Rothschilds.

CHAPTER IV

BATTLE

WILLIAM, after some breath-taking mishaps and after narrowly escaping capture at the hands of the invader, sufficiently recovered his composure to turn his horses in a northerly direction. Two weeks later he drove over the frontier into Denmark. There his younger brother, the Landgrave Karl, who like himself had married a daughter of King Frederick V, and who was now resident governor of the Duchies of Schleswig-Holstein, welcomed the bedraggled fugitive cordially enough and assigned him the royal suite in his palace at Gottorp as a temporary residence. The first man to visit him in his exile was the Director of the Hessian War Treasury. William was so happy to see him that he conferred upon him the title of Von Carlshausen. One half of Buderus's dearest wish was thus fulfilled: his children were nobles. All they lacked now was an independent income; the Rothschild connection would take care of that.

Buderus stayed with his master only a few days, noting down orders for the disposition of the great quantity of boxes and bundles of valuables left behind. Then he returned to Cassel with his newly-acquired halo to carry them out. William himself was too unhapy to remain long at Gottorp. To be at a court where others ruled and strutted while he was but a barely tolerated interloper, was not his notion of princely grandeur. Every time the Crown Prince-Regent came down to Gottorp the aged Elector must clear out of his royal suite, gather up his boxes and papers, seek a corner in his brother's apartments, and listen to everlasting reminders about the kindness and hospitality he was enjoying. When, therefore, some two months later, the agreeable Countess von Schlotheim,—"my best friend for whom I wait yearningly" as his diary describes her—followed him with their children into banishment, he set up housekeeping first at Rendsburg and later—Lawaetz having secured a suitable place—at Itzehoe, where he "felt almost at home again."

Back in Cassel meanwhile events moved swiftly and tragically. The French troops had completely occupied Hesse. The day after the flight, Governor General Lagrange had taken possession of the Landgrave's palace, packed the frightened old princess off to her daughter at Gotha, and two days later issued a proclamation confiscating all the former ruler's possessions in the name of the Emperor Napoleon and ordering all the state's revenues to be paid into the imperial treasury. In a panic Buderus and the secret regency council which William had appointed before his departure made haste to get their master's remaining treasures into hiding. Truckloads of coffers and boxes were buried under the walls and stairways of the palaces of Wilhelmshoehe, Sababurg and Loewenburg, one cartful of securities and other valuable papers was dispatched in the dead of the night to a warehouse in Frankfort, a number of cases filled with records found their way into the basement of the Judengasse home of old Meyer Rothschild. Subsequently it transpired that Lagrange had an itching palm, so that the greater part of the property safely reached its anxious owner at Rendsburg and Itzehoe, with the Governor General's connivance. The rest, consisting of eleven million thalers in bonds, coupons, cash, silver services and jewelry, including even William's prized rare-coin cabinet, which Meyer Rothschild had helped to fill, must be turned over to the imperial war chests. A round million francs went to Lagrange for his coöperation.

The Landgrave's sudden flight did not, as the Rothschilds had hoped, make an end of the bankers' war which had just previously broken out. It only delayed it for a space and shifted the fighting to another sector. Unquestionably the new alignment favored the Buderus-Rothschild side. So confident of this was Buderus that, far from endeavoring to pacify the enemy, he now boldly moved to eliminate the remaining competitors, all the way from the Jews in Cassel to the Van Nottens in London. On the very day of his master's departure he virtually appointed his associates sole bankers of the court of Hesse. They alone were henceforth to discount English and Danish drafts; they alone were to receive deposits of cash on hand. He instructed the Van Nottens to pay the interest on the Elector's English investments directly to Nathan in London. As everyone in Frankfort was aware that Buderus was in sole charge of his absent master's financial affairs, this practical Rothschild monopoly of the business could only come about through his orders. It was an open defiance of the great Frankfort houses, a frank avowal of his understanding with the Jewish concern, and a challenge to its competitors to do their worst.

The Bethmanns and Rueppell & Harnier accepted the challenge and carried the fight into Denmark, to the

Landgrave's exile. The older house deemed it beneath its dignity to do more than write; it wrote to Rendsburg often and vigorously; the other was not too particular to employ the same kind of weapons as their Jewish adversaries. Rueppell & Harnier, too, had friends at court. They were on the most cordial terms with a man—Lennep was his name—who stood as high in the Prince's esteem as Buderus. Lennep, too, was an honest courtier with a family to provide for. He had won the rank of War Privy Councilor long before Buderus had, and during those difficult days of the flight and the rescue of his master's possessions had shown the utmost courage and devotion. Best of all, he was now on a mission which carried him back and forth between Hesse and Schleswig-Holstein, so that he was in direct and frequent touch with All-Highest.

Early in March both partners journeyed to Rendsburg, accompanied by their friend Lennep, to lay their case before William. They brought with them an earful of news, part of it true, some of it fact grotesquely distorted, much of it pure gossip, all of it disquieting. Serenity's mistrust, never fully relaxed, was readily roused. He believed all that his visitors told him, and suspected a great deal more. So that was what his good man's much-made-of devotion amounted to! The moment his master's back was turned, he proceeded to rob him for his own enrichment. That was how he repaid his Prince for the faith reposed in him, for being raised from obscurity to titled rank, for the kindness and generosity shown him. Only lately he, William, had offered to double his Director's salary, notwithstanding the impoverishment that stared him in the face, though in truth Buderus had, out of regard for his master's late misfortunes, declined it. Oh, there was no loyalty in the world, no appreciation, no gratitude. ("Oh, Hessians, in what a light you show yourselves," wrote the exile in his diary on another occasion.)

Prince William had from the start looked with distaste upon the evident alliance of his most trusted business adviser with the Jewish firm. That Buderus, like every one else, should have the customary ties with one or another of the court purveyors, his master took as a matter of course. But why those upstarts of the Judengasse? Weren't there enough high-grade houses who would gladly coöperate with a man of Buderus's position?—The high-grade houses might, to be sure, be unwilling to go so far as a share in their profits, or the idea might not occur to them; but William knew nothing of that arrangement.—And, of course, receiving favors, Buderus must necessarily earn them. That was all right. But, after all, his chief duty was to his Prince, to the man upon whom he depended in the first instance not alone for his living but for the power which made him valuable to the others. What was the fellow thinking of? Couldn't he see that by giving his friends a virtual monopoly, he was making enemies for himself and exposing his master to the gravest dangers? This was no time to stir up bad blood. With the invader in occupation of the country, with loyalist conspiracies continually hatching for his expulsion and the restoration of the rightful ruler, with scores of boxes of valuables still far from safety and the foe's secret police hunting for them high and low, Serenity needed,—oh, tragically—the goodwill of every man in Hesse, in Frankfort, everywhere.

Though this was the aspect of things which principally

worried the Elector, the tales he was listening to disturbed him most profoundly on another ground also. He had, indeed, always found his man Buderus honest, loyal, dependable. Still, how could one really know? He was the head of a large family; his income was quite modest; his temptations, now especially when there was no one on the ground to supervise him, were enormous.—It was that thought, among others, that had moved Highness to suggest the salary increase.—Suppose, in these demoralized times, under the influence of the dreadful ideas issuing from France, suppose he were not to resist! There was no limit to the things he might not do, to the loot he might not take. There were a hundred unliquidated affairs of every conceivable kind that he could by collusion with the debtors wipe off the slate. Hundreds of thousands of thalers flowed monthly through his hands. There were countless transactions of which he alone knew anything. Come to think of it, his accounting for January and February had not yet come in—and Buderus was usually so punctual! It made William suddenly realize how utterly he was in his Director's power, and the realization made him profoundly uneasy.

So, partly to pacify his visitors, partly to administer a gentle snub to Buderus—a severe one he did not dare risk—he promised to look into their complaints. He promised it, and he meant it. He really must pull Herr von Carlshausen up a bit. Meanwhile, as an earnest of his esteem for the House of Rueppell & Harnier and for his man Lennep, he would forthwith entrust the latter with a financial transaction in Cassel of considerable importance, which should serve the double purpose of salving their feelings and sobering Director Buderus.

The bankers and their friend went on their way rejoicing. Their triumph was to be of short duration.

II

The longer the Elector reflected on the tidings he had received, the more he was disquieted and the higher soared his temper. When, therefore, he presently took action he proceeded rather more precipitately than he had meant to and than appeared necessary. He was in very bad humor with the world. His luck had deserted him; none of his affairs prospered any more. A revolt of the Hessian soldiery, from which he had expected great things, had ended in bloody failure. His endeavors to placate Napoleon and regain his throne—with Majesty superadded, the rascally go-betweens whispered to him—were apparently futile and certainly costly. The boorish disregard of his high station by the Holstein peasantry, who never so much as dropped a curtsy or lifted a hat when he went riding in his carriage, chafed his noble spirit beyond endurance. The unspeakable French were despoiling him without mercy. And now this fellow Buderus too, scheming heaven only knew what with those Jews of his! Well, he would stop that at least.

The explosion came the last week of June. In a letter, which by a sort of poetic fitness was sent through one of the Rothschilds, William suddenly decreed that, effective at once, the English and Danish checks, hitherto cashed by Buderus via Rothschild on the spot, be forwarded untouched to the Reserve Treasury at Itzehoe, the new seat of the captivity. "I shall expect from you," thundered His Highness, "an immediate acknowledgment of this decision and your compliance therewith (dass das Noetige besorgt ist)."

Coming thus without warning, this was an extremely unpleasant surprise. It not only knocked Buderus von Carlshausen's newly acquired knightly dignity askew, it struck terror and confusion into his and his associates' plans. Deliberate malice could not have chosen a worse time. A few months earlier such a blow, vicious as it was, might have been borne with resignation. But since the previous November things had been happening; startling, wonderful things. To continue happening, those English and Danish moneys of Serenity were absolutely indispensable. They were the concern's working capital. Their withdrawal spelled catastrophe.

The Elector had no sooner, by his sudden exit on the first of November, given the Rothschilds access to his money, than Napoleon, on the 27th, obligingly provided them with a profitable trade to employ it in. Having in the course of the summer thoroughly whipped Prussia and seized her coasts, the Emperor had on that day launched against Great Britain his memorable Continental Blockade. The Edict of Berlin, as it was called, prohibited all trade with England, declared all British merchandise contraband of war and closed the ports of the mainland to all ships arriving from the British Isles. This was the very thing that the Rothschilds needed. With Nathan in London to do the buying, with the Van Nottens handing him a monthly check for close to two thousand pounds, with Buderus in Frankfort supplying an equal or larger sum to the parent house, with cotton cloth and every other commodity from Britain or her colonies selling at famine prices, with four energetic, able-bodied, keen-eyed but close-mouthed young men on this side the Channel, the business of smuggling was as if made for the House of Rothschild. Nathan's connections in Manchester, his recent marriage into one of the most influential Jewish families in London, his evident command of considerable capital and his own great gifts as a merchant, had served to enlarge his credit over there. The family opened a receiving depot at the port of Hamburg, which was put in charge of old Meyer and one or another of the boys. By the end of June the imports from England had become by far the principal activity of the concern. The little shop on the Schnurgasse was still kept going, largely as a blind for the French police. The Rothschilds were doing a thriving commission business not only in cotton cloth but also in yarn, tobacco, coffee, sugar, indigo and other colonial wares, reëxporting to every part of Germany, to Holland and the Scandinavian countries and even into France itself. Things were going along swimmingly, and Nathan was once again spurring on his brothers, as well as doing his own bit, to get hold of further capital from the Elector—when, suddenly, the thunderbolt fell.

Worse things yet seemed to be looming. Throughout the summer Serenity kept ceaselessly ordering his Director to present himself at Itzehoe and give an account of himself. There were so many things he could not understand; he was all in a muddle about his affairs; besides, he was lonely and homesick for old faces. Buderus assured him he would be delighted to answer any question, from a distance. But he begged to be excused from undertaking that journey just now. He pleaded urgent and heavy duties at home, the hardships and the dangers of travel, the suspicions his departure would arouse in the watchful

French police. But William insisted. So early in September, his arguments and resistance exhausted, Buderus packed his bag and mounted the stage coach for Itzehoe. On the evening of the tenth he stood before his quizzical master.

He stood in the little house in Holstein with hat in hand and trepidation under his tunic. Yet, now he was here, he was almost glad. At last the long-threatened storm was about to break. Let it break; he could weather it. What had he to fear? He had done nothing he could not defend. Any other man in his place would have done as much, if not more. He was making the most of his opportunities, as a responsible head of a family was in honor bound to do, without in the slightest degree hurting his master's interests or betraying his trust. What was more, he had the inside grip on the situation; it would take months and a staff of auditors to check up on him. Highness might thunder. But so long as he kept his head he, Buderus, would hold the upper hand. Whatever happened, he was confident of the outcome. None the less he could wish it were behind him.

In three days it *was* over, and he was returning home triumphant beyond his rosiest hopes. He had beaten them all—the Cassel Jews, Rueppell & Harnier, Lennep, and the mighty Bethmanns themselves. The future of his children was assured!

The first encounter, on the evening of his arrival, was at best a draw. William, lofty, overbearing, injured and fussy, led off by demanding why his Director was so thick with the Rothschilds and so distant toward the Bethmanns. Exactly what was the reason that he so invariably favored those Jews of low antecedents and doubtful repute against the oldest and most honored Christian banking house in Germany? Buderus, a little disconcerted—he had expected a somewhat different opening—hedged and stammered. Why, there was no reason, other than the wish to do his best for His Electoral Serenity's interests. Devotion to his master was the tenderest, the only concern of his days and nights. William waved the generality aside with an impatient gesture. Then Buderus recovered some of his composure. The very superiority of the Gentile firms, he pointed out, counted against them at this time. Their high standards, their great past, prevented them from being useful in transactions which, since the French occupation, were necessarily of questionable legality. Indeed, the Bethmanns and the Christian houses generally, had shown little eagerness to risk their good name in the deposed ruler's cause. They were too much taken up with themselves to give a thought to Highness's misfortunes. The Rothschilds, on the other hand, precisely because of their humble origin, precisely because they had no ancient reputations to consider, were willing to do whatever was asked of them. They never refused a task, however difficult or dangerous, where his lordship was concerned. They were a god-send. He, Buderus, would hardly know what to do, or how to carry on his work, without them. They were Serenity's most loyal and devoted servants.

Buderus retired from the presence uncertain whether he had lost or gained ground. Alone in his chamber that night he went over the interview step by step. He decided that he had not acquitted himself as gallantly as he had expected. Without exactly losing the first round, he had let his master browbeat and confuse him. His choicest arguments were still unused. No, he would not risk another personal encounter if he could avoid it. He was too easily put out of countenance. Here in the quiet of his room he could think of any number of things he ought to have said. He would say them, now, in writing, away from that irritating, suspicious eye. He got up and went to work. The next day he handed William a long letter, categorically explaining his position. It was in effect a brief for the Rothschilds; and while it was by no means the last word that was to be said, it decided the argument.

Buderus began by frankly admitting that ever since the day of his master's regrettable departure, he had, with one or two exceptions, let the Rothschilds convert all the drafts coming from the Van Nottens in London. It had seemed to him good to do so because working through a single house was always more efficient and in these cruel times the only safe way. There was no need to dwell on the danger of too many people knowing his master's affairs just now. He had picked the Rothschilds for the reason already mentioned, as well as for the following:

Firstly. They were punctual with their payments. With money nowadays going out faster than it came in, this was of first importance. Indeed, on more than one occasion when there were pressing bills to pay, the Rothschilds had cheerfully settled up in advance of collection.

Secondly. They could be trusted absolutely to hold their tongues. When some disgruntled individual, unmindful of the injury to Serenity's interests, had recently informed against them, the police utterly failed to get a word out of them—not even after examining their books!

Thirdly. They always paid the exact rate of exchange prevailing on the day of sale.

Fourthly. They willingly attended to certain payments which need not be named and which were he to handle them himself would expose All-Highest to very serious consequences.

There were many other advantages about the arrangements that he could easily point out. However, he had said enough to show that, unlike certain people whose church affiliations were doubtless more commendable, the Rothschilds were loyal, discreet, business-like, honest, dependable and tireless in the service of the Most-High.

"And since," added Buderus sweetly, "I am unable to discover the smallest difference between a florin of Rothschild and a florin of Bethmann, I thought that I was doing everything for the best. It hurts me, however, to observe that Your Prince-Electoral Serenity, to judge by yesterday's verbal utterances, does not seem graciously to approve. I should, therefore, like to ask for definite instructions as to how the English checks are to be disposed of in future."

It was to him, he repeated, a matter of complete indifference. Only he must say right now in advance that after punctually carrying out highest orders, whatever they might be, he would not hold himself in any way responsible for any untoward consequences they might have. And this reminded him of something. His P.-E. S. doubtless recalled the sudden fit of mistrust that seized him earlier in the summer, when he issued that ill-timed order about sending on the checks here to Itzehoe. Well, it was no use now dwelling on the mischief that resulted in—the unpaid bills, the want suffered by interned Hessian officers and his own wounded pride. The one thing he was in duty bound to say was this:

"Had Yr. P.-E. S. been most graciously content not to interfere in my business, I could have sold 20,000 pounds sterling at 141½. Today they are worth at least six thousand florins less, and no human ingenuity on earth can now prevent that loss."

That thrust struck home. There was no fight left in William. He made a brave show of pretending that he was unconvinced at yet another conference. But he knew, and Buderus knew, that the battle was over. Serenissimus' religious preferences were not as extreme as all that. When it came to losing six thousand florins he was as open-minded as any French revolutionist. So he threw over Bethmann and the rest of them without much further ado. On the following day, amid mutual expressions of esteem and regret, peace was signed.

III

Returning home to Hanau—he had moved his headquarters to the little old capital, so as to be more accessible to his Frankfort associates and less in the way of the French usurpers at Cassel—Buderus went methodically to work to consolidate his victory. The Bethmanns were out. Lennep, as might have been expected, had during the summer eliminated himself by making a fiasco of the commission entrusted to him at Rendsburg. The man was not a financier to start with. In addition, he had had the ill-luck to lose a parcel of his master's bonds, which he insinuated certain Jews, including the Rothschilds, had stolen from him. Lastly, he had attempted to execute that commission without saying a word about it to Buderus; and that misstep had only given the latter the needed opening to crush him. That had done for him and for his patrons Rueppell & Harnier. The Cassel Jews need not worry anybody. They had no channels worth mentioning to Serenity's ear. They could be brushed aside without ceremony. So, competition all but wiped out, the Rothschilds had a clear field. The question now was, What were they going to do with their monopoly? No, even before that, the immediate problem was to see that they held it.

Buderus had from the beginning given much thought to that aspect of the situation. The Prince's flight, he perceived, was the greatest opportunity of his career and of his friends'. It not only made him all-powerful, so that he could put business into their hands to an extent which would have been out of the question in normal times; it enabled him and them to render services to the wealthy ruler in his hour of trouble and so to win his favor and gratitude, just when everyone was being cool to him. Before all else, then, there must be the strictest honesty and punctuality in money matters; everything they were entrusted with must be promptly and fully accounted for; he must never lose a penny through any fault of theirs. If losses occurred, they must suffer them themselves—and make them up in ways less obvious. But that was not enough. They must play the courtiers, wait on him and coddle him and cater to him in every way possible, regardless of time, effort or expense. They would find it worth their while. Highness loved flattery and attention; he was used to it and expected it; he would love it all the more now.

The keen young men knew wisdom when they heard it. It needed no urging from Buderus to tell them that this policy would be its own reward. All they required of him was a bit of prompting now and then as to the surest way to please the man he knew so well. When they opened their places in Hamburg that summer, they made the most of their nearness to Denmark to lend a hand with the transporting of the exile's treasures. One or two of the precious boxes were obligingly taken care of at their Hamburg premises till they could be safely moved further. A number of the coffers and parcels were relayed through them to Lawaetz, who saw them to their destination in Gottorp, Rendsburg, Itzehoe and subsequently in Prague. From their home base in Frankfort they disbursed the salaries of Hessian agents, soldiers and others in the former ruler's pay, sometimes deducting the outlay from Buderus's deposits, often uncomplainingly advancing the money out of their own pockets. Loans undertaken by William just before his banishment and partly liquidated but now threatening to turn bad, were taken over by them, further payments stopped if necessary, and the irate borrowers faced. No charge was made for any of these ticklish services. They were the unselfish Rothschilds' contributions to the comfort and peace of mind of their noble patron in his misfortune. Buderus had hardly overstated the case when he had told his master that without their support he would be helpless.

Buderus, however, did not intend to recline on his laurels. His victory at Itzehoe was a justification of his good counsel. So far, so good. But he knew his Prince too well to assume that any understanding with him was final. There would be other fusses no doubt, as the Rothschild-Buderus program went on toward its fulfilment. Serenity was not likely to submit to the very next step without a struggle. The competitors, temporarily routed, were bound to reshape their lines and attack again. This was little more than a breathing spell. It was the part of prudence to utilize it in preparation for future trouble.

The votive offerings to Highness must not only continue, they must be increased.

Waiting on William became henceforth a regular feature of the concern's business. To facilitate the work—and also to escape the excessive curiosity of the Napoleonic police—the Rothschilds bought a coach of their own. In it one member or another of the family was constantly journeying between Frankfort and the cities of refuge. Kalmann, the least gifted of the five brothers, who was by now a young man of nineteen, did most of the traveling. The eldest, Amschel, often remained within call for months on end, buying and selling and running errands for the Prince and the Countess von Schlotheim, advising him on money matters, bringing him news of home, of political events, of the activities of the French in Hesse—performing in short the combined functions of an ambassador, a personal manager, a secret agent and a courier. When William migrated to Prague the next year, it was the Rothschilds who helped dispose of the house at Itzehoe and secured for him the Zatory farm near the Bohemian capital. Their carriage was equipped with a secret compartment, in which reports from the Hessian regency council, bundles of securities and other bulky articles could be conveyed. Ordinary mail was concealed on the messengers' person.

The personal ties with the Prince were knitted closer in other ways as well. Occasionally old Meyer, as the titular head of the concern, wrote the exile a cheer-up letter, assuring him of his loyalty "to the last drop of my blood," advising him not to take too high and mighty a line with the conqueror, volunteering to interpose on his behalf with the Empress Josephine on her expected visit to Frankfort, and to use his influence with Governor General Lagrange by way of conserving the ex-ruler's property. The aged merchant knew, of course, that he was promising more than he could perform; but Buderus believed there was no harm in being hopeful. It would keep his master in good humor toward the firm; he rather liked feeling that people were exerting themselves in his interests, even if their efforts came to nothing. And it so happened that the Rothschilds did in fact play no small part afterwards in easing the rigors of the occupation for the Elector and his faithful. For that thanks to the interesting comradeship which grew up between a Catholic archbishop and the Jewish merchant family. Of the good prelate, more anon.

Just what use, however, all these ministrations were, is problematical. For the fact is that the peace made at Itzehoe did not last. Of course, renewed friction might have come sooner and gone further, had the Rothschilds been less thoughtful. There is no knowing. The Serene William was a difficult man, without a doubt. Hopelessly mistrustful certain people—Buderus, for instance—found him. He may have been. And then again, it is possible he was merely taking bankers' helpfulness and unselfishness at a discount. He had a shrewd and cynical streak in him. However all this might be, it was not many months after September 1807 that his suspicions woke again and the tension between Prince and Director quickly rose to the breaking point. And for this there appeared to be grounds.

Years and years ago it had become an established rule that Buderus render each month an account of his transactions. Upon William's precipitate exit there had followed such confusion, however, that Buderus was compelled to depart from custom. This was one of the agenda, it would seem, at the Itzehoe conference. With a reduced staff, with the French police watching his every step, with the administration divided between Hesse and Denmark, with the mails in chaos and less safe than ever, Buderus argued that in the interests of prudence, if for no other reason, he should be permitted to lump the entire year 1807 in a single report. Highness, surprisingly, agreed. He had his reasonable moments, at intervals. He realized what difficulties his man was working under, and he was not disposed to add to them. But he assumed that as soon as the year was over the report would promptly follow. When, therefore, 1808 came round and month succeeded month without a scrap of an accounting reaching him, he was first surprised, then annoyed and finally indignant. He urged, he pleaded, he became dangerous and threatened, he resorted to reprisals; the report did not come. It never did come till October of 1810, and then it was so tangled-up as to be unintelligible to the auditors. Thereupon William ordered Buderus to present himself at Prague and explain it. Buderus refused, and William made unprincely insinuations and held up the clearances on all the other accounts. In retaliation Buderus threatened not to dip another pen in ink till his reports were duly and formally acknowledged. So menaced, Serenissimus mended his manners and assured Herr von Carlshausen of his complete confidence. Only why not come to Prague? Now Buderus's tone also softened: He would be glad to take the trip, as soon as the political situation permitted. But alas! Napoleon continued to make war. And so the report for the year 1807 remained undeciphered till that triumphant day when, following the Battle of Leipzig, the Elector was carried into Cassel upon the shoulders of his jubilant subjects. Some of the clearances were still to be signed while the Emperor Napoleon was on his way to St. Helena.

There is no overwhelming reason for doubting Buderus's sincerity in this whole affair. There are only some remarkable coincidences. In the summer of 1808 when his master was becoming unpleasant, Buderus defended his delays quite convincingly. He must, he said, do every bit of writing and figuring with his own hands, attend to an enormous correspondence which in these times required the most painstaking care both in wording and posting, go on numerous journeys, carry on complicated negotiations with all sorts of people—and all this in the strictest secrecy. Besides:

> "It is surely most graciously known that my papers are hidden away, so that I could not (even if I had the time) possibly work at my accounts. I trust I shall soon be able to fetch them again, and then by taking extra time at night I shall try to relieve Your Electoral Serenity of uneasiness on this score, and prove that I have not a single penny of Your Highest Self's money in my hands."

Could anything be more straightforward? And yet—

Napoleon had no sooner seized Hesse than he went vigorously to work to collect the deposed ruler's loans. In those three and a half years between the spring of 1807 and the autumn of 1810, while William was waiting for his Director's accounting, repeated and ever-increasing inducements were offered the debtors to pay up what they owed to the imperial treasury. Concurrently the exiled Elector took steps, through Buderus, to have his money returned to himself. A large number of the borrowers settled with the usurper; many others preferred to redeem their bonds from the rightful lender. In some cases Buderus collected the sums in full, in others he must meet the terms offered by the French. Of all these complex transactions no accounting was rendered till three years later.

Interesting to note also is the fact that between 1807 and 1810 the contraband exported by Nathan Rothschild from England went on continually mounting. The biggest month was July 1810. By October of the same year Nathan had found more interesting ways to invest the Elector's funds, as well as other and larger ways of access to them.

Still it is not impossible that the two sets of occurrences have nothing to do with one another. The coincidences may be purely fortuitous.

CHAPTER V

POLICE!

THE French seizure of their country was accepted with resignation neither by the populace nor by its banished ruler. The Hessians were not exactly devoted to their miserly prince, but they loved the foreign usurper even less. Such is the curious sentiment of race. Napoleon and his royal brother Jerome and their lieutenants were no indulgent masters, it is true. They squeezed the last sou out of their German subjects, and carried the money out of the country, and in general conducted themselves as the victors in conquered territory always do. But the rightful and hereditary William and his predecessors, who had been governing Hesse for five centuries, had done precisely those things. The French made no abstruse distinction between public funds and the private purse of the chief of state, and governed by edict without so much as pretending to consult the pleasure of the governed, and when they wanted men for war, as they constantly did, they recruited every able-bodied male they could get their hands on and marched him off to wherever he was most needed, irrespective of his religious convictions on the subject. But it was by just such ideals of statecraft that the Landgraves had made William the richest money-lender that had ever sat on a throne. Nevertheless, the Hessians believed they could see a difference, and strenuously objected to the change. They addressed petitions to the Emperor for the restoration of their legitimate Prince, vowing that they had always been "completely happy under his rule;" and these being roughly dismissed, they took secret and solemn oaths to drive the foreigner out by force.

William's preference for the old régime is somewhat easier to understand. It was also rather more fervent and enduring. To exchange his lonely exile for dear, familiar scenes, the dethroned Elector shied at no weapon and scorned no ally. He prayed to heaven, to his subjects, to his supplanter. The most transparent charlatan could get money out of him by promising to use his influence at the Tuileries. Half a dozen such obliging diplomats were at one time exerting themselves in the cause. Simultaneously William, from his refuge, bombarded his accredited envoys at all the capitals, his poor wife, his daughter the Duchess of Gotha, the Austrian Emperor and no end of other people, likely and unlikely, to plead for him with Napoleon and to assure him of his loyalty and devotion. But as Napoleon had other plans in mind for Hesse, as he was, besides, more keenly interested in William's well-known millions than in his slightly tainted allegiance, and knew he could have only one or the other, he went after the cash and let the assurances go; so that nothing but snubs came of all these far-flung endeavors. The anxious Prince, for his part, was not quite so hopeful as to put all his wine in one vessel; wherefore, whilst his go-betweens were busy in Paris and elsewhere, he joined the various German liberation movements, went regularly to church so as to induce the Almighty to bless the hand of Napoleon's would-be assassins, and encouraged his agents at home to foment revolts which he undertook to subsidize, "in the event that they achieved their purpose."

It goes without saying that the imperial deputies and officials in Cassel, Hanau and Frankfort had more than an inkling of these latter enterprises, and kept a watchful eye open on all and sundry who still maintained contact, direct or indirect, with the absent monarch. And thus it came about that when the French, some two months after the occupation, upon ordering the Hessian military to don the imperial uniform and make themselves ready for service in Spain and upon being met with rebellious shouts of "Death to the invaders!" proceeded to ferret out the ringleaders and accessories of the plot, some good friend whispered to them that if they would go around to Number 148 Judengasse, to a house called "Zum gruenen Schild" but at present occupied by a family named Rothschild, they would probably find what they were looking for and maybe something more for good measure.

As a matter of fact, the information turned out to be mistaken. That is to say, the police did not find what they were looking for. They found, instead, a Jewish family of the middle class, consisting of an elderly pair, several daughters with their husbands, one or more married sons with their wives, and one or two unmarried younger members. The group was obviously worried and frightened; but, upon being questioned, gave what appeared to be a good account of themselves. They denied all knowledge of the soldiers' uprising and of the exiled ruler's affairs. They promptly, even cheerfully, produced their books when asked for them; and an examination of these seemed to prove that the family had told the truth. Not a trace of any dealings with the Prince or his agents could be found in them.

And that, for immediate purposes, was the end of the

AMSCHEL
VON ROTHSCHILD

first encounter of the Rothschilds with the Napoleonic authorities. All in all, it was the family's inning. They had had a scare, it is true; but even that was not an unmixed evil: it gave them confidence for future searches, if there should be any. Their skilful conduct throughout was, moreover, likely to avert suspicion later on. Most important of all, they had not slipped up on a thing. The police seemed to have gone away no wiser than they had come. His Serene Highness would be delighted when he heard that; it should strengthen his belief in their ability, their discreetness, their loyalty. He should hear of it, of course, at the first opportunity. The good Director Buderus must see to it.

This was in the summer of 1807. A month or so later, as might be recalled, Buderus was facing his master at Itzehoe. In defense of the Rothschilds and of his close relations with them, he did surely enough cite the incident with the French at Frankfort. It was one of the things that impressed the Prince and ended the discussion.

But the Napoleonic police, as it turned out, took a lot more convincing than that.

II

It would have been little short of a miracle if the curiosity of the occupation authorities had been appeased by that initial visit. Their failure on that occasion to connect the house with the Elector's plots had been disappointing, but it did not allay their doubts. They drew from it the simple enough conclusion—the firm was keeping a double set of books. It was an irritating device; however, there was no help for it; the merchants would use it, to escape taxes and cover up doubtful transactions. The Jewish family's resort to it was anything but reassuring; it only indicated that there were aspects of their business which they wanted to keep dark. The house of the Green Shield with its dependencies on the Schnurgasse, the Kurtrierplatz and elsewhere would bear watching.

Exactly what those very busy young men were up to remained, for the time being, to be found out. Nor did it look as if it were going to be easy, even afterwards, to bring them to book. They were about as keen and tough and slippery and uncommunicative a lot as any police officer in His Majesty's service would care to meet. For all that, no amount of shrewdness could possibly keep their hand concealed forever. They were much too active, their enterprises were too varied and numerous, for that.

There was, to begin with, the refugee Prince with his millions. An undetermined but certainly a huge part of his fortune was known to have been left behind, in the form of outstanding local loans, in securities of every sort, in jewelry, silver and what not. Gossip had it that this entire treasure had on the night of the flight been rushed to the Rothschild premises and that it still remained in their care. However that might be, a lively commerce between him and them was obviously going on. For the longest time every one in Frankfort had been suspecting that Buderus von Carlshausen was on a certain footing of intimacy with the Jewish merchant family. After October 1, 1807, that suspicion had turned into fact. This Buderus was by common knowledge the man whom the exiled William had left in charge of his financial affairs. It was clearly his job to rescue his master's loans from the imperial grasp, to gather up the tangible property and get it across the frontier to its owner, and in other ways to look after the ex-ruler's pecuniary interests. But Buderus was keeping mouse-quiet at Hanau and on his little country estate of Carlshausen nearby, while his associates the Rothschilds were working like beavers and their carriage was uninterruptedly on the road. It was as simple as two and two: The young bankers were the link between the flown Elector and his man on the ground.

That was one thing. Then there was another. William, as the police had long ago found out, had left behind him in Cassel a secret ministry, or regency council, to represent his political interests. It was they who directed the agents and conspirators in Hesse, who kept the communications open with the League of Virtue and other German liberation societies, who watched over the disbanded army chiefs and their subordinates, and who inspired the petitions and the popular patriotic fervor. The council, the agents, the old officers and soldiers must live. Their master, through orders on Buderus, saw that they did not starve. And the Rothschilds were Buderus's bankers.

Then, again, there was the Continental Blockade, which prohibited trading with Napoleon's arch enemy, England. The Rothschilds not only had a shop in which English cotton and English colonial wares, such as coffee and tea and indigo, were sold; one of their number was residing and doing business in London; his father and brothers on this side of the Channel kept in touch with him regularly both from Frankfort and from a branch office which they had latterly opened at the port of Hamburg. This absent member seemed in effect to be one of the firm, its representative in the enemy capital. And meantime the blockade was being patently violated by somebody; for the Continent, notably Frankfort, was filling up with contraband. It looked rather as if the concern might be having a hand in the smuggling trade.

In sum, even without anything unusual happening, the sheer complexion of the Rothschild affairs and contacts had a suspicious color. In disturbed times like these, when extraordinary events were crowding one another off the calendar, when even the most peaceful citizen of an occupied country had all he could do to keep off the police blotters, a great firm on the make such as the House of Rothschild could hardly expect to escape attention. That first little episode in the summer of 1807 was nothing but a prelude. Between that year and 1811 no fewer than five actions were taken, four of them in their raids on the premises or summonses to headquarters. The French authorities had scented blood and meant to trail the quarry to its lair.

To make it easier for them, there were the coreligionists of the Rothschilds, to whom the progress of the brothers was not an agreeable sight.

III

On the 7th of July, 1807, Napoleon and the Tsar of Russia signed at Tilsit a treaty of peace and friendship, whereby the two emperors agreed to divide Europe between them. Five days later the Electorate of Hesse along with some other fragments of the Confederation of the Rhine was transformed into the Kingdom of Westphalia. At Cassel preparations were at once begun for the entry of the new monarch into his new capital. Two weeks before Christmas Jerome Napoleon I ascended the throne amid the cheers of his loyal Hessian subjects.

Governor General Lagrange, who had hitherto ruled the province in the name of the Emperor, and who had proved so obliging in the matter of dispatching Prince William's coffers out of the country, became Minister of War in the royal cabinet. He had hardly taken office, however, when rumors of the unkindest and most disquieting sort began reaching the palace on the Wilhelmshoehe. If they were to be believed, Lagrange had as Governor General not performed his duty as faithfully as could have been wished. Thus, among other things, he had confiscated eleven million thalers of the Elector's money, which had been duly delivered to the imperial exchequer in Paris. This he had reported to be the sum total of the former ruler's fortune still within reach. It now appeared, however, that at least an equal amount, consisting of negotiable securities and other things of value, had somehow slipped through the lines into the hands of their outlawed owner; that, in addition, a great assortment of loans to princes, merchants and others of the vicinity had by the General's indulgence been permitted to be repaid to the original lender, instead of being collected for His Majesty in accordance with the Decree of St. Cloud and other decrees; that a not inconsiderable number of such loans were still outstanding; and that, lastly, the grateful ex-Elector had rewarded the amiable Lagrange with a little gift of one million francs, besides gallantly presenting a memento to Madame Lagrange in the form of a necklace valued at 30,000 francs.

In view of these rumors, which inquiry showed to be not unfounded, it became the painful duty of King Jerome Napoleon I to offer the portfolio of War to some incumbent of sterner composition and to banish the good

Lagrange from his royal presence. It seeming improbable, moreover, that the negotiations between the refugee Elector and the late Governor General had been conducted without intermediaries on the ground, or that their execution had been effected without the aid of subordinate French officials, the inquiry was widened with a view to discovering such possible accessories. The trail led, on the French side, to certain of the former Governor's immediate aides, and, on the Serene William's, to Buderus, his preferred bankers and one or two others. Lagrange's dismissal occurred in January 1808, only a few weeks after Jerome's arrival in Cassel; the supplementary investigation lasted till mid-summer of the same year.

The upshot of it all was that Buderus as well as his old rival Lennep was arrested and taken under guard to Mayence. Buderus freely admitted his continued loyalty to his banished master and his concern with the latter's affairs, but no amount of grilling or threats would produce anything more. He was, he insisted, merely His Highness's bookkeeper and factotum; there was nothing illegal about that. Yes, he was sending reports and balance sheets and that sort of thing by post to Denmark, to his employer's present address. If the authorities had anything against his doing so, he would, of course, have to stop. No, the police were quite willing to have him continue. Only he must submit all papers, before posting them, to His Majesty's servants. With this warning, suggestive of future interviews, both men were allowed to go.

The Rothschilds' turn had come earlier. Old Meyer being ill in bed, Salomon responded to the summons by appearing at the court house in Frankfort. He entered a sweeping denial, of course; his firm, he declared, had had nothing to do with the Lagrange bribery episode. It happened to be quite true. That entire affair had been handled by William's political representatives, not by his financial agent. The secret regency council had seen the Governor General, had come to an understanding with him as to terms, and had then merely asked Buderus to provide the wherewithal. Partly because Highness was just then in bad humor with the Rothschilds—it was the time of the Bethmann and Rueppell & Harnier insinuations—and partly because the Jewish bankers were likely to arouse jealousy in mercantile circles and suspicion in official quarters, the Prince's ministers directed that the payments be made through a concern of their own choosing. The Rothschilds' hands were thus clean. Salomon, however, could not deny that certain correspondence from Holstein reached Buderus through his address; and upon being ordered to deliver the same to police headquarters in future, he was excused.

No more enlightening was the examination of Bansa & Son, bankers, the concern above alluded to. They, too, entered a general denial, they likewise cheerfully submitted their records, and these, equally with the Rothschilds', contained not a solitary mention of Governor General Lagrange. The Frankfort schools of business taught double-entry bookkeeping as a regular part of the curriculum, clearly.

The Royal Westphalian police were sure they were on the right trail. Their failure to bag their game baffled them. Their doubts increased, and so did their vigilance.

IV

The erection of a kingdom upon the ruins of his beloved Electorate, the Majesty whereof adorned not himself but the son of a Corsican lawyer, was a cruel blow to William. "Most terrible of all days!" he moaned in his journal. "I am deposed. Hesse, my dear Hesse, knocked down to the Kingdom of Westphalia. . . . My house has reigned uninterruptedly for 542 years, since Henry the Child, through twenty-one rulers, attained with me its highest peak, and now has totally ceased to be! O God, give me strength to bear this misfortune as thou wouldst have me, without whimpering."

The prayer must have been granted; for though he never ceased complaining, his courage did return after a time. The wretched fiasco in which the Christmas soldiers' rebellion had ended had not disheartened him. It had on the contrary given him much hope. For the lesson which he drew from it was, not that the usurper was invincible, but that his people were ready to die for their Prince. Logically, therefore, he buckled on his saber for fresh efforts. How very much in earnest he now was may be judged from the fact he no longer insisted on bartering Hessian troops for English subsidies (as he had obstinately done before his flight) but volunteered to put an army corps of four thousand men into the field at his own expense, as his contribution to the anti-French war then brewing, and even to help with money in the ambitious plans for a general revolt in Northern Germany which were being fostered by the Prussian minister Von Stein. The corps, to be sure, subsequently shrank to thirteen hundred men and not quite three hundred horses; but he did design the uniforms himself, and anyhow it was nobody's fault that recruiting was so slow.

The whole adventure misfired, unfortunately. A letter of Von Stein's dealing with the projected war and uprisings fell into the hands of the French, and this caused Napoleon to demand that the Prussian king dismiss and banish his minister. In April (1809) the Austrians were beaten at Eckmuehl, by way of a prelude to the crushing defeat at Wagram. On the same day French artillery scattered the premature rebellion of the under-armed and badly-led Hessian peasantry.

As might have been expected, the royal police at Cassel once again determined to hunt down the financial agents of the plot. Poor Lennep was at once taken into custody, and locked up in the fortress at Mayence where for weeks he was treated like a common criminal. Then, on the 9th of May, a detachment of soldiers commanded by a police officer showed up at Buderus's home in Hanau with a warrant for his arrest. Buderus happened to be with his family at his country place in Carlshausen that day. A sister of his was alone in the town house. Pointing a gun at her head, the officer demanded to know where her brother was hiding. After much rough-handling of the lady, breaking open of desk-drawers and rummaging through files, they were persuaded to leave. They then proceeded to Carlshausen, seized what papers they could find, and marched Buderus as their prisoner back to Hanau. There he was severely grilled for two days and finally released under bail.

The Rothschilds came off rather easier. Residing in Frankfort, they were not within the jurisdiction of Jerome's kingdom. To be sure, Frankfort was, like Hesse, part of Napoleon's empire; it was, however, a separate unit, and was governed by a gentleman of quite another stripe. Archbishop Carl von Dalberg, sometime Elector of Mayence, had found favor in the imperial sight by doing the preliminary diplomatic work in the formation of the Confederation of the Rhine. A good Teuton, an easy-going, kindly man, an ambitious prelate, he was convinced that Napoleon was destined to do infinitely more for the advancement of German unity than all the petty, selfish, mutually distrusting native princelings. For his services the Emperor appointed him primate of the Confederation, and assigned him the City of Frankfort as his more or less sovereign domain. His bailiwick was left intact even after the anointed Jerome entered his kingdom. In 1810 Napoleon named him Grand Duke of Frankfort and gave him Hanau for his capital.

Thus the Rothschilds, though in fact subjects of imperial France, came directly under the allegiance of Archbishop Dalberg; and he and they were the best of friends. The Jewish firm had from the beginning made a point of cultivating the good prelate. His cloth notwithstanding, he was a man of the most liberal views; also, he was ambitious and hard up. The bankers, on the other hand, had ample funds, and their affairs just then were of such a nature that influence in high quarters was desirable at any cost. As time was to prove, Dalberg's friendship was decisive in at least one crisis in the family's history.

It surely was a life-saver in the spring of 1809.

Having disposed of Lennep and Buderus, the Westphalian Commissioner of Police, Savagner, gave his attention to the Jewish banking house. He made up his mind, now once and for all, to finish with those bright young men. He had had enough of idle hearings and farcical examinations of their dummy books. He wanted the lot of them jailed. He wanted them jailed, and he wanted their places, all of them, thoroughly ransacked. Evidence that they had played any part in the recent revolt was, to be sure, lacking. No matter. It was manifest to everyone that they had their hands in a dozen unlawful operations. Well, this was the time to bring them to book. The late uprising was merely the needed pretext.

But Dalberg, it appeared, was of another mind. He was sorry to seem unobliging to a friendly neighbor state; but really he could not have his subjects annoyed, let alone imprisoned, on mere suspicion. He refused the warrants, therefore, for which Savagner asked. He did something more: he quietly let the Rothschilds know that trouble was brewing for them, and that though he was doing his best, he might be unable to avert it altogether. With this timely warning, the energetic young people set about preparing for the worst. The boxes of documents belonging to the Prince were during the night hauled out of their hiding place in the house cellar and laboriously transferred through a subterranean passage to the long-disused space underneath the court which in times gone by had served the dwellers of the Judengasse as a refuge from rioting mobs. Papers of their own which were likely to arouse embarrassing attention were similarly disposed of. The merchandise, which just at this time came in especially large shipments from certain countries unapproved of by the French, it was, of course, impossible to whisk out of sight. The most one could do was to remove tell-tale wrappers and tags. That done, the family carefully rehearsed the threatened interview, and sat down to pray for more power to the Archbishop's elbow.

Events showed the wisdom of these preparations. In the next day or two the good Dalberg was rather forcibly reminded that there were limits to his sovereignty. Pressure exerted from Cassel via the imperial envoy at Frankfort could not be ignored. A point had, therefore, to be yielded. Of the arrest of the bankers Dalberg still would not hear. With no more evidence than Savagner had to offer, it would be unconstitutional and outrageous. However, if the Westphalian authorities really believed it would be of any use to them, why, of course, they could have a search warrant. But propriety and due respect for the sovereign dignity of Frankfort demanded that an officer of the city state assist at the proceedings. He must insist on that, naturally.

So Dalberg's man assisted, and did what he could as public defender. None the less, the visit was by no means an empty formality. The search, begun at the house on the Judengasse, was carried into the merchants' dependencies in town. Old Meyer, though again ill in bed, was questioned and cross-questioned most thoroughly, and so was Guetele, his wife, their daughter Jettchen, who was in charge of the cash box, two sons—the others being on the road—and their wives. Perfunctorily, too, the visitors glanced at the books. They had learned by this time how little they must expect from that source.

A certain directness and self-assurance marked the authorities' conduct of the personal examinations. The questions had not only been written out in advance; they seemed to be based on information of a peculiarly intimate nature, as if someone on the inside of William's affairs had had a hand in their preparation. It disconcerted the family not a little.

Old Meyer especially was upset by this unexpected development. The apparent omniscience of the police played havoc with his poise. A sudden question brought from him the admission that Buderus had earlier in the year deposited twenty thousand florins with the firm. It had been drawn out again, however, by checks payable to a number of persons. Who these persons were, he could not remember, nor anything about them. He was an ailing aged man, and his memory was not what it used to be. Could he at least explain how it was that the transactions had not been entered in the books? Yes, he could do that. The whole matter was in the nature of a friendly personal service, and Buderus invariably made good each disbursement; thus the account remained constant and did not have to be kept track of. Thereupon his inquisitor pounced on him. That being the case, Savagner demanded, was it not true that the bank still owed the ex-Prince's man the full twenty thousand florins? The confused old man conceding that it must be so, was commanded to hand the sum over to the imperial treasury, in accordance with the Edict of St. Cloud.

This, after all the warnings and rehearsals, was a sad slip. It hit Buderus particularly hard. Here he had been harping for three years on the discreetness and self-sacrifice of the Rothschilds, and now he must report that! He would have to do a deal of explaining, and stress the far greater losses which the faithful bankers had prevented.

The unerring intelligence that guided Savagner's men

in the questioning seemed also to inspire their search through the buildings. To the riot cellar, where William's boxes lay interred, they miraculously did not penetrate. But the way they hustled through the stores of merchandise and eyed each piece of English stuff betrayed a remarkable expertness. With every identifying mark removed, they could naturally do no more than think things. But their discoveries and the Rothschilds' halting explanations forebode trouble in the future. It came the following year, and hit many other people besides the Rothschilds.

Meantime it transpired by whose hand the police had been so ably directed on this occasion—as well as on some previous ones no doubt. The questionnaire had actually been prepared and the constables coached by one of the Rothschilds' old friends among the Jews of Cassel. The little group of merchants in the Hessian capital had never forgiven their Frankfort rivals for grabbing off Herr Buderus and his flesh-pots. When they saw, however, such powerful houses as the Bethmanns' going down in defeat before them, they abandoned all hope of redress through appeals to Highness direct, and adopted the purely negative tactics of trying to injure the upstart concern through the new régime. They were aware, of course, that by so doing they would strike quite as much at Buderus's master as at his Jewish associates. They did not mind taking that risk. They were, to begin with, half-convinced that the Electorate would never be restored, not at least in William's lifetime. The Bonapartes were growing stronger every day, and the exiled Prince was a gouty old reprobate. Besides, the more of his money fell into the hands of his conquerors, the less would there be for the Rothschilds to play with. Lastly, though they were careful not to come out into the open, they rather felt that a bit of quiet intimidation would have the desired effect on the faint-hearted refugee.

A gentleman named Levi was especially active in the pursuit of this policy. Son of a merchant with whom old Meyer had clashed years ago, married to a daughter of Michel Simon (later M. S. Meylert), one of the leading bankers in Cassel, and associated with the latter's firm, he had good cause for viewing the rise of these once negligible competitors of both his houses with ill-feeling. With his knowledge of the Elector's affairs, his wide acquaintance in the Jewish community of Frankfort, and his former dealings with the Rothschilds themselves, he was in a first-rate position to help the police where the bright young brothers were concerned. He was a little too confident, however, this time; and his part in the proceedings, thanks to Archbishop Dalberg's good offices, became known. It helped Buderus to eliminate the house of Michel Simon from the Princely finances for good and all. Moreover, as this raid on the Rothschild premises led to much unpleasantness for other merchants in due time, Levi succeeded in bringing upon himself the execration of the Frankfort business community as well. It taught him to coöperate with the French authorities more cautiously in future.

V

The customs authorities in Paris had been aware all along that a lively trade in contraband was going on across the Channel and the North Sea. Some of Napoleon's advisers had for some time, therefore, been in favor of modifying the Edict of Berlin. The blockade, obviously, did not prevent Britain from selling her own and her colonies' products on the Continent; it merely robbed the imperial treasury of much needed revenue. Would it not then be wiser to open the coasts to a limited list of articles, tax them heavily, and use the money to tighten the restrictions on the rest? The Emperor, being a soldier, not an economist, was not moved by this logic. He was determined to strangle the "nation of shopkeepers;" besides, though there was doubtless considerable smuggling, the extent of it was, he thought, much exaggerated.

The police news from Frankfort, however, in the summer of 1809, obliged him to change his views. It was not so much that the premises of a particular merchant family named Rothschild had been found to be crammed with goods of suspicious origin. It was the inescapable conclusion to be drawn from that accidental discovery that was disquieting. Frankfort was a great, bustling commercial center. People of all kinds were getting rich there every day. Never in all its history had it been as prosperous as in these last two years since the Continental Blockade. Was it not evident that others besides the Rothschilds were engaged in the forbidden trade? And Frankfort was only one town.

It was many months before this reasoning could reach the Tuileries. Napoleon was that year divorcing Josephine and marrying Marie-Louise, as well as winning fresh victories on the battlefield. In August of 1810, however, he took action. The Edict of Trianon, dated that month, left the restrictions on British manufactured goods unchanged, but declared colonial products admissible under duties averaging about forty-five per cent. At the same time a secret agent named Thiard was sent up to Frankfort to see whether the suspicions about its merchants were justified. Early in October Thiard sent in his report. Its nature was such that Napoleon immediately framed a new decree especially addressed to the affairs of that city. It charged that Frankfort was full of contraband and ordered the unlawful goods seized. Though the document was at once communicated to the authorities there, it was not to be published for several days, lest the smugglers take warning. On the 30th two regiments of infantry marched into the city and began a general raid on shops and warehouses. No fewer than two hundred and thirty-four merchants were caught unawares. Several millions in taxes on colonial goods were collected by the French, and a quantity of English manufactured goods was seized and publicly burned. By a lucky stroke, however, the Rothschild stocks were just on that day all but depleted of contraband. Though Nathan had only some weeks earlier sent over from London his largest shipments, the raiders found no English goods whatever and a mere trifle in indigo and some kindred substances. On these they willingly paid the demanded imposts.

It is a fact, however, that from this time forth the smuggling of goods ceased to be a part of the firm's commerce. Whether this was because they had tired of being eyed with suspicion, or because the blockade was too efficiently maintained, or because they found some new outlet for their energies, remains to be seen.

Certain it is that the authorities, aided as usual by

jealous people in Cassel and Frankfort, continued to burden the house with its attentions. Indeed, the most irksome display of French mistrustfulness toward the family was not to occur till a year later. But of that in its place.

CHAPTER VI

THANK GOD FOR NAPOLEON

YEARS later—it was in 1834, to be precise—Nathan Rothschild told friends at a dinner party in London how he had got his start. He said, among other things:

> "The Prince of Hesse-Cassel gave my father his money; there was no time to lose; he sent it to me. I had £600,000 arrive unexpectedly by post; and I put it to such good use that the Prince made me a present of all his wine and linen."

This bit of reminiscence has had a curious destiny. The many authors who have since written about the history of the family have treated it either as literal truth or as an out-and-out invention. It is really neither. It is simply fact, slightly embroidered. Nathan did receive £600,000 of the Prince's money—and a little bit over—and he did put it to excellent use. Only it came to him neither unexpectedly nor in a lump. Whether the Prince was so grateful for the *way* Nathan used it as to make him a present of anything, appears more than doubtful. Several barrels of wine from the palace cellars were during the exile actually stored with the Rothschilds, but His Highness not only asked them back on his return but was rather horrid about it. Of linen the records say nothing at all.

The plain truth of the matter is that Nathan begged and schemed for that money, and left no stone unturned to get it, for all of two years; that it was two years more before he got anything like the entire amount; that, though he invested it so skilfully as to make the fame and fortune of his whole family, the Prince was so little pleased with the relationship that he threatened to withdraw from it altogether; and lastly, that while William lost little money by the transaction, he worried and fretted himself almost into the grave over it, and had to wait years before Rothschild even began to give him the accounting he demanded.

As far back as the spring of 1807 Nathan had begun casting covetous glances at the more substantial reserves of the Elector's fortune. William, as he knew, had many years before invested some half a million sterling in the British "Funds" or Consols. He knew it, because his father had away back in the 'eighties begun discounting the London dividend checks for the Prince, and because he himself was now collecting those same remittances for him through the London bank of Van Notten & Company. It occurred to him that perhaps the surest way to get access to those reserves would be to have his brothers persuade Buderus to induce Serenity to put through him, say, an equal sum into the same securities. There could not be a safer investment than Consols, and there could not be a better time to buy them than right now. What was more to the point, Nathan needed the money in the worst way. In London, where he had now been for three years, he saw men not half as clever as himself making fortunes every day on the bullion market, in the cotton trade, in war supplies, in stock exchange operations and what not. He could do as much and more; but his hands were tied for lack of capital. What, he asked, his brothers, was the good of having Buderus in the firm if he could not do a little thing like that?

But the cautious Buderus, on being approached, counseled patience. Therefore Nathan was obliged to see what he could accomplish through other channels. In London was the Elector's chargé d'affaires Lorentz. Nathan secured an introduction to him; and so ably did he present the case for Consols and Rothschilds that the diplomat was won over, at least to the extent of conveying the idea to his sovereign. Unhappily, the démarche proved worse than useless. Nathan was no doubt right in thinking 1807 a good time to invest in the "Funds;" but he overlooked the fact that it was equally the worst possible time for any Rothschild to approach Highness with any proposition whatever. For it happened to be the inauspicious month of August, when the Frankfort rivals of the family were bombarding Itzehoe with rumors and insinuations, and when Serenissimus was peremptorily summoning Buderus to explain what in heaven's name he meant by being so thick with those unspeakable people of the Judengasse. So the upshot of Nathan's efforts was that William, replying to Lorentz, wrote that should that fellow again dare inquire about All-Highest's affairs he was to be unceremoniously shown the door. "For it is the farthest thing from My intentions to have any dealings with him."

Almost immediately after this cold rebuff, however, the prospect brightened. The very next month, as will be recalled, Buderus did journey to Itzehoe and succeeded in calming his master's fears. The effect of that reassurance was—not, indeed, to evoke the hoped-for half million sterling—but at least to dispose the Prince favorably toward the firm in case he should some day decide to put more money into Consols. Hardly had that preliminary been disposed of than along came Napoleon to attend to the rest. In the ensuing fifteen months or eighteen, political and military events so shaped themselves as to destroy virtually every other investment market for the Prince's millions and to leave him scarcely any other choice.

II

The years 1806–08 were a period of uninterrupted catastrophe for the Electoral finances. One after another Prussia, Denmark, Austria, Russia—all the smiling lands where he had for long years been reaping such rich harvests—became submerged. The Bonaparte inundation gradually spread over and engulfed them. Some were conquered outright, others succumbed to alliances with the usurper, the rest were driven into bankruptcy.

The greatest of these calamities was, of course, the seizure of his own beloved Hesse and contiguous lands. Yet so long as the reasonable Lagrange Governor-Generaled it there, some hope remained of an arrangement whereby investments at least might be made secure. But then, with tragic swiftness, came King Jerome, Lagrange was bidden to go elsewhere, and Napoleon—whose inexorableness toward William was mainly an affection for his money—redoubled his efforts to collect the refugee's loans. By offering the borrowers increasingly tempting rebates, by threatening them with penalties if they failed to pay up, and by promising rewards to all and sundry for informing against recalcitrant debtors, the Bonaparte brothers succeeded in collecting a round six million thalers, in addition to the much larger sum which Lagrange had previously been obliged to turn over.

That did for Hesse and vicinity. It did also for Russia. For the same treaty which had made Jerome king had tied the Tsar by an alliance to the Napoleonic chariot.

Next came the turn of Denmark. When William fled there in the autumn of 1806 that country was still neutral. A year later, however, England had in self-protection found it necessary to bombard Copenhagen and seize the little kingdom's fleet; with the result that Denmark was likewise driven into the arms of the enemy. Thereafter William's unhappiness over the Holstein peasantry's boorish manners was aggravated by a vague feeling that his continued presence on Danish territory was both dangerous to himself and embarrassing to his hosts. The king, who was both his nephew and his debtor, was polite to be sure, but in subtle ways he made it evident that his uncle's departure would be viewed with relief. So William found it prudent to collect his boxes and things and go wandering again.

At this juncture it was that Prussia too fell from grace. As a field for investment that kingdom had in fact hardly counted since she had been bagged by Napoleon at Jena two years before. But now she added insult to insecurity. At the time of his flight the Prussian king had invited the Elector to come and occupy one of the royal palaces as his guest. In his present quandary William bethought himself of that offer and reached out a feeler with the intimation that he might now be persuaded to accept; to which His Majesty replied that nothing would make him happier—if Serenity would first obtain the consent of the Emperor Napoleon! Surely no self-respecting Prince could consider lending money on any terms to people who insulted one that way.

The Emperor Francis of Austria, it was true, had shown a more hospitable spirit, and had willingly let the homeless Prince find asylum in the capital of his Bohemian kingdom. But Austria was a bad risk. William had had no end of annoyance in his dealings with her. Already five years before her finances had come to such a pass that she must stop paying interest on her debt. Since then continuous war and invariable defeat had all but ruined her. The Austrian paper currency was almost worthless and the state was on the verge of bankruptcy.

The result of it all was that by the end of the year 1808 William found himself with money accumulating on his hands, loan after loan coming due, and no place to put a thaler safely out to interest. Next to the loss of his throne, this was about as distressing a situation as he could imagine. Then it was—but not till then—that Buderus came forward with a bright idea. Why not Consols? In these dreadful times, they had proved almost the only safe investment. They were now cheaper than they had ever been in their history or were likely to be at any time in the future. . . . And, in passing, why not commission the House of Rothschild with the deal? They were anxious to be of service, they were as always willing to work for less than others (like the Van Nottens, for instance) and they had a capable man right in London. The Rothschilds, like the Consols, had been a rock in adversity for Serenity. When fair-weather friends had run to cover, they had stood by loyally, dependably, unselfishly, without a thought of the risks to their own lives and fortunes.

III

For once William agreed promptly and without dickering. There was really nothing else to do. Those idle thalers were worrying him nearly as much as those much too active Bonapartes. He grasped at Buderus's suggestion gleefully. In the two years between February 1809 and December 1810 he authorized three purchases of "Funds" amounting in all to £550,000. As the accruing interest was also to be invested in the same security, the grand total came up to considerably more than the figure named by Nathan in his after-dinner reminiscence of 1834.

The Rothschilds, too, were as good as their word. They had said they were going to do this business for their noble patron without a thought of self, and they meant it. They waived commissions entirely. All they asked was a nominal brokerage fee of 1/8%, based on the face value of the bonds, to cover portage and incidental costs. They did not care to make any profit whatever. As the securities were bought at an average of 72, their services cost the investor the altogether negligible sum of a thousand pounds. A mere thank you. William was delighted.

To Buderus, likewise, the bankers behaved handsomely. They had intimated that if he would put through that long-coveted deal, they would show their appreciation in a large way. The very day the Prince's consent was received Buderus was presented with a generous block of stock in the concern and the old verbal understanding was formally reduced to writing. The document is dated February 17, 1809, and reads thus:

"The following agreement has this day been concluded between the War Privy Councilor Buderus von Carlshausen and the mercantile firm of Meyer Amschel Rothschild in Frankfort:

First. Buderus has invested with the banking house of Meyer Amschel Rothschild the sum of twenty thousand florins and has promised to assist the said firm with counsel and in other ways to the best of his ability.

Second. The House of Meyer Amschel Rothschild promises, on its side, to give the said Buderus a faithful accounting of its earnings upon the above-named capital stock of twenty thousand florins, and grants him the right of access to all the firm's books at all times, to the end that he may be sure of the most equitable treatment."

William's rejoicing gradually sobered down as time passed. He had expected, it would seem, that the London Rothschild would the moment Serenity's order reached him hurry to the nearest broker's, buy the bonds, rush with them to the Bank of England, and having duly registered and deposited them, forward the certificates to Prague by the first boat. It was, on several counts, a vain hope; and only goes to show how naïve a great capitalist (and Fuerstlichkeit into the bargain) may be. In the first place, Nathan did not actually receive any such thing as £600,000, nor even £150,000 all at one time. William sent him his order, and then took his time to furnish the wherewithal; he was relying for the funds on maturing loans, and dribbled them out in monthly instalments as they reached him. For Nathan to have executed the commission immediately and in full would have meant that he must tie up his own capital. He had no capital. It was to secure that commodity that he had prayed for this business all this long while.

Then there was another, even more persuasive reason why Serenity must be disappointed. By the terms of the contract the exchange rate for sterling as well as the price of Consols was fixed at a definite figure, win or lose. Now the Napoleonic wars had already brought both the English currency and the English "Funds" to a lower level than they had ever known; and more wars were coming. The chances of a further drop were therefore excellent. A little waiting was likely to be worth while. As a matter of fact, Consols did fall approximately ten points before Nathan got around to buying them, or at least to delivering them.

Lastly, what did that pig-tailed innocent back there in Prague imagine the Rothschilds were doing this thing for? Did he really suppose that six able-bodied and agile-minded men (not counting Buderus) were going to give their time and labor for a brokerage fee which would hardly feed their horses and keep their carriage in repairs? Or did he imagine that *they* were so naïve as not to know what to do with money when they got it into their hands?

Well, William had not stopped to consider all these questions before he gave his orders. He began to wonder a little now. Months passed, a year, two, three, and no certificates came—not a scrap of a receipt from the Bank of England to show that a man named Rothschild had deposited Consols there in the accustomed way. He became a bit uneasy. A doubt arose in his mind: Was his money safe at all? To be sure, communications were chaotic. The blockade did make travel unsafe; and entrusting valuables to the mails was out of the question. And yet, the money from this end seemed to be reaching London somehow. Was there any more risk in one direction than in another?

He began regretting Denmark and giving ear to Austria. Come to think of it, he had never quite got it straight in his mind why that last affair with Copenhagen had come to nothing, away back in '07. Odd! The Danes wanted the money, and heaven knew he was ready to give it to them. The differences that had come up were trifling; the usual sort of thing. He held out for a long term loan; they were for a short term one. Surely that ought to have been ironed out. But the most curious thing happened. The Rothschilds, who naturally should have stood with the borrower on such a point (the shorter the period, the greater the turn-over and the larger the bankers' commissions) took a determined stand with the lender; and then before he knew it, they reported the negotiations broken off. At the time he had written it down as a striking instance of the well-known Rothschild loyalty. Well, was it? He now wondered whether they had not been moved by some more human motive. Hadn't they already in those days begun clearing the field for the English business, and discouraging every other borrower? It seemed that way. They surely were endowed with long sight, those people! Was it not that very summer Lorentz wrote that their London man had made overtures to him?

Austria now—true, she was in a muddle. But at least she was not away off at the other end of the world like London. And could anything be less safe than Consols with such brokers? Moreover the Emperor Francis had been a magnificent host; had given him an honor guard and otherwise treated him as a visiting sovereign. All in all, Prague was the nearest thing to a home that he, William, had had since he quit Cassel. Besides, Consols brought 3½%, while the Austrians were prepared for almost any terms; they needed the money so badly. No, he would think twice before he declined their proposals.

So he wrote Buderus to ask what he thought of the matter. Buderus, of course, informed his Frankfort associates of what was brewing; and these, terrified at the menace to their London enterprise, were at first for vetoing the Austrian plan out of hand. Upon deliberation, however, a subtler course was adopted. Let Serenity meet his hosts half way, by all means. There were some six million thalers outstanding among thirty-odd debtors here and there and everywhere, which for a variety of reasons—chief among them the long arm of the Bonapartes—were uncollectable. Why not have William suggest to His Viennese Majesty that he take them over? In that way Austria would have what she wanted; Serenity would get his bad debts into a single, relatively safe, place; Nathan's operations in London would continue unembarrassed; and everybody would be happy.

That strange man in Prague actually took up the scheme. He saw nothing ridiculous about a Hapsburg turning sheriff for his benefit. So he informed Vienna that he would be most happy to tide over His Majesty, if the latter would persuade his son-in-law Napoleon to let him collect certain loans due the Elector of Hesse-Cassel, a list of which was herewith appended. The proud paupers in the Austrian capital, however, did not seem to take kindly to the idea; for the Emperor had his treasury people write back, a bit ironically, that he appreciated the Elector's thoughtfulness and goodwill, but felt the offer did not quite comport with the dignity of the imperial and royal state.

This was in the spring of 1810. All through the summer, consequently, William saw with a heavy heart his strong-box filling up and no outlet in sight. By September he must therefore again listen to Buderus's counsel and authorize the London Rothschild to invest for him a third £150,000 in Consols.

IV

And all the while no sign of a Bank of England certificate, not even for the first purchase, ordered now nearly two years ago.

He gently prodded Buderus. "I am not unaware," he wrote, in effect, "of the grave risks involved. I have the fullest confidence, too, in the wisdom and loyalty of the Rothschilds. Yet here it is more than a year and a half now since that first contract was signed. Don't you think that in all that time a way might have been found to forward that document to me? It seems to me odd that there should be so much hesitation and delay, when the remittances from this side reach England month after month without loss. Would not the same precautions, whatever they are, serve also in an easterly direction?"

Buderus began to be nervous. He warned his Frankfort people that the air was becoming electrical, that a storm was gathering, and that something had better be done about it soon.

At this juncture the diplomat of the family had an inspiration. Short of handing Serenity the certificate itself—which obviously was impracticable so long as the Consols were unbought—there was nothing in the world would so delight his soul as a little concession on the new contract. The firm could afford it—it need not be more than a trifle anyhow—and it would relieve the tension. In October, therefore, Buderus was able to write: "After much persuasion and effort I have succeeded in cutting down Rothschild's price on the third Funds investment one-quarter percent, thus saving Your Serene treasury 4521 pounds." Nevertheless he felt it desirable to add: "The certificate for the first investment will be brought over by young Rothschild as soon as there is the slightest chance of safety."

And William was even more pleased than had been expected. He not only did not cancel his recent order; he raised it to a quarter of a million! That, however, did not prevent him from reminding Buderus that he was still waiting for his receipt. "I instruct you at the same time to see to it that the document for the first investment reach me now without delay and that the others follow as soon as possible."

Just then, however, Buderus was obliged to report some unpleasant news. No more than a fortnight after his last letter came the great raid on the Frankfort business houses. He gave William a terrifying account of the event. "The Court-Agent Kalmann (Karl) Rothschild was about to start for Prague when several French regiments marched in with artillery and a great number of customs men, seized all the City's gates and ordered no one to leave . . . I have taken all conceivable care and I can only give the highest praise to the sons of the Superior Court Agent Rothschild for the indefatigable concern and zeal with which they have shown their devotion to Your Electoral Serenity."

Moreover: "New incentives have been offered informers and borrowers to bring about the liquidation of Your Electoral Serenity's loans, by assuring them of a reward of fifteen percent, and the quantity of spies and traitors under every disguise is so great that no one can be trusted any more."

Finally: "As soon as it is possible I shall see that the Court-Agent Kalmann Rothschild leaves Frankfort with the packs."

Without saying so outright, Buderus evidently meant to convey that the Bank of England certificate would be contained in those delayed "packs." But five months later, nothing of the sort having arrived in Prague and William having again made inquiry, Buderus tells him: "Young Rothschild is really going to London to fetch the receipts for the Funds investments." Incidentally: "His father has, without my asking him, succeeded in collecting 160,000 florins from Copenhagen. Will Serenity permit me to express to him Your satisfaction at his manifold endeavors in this connection." Then: "I am notified by Rothschild that the police in Prague have discovered the secret drawers in his carriage. I have therefore thought it prudent not to send along my accounts for last month and enclosures. These cannot be concealed in the clothing like letters."

Whether or not young Rothschild went to London, he did not fetch the receipt for the Consols. At any rate six weeks more passed without any such document reaching its anxious owner. Wherefore, though William obligingly forwarded the requested thanks for Rothschild, he must say: "I had no idea that the police here have found out the secret hiding places. There is in any event nothing to fear at this end . . . I am looking forward with genuine longing and justifiable eagerness to the Funds documents."

The summer was half gone and still nothing had arrived. William, despairing of ever accomplishing anything through Buderus, bethought himself of another channel. He instructed his envoy in London to make direct inquiry. What was his astonishment to learn that this was the first Lorentz had heard of the whole matter! Buderus had never said a word to him about Consols. And not only that: The Funds were down to 62 and still falling!

Then the dykes gave way. "I am distressed beyond words," he notified Buderus, "and am looking forward with genuine yearning to your explanation.

"Till then please stop all further payments against the Funds.

"Neither are any more interest moneys to be reinvested therein.

"Lorentz must be kept informed of all My English financial affairs. Especially must he know about the capital invested for Me by Rothschild so that he might as My chargé d'affaires keep an eye on it.

"I request you to attend to this without delay."

The effect produced by this bombshell in Frankfort may well be imagined. Buderus wrote often and sorrowfully of the already well-known dangers of carrying valuable documents across the Channel, of the tireless efforts of all the Rothschilds to satisfy Serenity's genuine longing, and of the inadvisability of confiding business secrets even to accredited chargés d'affaires. Kalmann went to Prague and argued and pleaded in person. But William was adamant. For the better part of a year nothing would induce him to authorize the payment of a solitary thaler to London. There is no telling what might have been the consequence of this obstinacy, if by a rare piece of luck Buderus's deposits in the Rothschild bank had not just during that period risen to quite unusual figures. Whereas in September (when the stoppage order reached him) his account showed a balance of less than 30,000 florins, it now gradually began increasing so that by spring it was 360,000—which was slightly over the normal monthly instalment remitted to Nathan.

The embargo was at last lifted in May. For though Buderus had repeatedly assured his master that no pressure would or could in the slightest degree affect the blockade, the first certificate did brave the Channel that month, after nearly three and a half years of faint-hearted hesitation. A second followed within less than a year.

By 1813, however, the House of Rothschild could afford to be indifferent to both the millions and the wishes of the Elector of Hesse-Cassel. How this consummation was effected in so brief a time will appear in the pages immediately following.

PART II

GLORY

CHAPTER VII

AID AND COMFORT TO WELLINGTON

INTERESTED people in Frankfort observed a curious phenomenon toward the end of 1810. The young Rothschilds had scattered and vanished from sight. In the last four years one had become accustomed to their periodic disappearances, one at a time; and one could even make a fair guess at their destination. This was something new; it looked for all the world like an emigration; it was a shift of base. What and where might the new enterprise be? That was what puzzled competitors and old rivals. The refugee Prince? That was an old story; his affairs could hardly absorb the entire lot of them. Nor did it seem to be blockade running. That once thriving business had gone lean of late; and the Rothschilds had, like most other merchants, given it a wide berth. Their export and commission undertakings, as a matter of fact, were decidedly languishing. The shop and the warehouses were in charge of an aged man and a young girl. Yet, far from declining, the prosperity of the family seemed to be flourishing more luxuriantly than ever. They had lately acquired two parcels of land on the Bornheimerstrasse on which they were planning to erect a bank building of their own. Old Meyer and the women-folks were in the most cheerful of moods.

What might it all mean?

The phenomenon remained a mystery. No Frankforter

had the remotest inkling of the Elector's recent English investments, still less that the Van Nottens had gone the way of the Bethmanns, least of all in what manner their successors were employing the enormous wealth thus suddenly dropped into their laps. Even those who were in the secret were scarcely aware of all that was happening. Buderus, for instance, who had had some little part in the initial proceedings, might have found it difficult to expound their present ramifications with anything like certainty. It is doubtful whether the titular head of the House of Rothschild himself was abreast of the details. The business was much too complex and confidential and far away for Frankfort to follow. And the young men were much too preoccupied to report back with any frequency.

In the beginning Nathan's thought in reaching out for a bit more of William's surplus had been simple enough: he could use it advantageously in expanding his contraband operations. If he got all he hoped for, he might, indeed, discover a few things to do on the Royal Exchange. But that miser back there in Prague hung on to his thalers with the grip of death. He sent him authorizations—as if one could do business with a scrap of paper—and then tremblingly dribbled out instalments. For the better part of two years, therefore, anything more ambitious was not to be thought of. Besides, defying Napoleon had its rewards. Then just as the monthly remittances had accumulated to a sizable sum came the Edict of Trianon and emasculated the blockade to a tame, more or less legal and not especially remunerative business. Some months later followed the great raid on Frankfort. That was the final blow. Willy-nilly something must be found to take the place of contraband.

Nathan did not have to look either long or far. England had other irons than the blockade in the Napoleonic fire. There was, for instance that obscure struggle in Spain and Portugal, and the muddle it had got into. Everybody in England knew there was a Peninsular War, that its aim was the invasion of France by land, that for a long time past the expedition had not budged, and that the reason was the inability of the government to get provisions to its forces. Everybody knew it; yet nobody seemed to have thought of exploiting it. What, now, did the situation offer? The failure to keep the army supplied was due to the unimaginative efforts of the government to reach the Peninsula direct from the sea. More than once ships carrying money had been captured or sunk. Therefore Wellington, the commander, rather than see his men starve, had been obliged to take the bull by the horns. He had in effect set up a small bank of issue of his own right in Portugal. His drafts—being nothing but paper money drawn against reserves which, though solid enough, were inaccessible—could only be circulated at a fantastic discount. The government was scandalized, but it must honor the drafts just the same. And a group of scalpers—Spanish, Maltese and Sicilian—were, clumsily and with no more imagination than the London authorities, reselling Wellington's paper to bankers near home, away below its face value, of course. Before the notes reached England they had gone through half a dozen hands and the originally enormous profit had been largely frittered away.

Obviously the whole performance was silly from beginning to end. So long as there was a land route between Portugal and London it was sheer incompetence to try to send money by water and take all the risks. That, however, was the government's affair. What interested Nathan was the brainlessness of those scalpers, "The Cab," as they were called. Their paper eventually must find its way to London, or it would not be worth buying at all. And so long as it arrived eventually, there was no good reason why it should not get there directly and the proceeds stay in one hand.

Well, he had the organization, he had the capital, and he was willing to give the game a try. It was an enterprise exactly to his taste. It afforded all the adventure and rewards of the late lamented contraband trade. Why, it was in fact really nothing but smuggling of a new and peculiarly interesting kind. His Continental brothers would take to it as fish to water. Their five years of blockade running had them left as fit and agile as athletes. Add to that the equally ticklish courier work for His Highness, and there was not a more competent or better trained staff for the job anywhere between Lisbon and London. False papers, disguises, bogus names, secret caches, official-bribing—all the tricks and dodges of the spy—were old familiar things to them. It was not by prayer that they had become successful men of affairs in time of war.

II

Quiet, home-loving Amschel was persuaded to relieve Kalmann (Karl) of the Frankfort-Prague route. Father took over the diplomatic mission of contracting Buderus. The goods trade at home, stripped down to a bare skeleton, became the province of the unmarried girls, Gotton (Julie) and Jettchen (Henriette), flanked by their sisters-in-law.

And mother Guetele kept house for her family as usual, leaving business to those who fancied and understood it. Thus liberated, the three youngest and ablest male Rothschilds could dedicate themselves to the new venture. Blessed by their parents and their women, they pushed off silently while Frankfort slumbered. Ignorant of any language but Jewish-German, they threaded their way across frontiers, over hostile country, through armed outposts; paying when they must, dodging where they could, confident of their well-filled purses and their own stout hearts; and presently bobbed up on the Western rim of the Continent to keep the tryst with Nathan.

The two youngest men took the ends of the line—Kalmann the Pyrenees, Jacob the Channel coast. Salomon, the persuasive and diplomatic, stationed himself between them, in Paris. In the nature of the case, London remained the headquarters and terminus, as it had been the originating source, of the enterprise. The chain complete, the machinery could begin to function. Kalmann speedily entered into relations with the merchants along the Franco-Spanish frontier, offering to buy from them whatever notes of the British commander they might acquire in trade. Mutual safety required that the commerce be kept dark; the Spanish shopkeepers understood that. They may or may not have understood, further, that too much advertising tended to force up prices. As soon as Kalmann had got together a sufficient quantity of Wellington's paper, he headed north with it; Salomon at the same time quit Paris; along the route somewhere the brothers met, exchanged satchels, and then faced about. Avoiding the capital, Salomon journeyed on toward the Channel, found Jacob at an appointed spot, and the performance was repeated. From Dunkirk or Gravelines London was but a jump, and in London the almost worthless drafts became legal tender acceptable at par. The water-stage was at first attended to either by Nathan traveling south or by Jacob going north; later on dependable English sea-captains were commissioned with the task.

This was the colorful and exciting aspect of the venture. Danger of the most breath-taking variety attended every link of the chain. It was espionage and commerce with the enemy, and the penalties for these offenses were, then as now, brief and final. The smallest slip of eye or foot brought one face to face with the guillotine. Of course, the brothers were not so reckless as to neglect precautions. Itching palms were generously greased all along the route from the mountains to the sea; on the Narrows the prefect of police of the Pas de Calais Department himself lived so prosperously on the Rothschilds' bounty as to attract the critical notice of his superior in Paris.

But the business was not all poetry. The pedestrian element was to find the shining metal cash, which alone was of any use to Wellington. Toward this consummation Nathan contributed more than his share, both with substance and ideas. He had anticipated the problem from the beginning and had arranged to meet it. Each man in his territory was between trips quietly picking up all the yellow loose change he could get his hands on. The light-footed Jacob was particularly active, not only in France but also in Holland and elsewhere; Salomon helped out from Paris and the larger towns of his route; and Nathan himself did his best to turn Wellington's drafts into guineas. Kalmann, at the extreme end of the chain, had his hands full collecting the paper. All of them had to work with the utmost circumspection, not alone because exporting gold was everywhere forbidden, but principally because of the influence on the exchange.

Sooner or later, however, the traffic was bound to hit a snag. After half a year of combing the world for gold there was no gold left to comb. Every country in Europe was on a paper basis; what little coin was still in circulation was, as always in times of inflation, being hoarded; the rest had, by the Rothschilds' own efforts, rolled down into Spain. The difficulty seemed insuperable. The British authorities ought, of course, to make things easy; the Rothschild consortium was doing their work for them, and rendering a patriotic service to England besides, in the face of the gravest danger to themselves. But those complacent and unimaginative men at the royal exchequer knew nothing about the consortium or its work, and if they did know they might take it into their heads to spoil the game. It would be not unlike them.

But Nathan still had a shot in his belt. He took to haunting the curio shops, the old metal-dealers, the junk yards and the bullion market. It was not long before the trade came to know the paunchy young man with the inscrutable face as a buyer of unlimited capital who paid the highest prices for everything made of gold. When therefore the East India Company brought in a large shipment of gold bars, Nathan was one of the first to get wind of the event. The lot was to be sold at auction at the Company's offices. Nathan showed up early and bid so lustily that the entire shipment, valued at close to a million pounds, was knocked down to him. Thereupon word went out over the Channel to Dunkirk that all was well.

III

But the good news proved to be a little premature. Before Nathan had had time to remove his treasure, let alone get it across to his brothers, a very official-looking document was brought to him. It was a letter signed John Charles Herries, Commissary General, inviting him to be so good as to present himself at that gentleman's office for a conference. Mr. Herries, who had expected a rather impressive personage of the customary City dimensions, was not a little taken aback to see this very unprepossessing, ill-groomed Continental being ushered into his presence. His surprise was heightened when the visitor began speaking. Could this be the man at all who drove bargains involving hundreds of thousands of pounds? Never before had the English tongue been spoken with such an accent in His Majesty's offices. But as the interview continued Herries found himself listening with close attention to what his guest was telling him and forgetting altogether the oddity of his idiom.

The Commissary General began by inquiring whether it was true that Mr. Rothschild had acquired a certain quantity of gold from the East India Company, and upon receiving an affirmative answer, went on to say that His Majesty's Government would consider its repurchase at a given figure. There happened just at that time to be a military expedition on the Iberian Peninsula; it was the duty of the Commissary General to supply the army engaged in that enterprise; owing to the blockade great difficulty had been encountered in shipping provisions *in natura;* and according to the officer in command, he could readily live on the country providing he had the necessary funds. The government, therefore, desired to secure the bars in question for that and kindred purposes. Mr. Rothschild, being a British subject and patriot, was entirely ready to comply, for a consideration. If he might be permitted, however, he would like to ask just how the authorities proposed to reach Spain. He had no wish to pry into state secrets; only as it happened he had acquired the metal for that identical purpose. He had, if the truth must be told, been doing his humble part in keeping the Peninsular forces alive for some little time past. Naturally, he had not attempted to ship by water. As the government had doubtless found out for itself, that route was not quite safe. Fortunately there were other ways, which, if the Commissary General cared to hear of them, he would be glad to explain.

Nathan sketched in outline his organization, his methods, and the recent hardships he had had to face in consequence of the growing scarcity of gold coin on the Continent. As a private person, he could not, of course, honorably do the things that the situation demanded. There was, on the other hand, no reason why the state should stop where he must. It could, for instance, in a time of national peril like this, produce French napoleons and Portuguese ounces in its own mint without asking the permission of the governments concerned. There were other short-cuts, too.

Herries not only cared to listen; he was so hugely impressed with what he heard that he invited Mr. Rothschild to put himself and his organization at the service of the British government. Nathan was aware that the East India gold, purveyed down to Wellington in the old way, would have brought many times the returns he was getting from Herries. Still, low profits never yet ruined a merchant; he was disposing of the whole thing in a lump, without effort or risk or worry. And, lo! he had made a priceless contact with the English Treasury into the bargain. In that 1834 after-dinner reminiscence, already quoted, he described this day's adventure as the best piece of business he had ever done. Well he might! Nothing that had ever happened to the Rothschild family, since the Elector's flight five years before, was destined to mean so much for its future.

IV

While these happy events were occurring in England, the mainland was becoming uncomfortably warm under the other Rothschilds' feet. The curious Frankforters, though still baffled as to the nature of their young fellow-townsmen's affairs, had traced their whereabouts. The locale seemed to them suggestive. Enterprising business men did not go to French seaports for the salt and the bathing. Therefore the imperial authorities began receiving hints, in writing and otherwise, that the undefined activities of a certain trio of brothers would in all likelihood repay looking into. The communications in due course were forwarded to police headquarters in Paris, and thence to the prefect of the Pas de Calais department. It became the unpleasant duty of this well-disposed official to warn his young friend Jacob that matters were passing beyond his control and that it might be best to go while the roads were still open.

Jacob had rather been thinking so himself for some little time past; so he took good advice when it was given him.

Early in March, 1811, he therefore dropped everything and sank out of sight. Much as he disliked saying anything about his movements even to the discreet Frankfort authorities, he felt it necessary to regularize his status; and it was better to confide in the good archbishop than to risk unpleasantness in Dunkirk. Dalberg, as it happened, was himself getting ready for a journey to France. Marie-Louise was about to present Napoleon with an heir to his throne; and throughout the empire and its dependencies well-disposed chiefs of state were arranging to assist at the grandiose ceremony with which that long-awaited event would be attended. The pope himself was to baptize the eaglet; and Dalberg, apart from wishing to pay homage to his secular chief, deemed the occasion good for bringing certain matters in which he was interested to the attention of his spiritual overlord as well. But going to Paris in such circumstances required money, a great deal of it. Old Meyer Rothschild, the moment he learned of his friend's difficulty, cheerfully offered him a loan of eighty thousand florins.

Naturally, therefore, when, as chance would have it, a son of the generous lender needed a little favor at that very time, the grateful Grand Duke could hardly refuse it. James obtained not only a passport duly visaed with which he could return to France openly; he got something in addition which, as time soon proved, was infinitely more valuable still. Dalberg gave him, namely, several letters of introduction to important Paris banking houses, including one to Count de Mollien, the imperial minister of finance.

Noblesse oblige. It would not do for one coming so highly recommended to slink about in the dark. Consequently James laid his cards before de Mollien with the most engaging frankness. He had, he confided, a brother in London, with whom he was in constant touch, and from whom he received at intervals shipments of English gold. As to the ultimate destination of the metal he was a bit reticent; but he communicated enough for de Mollien to draw his own conclusions. And Napoleon's minister of finance who, it seems, did not quite measure up to his generals, perceived at once that a country which was so stupidly governed as to let a thing like that happen could not but be on the brink of economic disaster. He so told the emperor. He only prayed that this brilliant young Frankforter might be correctly informed. To doubt James's truthfulness did not occur to him. The Frenchman, indeed, was so convinced of the boy's sincerity (James was only nineteen years old) that he took him under his wing and shielded him from annoyance at the hands of other officials.

Savary, for instance, the imperial minister of police, was inclined to be skeptical. Here, he figured, was a much too plausible stranger from a conquered province who, while pretending to have nothing to hide, was carrying on a very doubtful kind of commerce with an associate in an enemy country. He might be harmless; yet it would be as well to keep an eye on him. So Savary quietly put his subordinates on guard everywhere from Mayence to Paris and the Channel ports, ordering that the goings and comings as well as the mail of all Rothschilds from Frankfort to London be given the closest attention.

Unfortunately for this loyal and astute servant of Napoleon, the Rothschild movements, and especially the Rothschild mails, were not as susceptible to observation as he imagined. There was, as a matter of fact, no such thing as a Rothschild mail. Between Frankfort and Prague they had for six years past been their own post office, as well as the Elector William's. Across the Channel their trusted sea captains brought and carried whatever was needed. And from Dunkirk to the Pyrenees, the brothers attended to major matters themselves and delegated the remainder to safe couriers in their pay. Moreover, even if by some remote accident a letter of theirs were to fall into outsiders' hands, it would convey precious little. The correspondence of the firm and of those with whom they did business was carried on in a code, no names were either signed or mentioned, and the key to both was frequently changed.

On the first of November, a letter of mysterious origin, bearing the signature "O. H." was in fact intercepted by the French secret service in Hamburg. Had those functionaries known a little more about the Rothschild way of doing things, as above outlined, they would readily have recognized their catch for the *canard* it was, if for no other reason than that it revealed so much. "O. H.", who appeared to enjoy a high position in the absent Elector's entourage, was addressing the latter's brother in Gottorp, and telling him the latest news about the progress of the secret political movement for the liberation of Germany. The letter, incidentally, mentioned Lawaetz and the Rothschilds by name and Buderus under the somewhat thin disguise of "Bravo." The communication left no doubt that all these people were deeply involved in the Elector's treasonable schemes and their financing, and was patently designed to cast suspicion upon the Rothschilds and their associates.

But as Monsieur Citiz in Hamburg was informed neither of the family's methods nor of its enemies in Cassel and Frankfort, he took the intercepted document at its face value and promptly forwarded it to his chief in Paris. Thence a hue and cry went out to secret police headquarters in Mayence, to ambassador Bacher in Frankfort and to the coast guard at Dunkirk and Gravelines urgently requesting that the affair be pursued to the limit and the various persons named taken under close surveillance. Bacher, in his reply, suggested proceeding cautiously, lest the suspects take warning. Dalberg, as usual, made light of the whole matter, and gave the meagerest coöperation. From Mayence the report stated that the House of Rothschild had since the raid of the previous year apparently given up smuggling and now confined itself to trade in legal merchandise and banking; that their sentiments toward France, while correct on the surface, were far from loyal at heart; and that Dalberg was for some unaccountable reason so thick with them that he refused nothing they asked of him.

The correspondence on the subject was kept up with undiminished zeal for several months. Every day, it seemed, the French net was about to close on the elusive gentry. It never did, however; and in the end, the pursuit which had so hopefully begun was abandoned for lack of results. It would, in fact, have been given up sooner, if in the midst of it, one or two even more suspicious looking letters had not been picked up on the coast as well as, again, in Hamburg. This time the internal evidence showed unmistakably that the police had in their hands genuine correspondence between one Rothschild and another. What was especially noteworthy was the circumstance that one of these documents was discovered not in the mail bags but on the person of a courier. If these gentlemen's operations were as pure as they pretended, why should they try to avoid the regular postal service? Their excuse that the letter had missed the mail and had been rushed to the port so as to catch the boat, was patently specious. Besides, the contents were hardly reassuring. James was telling his brother in London that he had duly received several shipments of English and Portuguese gold coins, and that he had got drafts for them from the bankers in Paris!

Savary and the military governor at Hamburg were, therefore, in favor of speedy and summary action. They wanted James arrested, and at the very least expelled from France. They were so sure of the treacherous character of the brothers' activities that they carried their conclusions to the emperor himself. But Napoleon dismissed their fears with a wave of the hand. Why, de Mollien had been aware of the traffic all along. It was quite all right.

And all the while Nathan sat at a desk in Commissary General Herries' office in London, or traveled under his orders on the Continent, to all practical purposes an official of the British government; and hundreds of thousands of pounds in gold—English guineas, Dutch ducats, and French napoléons-d'or, the latter either collected in France itself or minted in London—were quietly, unobtrusively, without disturbing either the bourses or anybody's blockade, rolling down into Spain to feed and clothe Wellington's Peninsular army. Suddenly, upon returning from his disastrous expedition to Russia, Napoleon woke up to learn that the British general—the man who was so soon to crush him at Waterloo—had somehow extricated himself from the impasse that had so long held him fast beyond the Pyrenees and was marching his well-fed and well-equipped forces into the southern provinces of France.

V

Meantime in Frankfort Meyer was nearing the end of his days. A man of over sixty at the time of the Elector's flight, these years of unwonted toil and anxiety had sapped his declining vitality. Already in 1808 he had had to undergo an operation for an internal malady. He was pronounced cured; but as a matter of fact he never quite recovered from the shock and his wound gave him almost continuous pain. Toward the end of the year 1811 he was once more obliged to take to his bed. After an illness of several months he again rallied. On the Day of Atonement (September 16, 1812) he insisted, despite the warnings of his physician and the solicitous objections of his family, on fasting the full twenty-four hours and on spending the entire day kneeling in prayer at the synagogue. On the morrow his old wound burst open and it was evident to those standing about the bedside as well as to the sick man himself that a crisis was approaching. A notary and witness were hurriedly sent for, and in their presence Meyer dictated a new will to replace the one he had made four years earlier. He had barely enough strength left to sign the document. Summonses were dispatched to his scattered sons, but only two—Amschel and Kalmann—arrived in time. Early on the evening of the nineteenth all was over. He was buried in the ancient Jewish cemetery of his birthplace, aged sixty-eight years and seven months.

There seven generations of his ancestors rest with him, but not a single one of his descendants.

Did Meyer as he lay dying see in his mind's eye a vision of the greatness that was so soon to come to his house? From beyond the northerly entrance to the Judengasse he could dimly hear the sounds of the workmen erecting the structure in which the business he had begun so long ago was to be housed. Meyer Amschel Rothschild had labored and striven and brought forth sons, and now the time had come for him to take permanent leave, but the firm of M. A. Rothschild & Sons was going forward. How far would it go? It seemed a miracle, when he thought back over the years, that it had come as far as it had. A bare dozen years ago he had been a small tradesman and money-changer, with the most modest capital, credit and prospects. Before that the rare-coin case, the second-hand shop with Moses and Kalmann in the back-yard of the Saucepan, the clerk and the messenger boy at Oppenheim's in Hanover, the penniless orphan, the Talmudic scholar at the Yeshivah of Fuerth. And now! No one knew better than he how much of this extraordinary growth was owing to his remarkable sons. Still, it was on his foundations they had built. But they would go on building, and he must do all he could not to hamper them.

Meyer's will was designed not so much to dispose of his estate as to secure the future. The business was left absolutely in his sons' hands. To make sure that his daughters and their husbands would not interfere, he went so far as to sell out his own share to his male heirs. The hundred and ninety thousand florins thus realized, were, apart from his home, distributed between his wife and his ten children. "I direct and desire, therefore, that my daughters, my sons-in-law and their heirs shall have no part whatever in the existing firm of M. A. Rothschild & Sons, and that still less shall they, on any pretext whatsoever, . . . claim the right to examine the said business, its books, papers, documents, inventory, etc. . . . And I shall never forgive any of my children if they should against this my paternal will take it upon themselves to disturb my sons in the peaceful possession of their business." Moreover, the entire inheritance of his wife and daughters must remain in the sons' keeping, to be used as capital in the firm and to receive interest at five per cent.

Guetele was more fortunate than her husband. She survived him thirty-seven years, and lived to see the culmination of her sons' careers. But she remained throughout her long life the same simple, unassuming, pious housewife she had been from the beginning. Though Amschel presently built himself a palace and gave banquets to statesmen and diplomats, she refused to give up the humble home in the Judengasse where she and Meyer had spent so many happy years. Her sons would send her jewels and costly lace kerchiefs from Paris, London and Vienna, and she accepted them with pleasure, but nothing would induce her to eat at their tables because their French chefs did not conform to the Jewish food ritual. She reveled in pride at her boys' achievements. When many years later a poor woman came to her crying because her only son was to be sent to the wars, Guetele reassured her. "Never fear," she said, "there is not going to be any war. I shall tell my boys not to lend them the money." Like Letitia Bonaparte, she enjoyed the rare destiny of seeing her sons the most powerful men in Europe, and her glory was marred by no St. Helena.

CHAPTER VIII

THE GOODNESS OF MR. HERRIES

JUST what had the trusteeship of William's English investments netted? No one, perhaps not even the brothers themselves, could have said exactly. Certainly those six hundred thousand pounds had been productive in their competent hands. Had they multiplied five or six times, eight or ten, in those four epochal years? Had the capital (costing three per cent) earned a hundred and fifty or two hundred and fifty per cent? They did not take the time to figure it out. They were too busy, their holdings were too scattered; and anyhow what mattered a few hundred thousand more or less to men who had overnight become millionaires in sterling? Besides, they were not quite such materialists as to miss the essential point, which was that the cash dividend was a small thing beside the friendship of the British Commissary-in-chief.

With the entry of Mr. Herries, indeed, the center of gravity had shifted from Frankfort to London. Nominally the concern still rotated about the old home office; and Amschel (renamed Anselm), as the eldest of the five, was chief. In reality the leadership had long since passed to Nathan. It was he, to begin with, who had conceived the great plan which had enriched them all, and had set up the organization to carry it out, and it was he who had made the contact with Herries and must go on cultivating it. For a good while to come, clearly, Herries was destined to play a part roughly resembling that which Buderus had lately filled. Hesse-Cassel had served its time, and would henceforward fade out of the picture, to be supplanted by His Britannic Majesty's Treasury Department. Therefore, regardless of age and priority, and quite apart from natural talent, the man who sat in London would inevitably be *de facto* head of the firm.

Nathan and his brothers did not have to be trained statesmen to foresee, in outline at least, the history of the next few years insofar as it concerned their interests. So long as Napoleon remained emperor of the French, England would go on making war on him. The difficulties she had hitherto encountered in supplying her forces were not likely to diminish; and that being the case, there was no reason why Herries, or whoever was charged with his duties, should not continue using the Rothschild plan and the Rothschild organization which had proved so effective in the past. In reality, these calculations erred on the side of conservatism. As the Napoleonic interlude approached its final phase the problem of transferring British funds to the Continent became graver and more complex than ever.

Ever since Austria had signed the Treaty of Vienna in 1809, the German states had been at peace with France. It was not a matter of choice. Nor was it resignation. Prince Metternich, for all his sacrifice of Marie-Louise on the altar of the conqueror, was straining to be at it again. So was the ineffectual Frederick William III of Prussia. So, of course, was the banished Elector of Hesse and the great majority of the lesser princelings. What cooled their enthusiasm was partly an almost superstitious awe of Napoleon and chiefly lack of money. Their economy, antiquated and ill-administered at best, had become hopelessly disordered under the stress of war. Defeat, inflation and extravagance had ruined their credit. In Prussia things had come to such a pass that the king was unable to meet his private expenses and was continually harassed by tradesmen and bill collectors. The case of other German sovereigns was at least equally trying.

Napoleon's disaster in Russia in the winter of 1812–13, followed as it was by the virtual annihilation of the Grande Armée, put fresh heart into the German liberators. It did not, however, solve the problem of finance. The Prussian Chancellor Hardenberg no doubt expressed the sentiments of all the Continental Allies when he told England that without pecuniary assistance it was out of the question for his country to fight. Fortunately England was, under her new treasury head, prepared to return to the policy of Pitt and grant subsidies in exchange for soldiers. The very year of the retreat from Moscow Chancellor of the Exchequer Perceval had been assassinated. Vansittart, his successor, managed to convince the Government of Lord Liverpool that the defeat of Britain's great enemy would be cheaply bought at such a price, and that it was in any event unlikely to be had any other way. In the years 1813–15 Parliament appropriated fifteen millions sterling for the support of the Continental Allies, more than two-thirds of the sum going to Austria, Russia and Prussia.

Now arose the old question of remittances. In the past the British authorities had known but two ways of making payments on the mainland, one more costly than the other. They either shipped silver bars or gave the payees a free hand to draw on London. The insurance rates on bullion however, were prohibitive; besides, there was no such thing as fifteen million pounds' worth of silver, or any approach to it, in the whole of Britain. Drafts on London, again, in such enormous quantities not only played havoc with sterling exchange, causing terrific losses to both Britain and her friends; the markets of Europe became so swamped with the paper that after a short time it was nearly impossible to cash it at any price. Thus, in all Berlin Hardenberg could only with the greatest difficulty and at heavy discounts dispose of twenty-five thousand pounds' worth of his English checks, at a time when he had two-thirds of a million to realize. In Vienna the offer of drafts on London in the sum of eighty-three thousand pounds resulted in depressing sterling by several points. The operations must be carried out with the utmost secrecy, and that involved paying commissions to numerous agents, as well as competition on the exchanges between states fighting in a common cause.

At this juncture Herries laid before Chancellor Vansittart the Rothschild plan which had proved so workable in Spain, with the suggestion that it be extended to the subsidies problem. He put stress on the advantages of the new method: it was economical, and it virtually was not felt on the exchanges. What was more, there really was no other way in sight by which any large sums could be transferred to the Continent. Vansittart did not take much urging, and Nathan was sent abroad as the secret agent of the British Treasury to do for the coalition what he had now for some time been doing for Wellington.

In the interval, however, the situation had greatly improved, and it was no longer necessary to go to the danger and trouble of collecting coins. The French were in retreat on all fronts,—it was after the decisive Battle of Leipzig—

the Allies were pursuing them across the Rhine and through Belgium, while Wellington was rapidly moving across the Pyrenees into the southern provinces. The Continental Blockade was a ruin and smugglers were more active than they had been since the summer of 1810. In the ports and commercial centers of Holland and Germany merchants were struggling with the question of how to pay for the British merchandise they were receiving. It was, as the Rothschild brothers rather simply perceived, the reverse of the problem with which the governments were troubled. Here, on the one hand, were state treasuries bursting with drafts on the British capital which could not be cashed; and yonder, on the other, were the contraband carriers wondering what they were going to do in London with all their checks drawn on Frankfort, Amsterdam and such places. It seemed to the Rothschilds that they and their father had long ago dealt with a situation not unlike this. They had ample funds on the mainland. Why not relieve the smugglers of their paper, exchange it with the governments for theirs, solve both sides of the difficulty in one simple operation, and without one party knowing what was happening to the other, gain the thanks and the discounts of both? It was legal, safe, easy and every bit as profitable as the old way.

The chancelleries could not quite figure out how it was done, but they were delighted to find that somehow and suddenly their checks were being accepted without demur and credited as bank deposits wherever the money was needed. And when Nathan returned to London and related his success, Herries sent a secret report to Vansittart glowingly praising the astuteness of the man who had not only carried out his commission without a hitch, but had in addition secured seven hundred thousand pounds' worth of checks on Frankfort and Holland for future use; and all this without in the slightest degree affecting the exchange on London! He was quite sure, added Herries, that an operation involving a mere fraction of these sums, entrusted to treasury officials or British diplomatic representatives on the Continent, would have had ten times the adverse effect on sterling.

II

Traders on the Royal Exchange began to take notice of Nathan Rothschild. This pudgy foreigner with the baggy clothes and expressionless eyes seemed to have sources of information inaccessible to anyone else. At least he was acting as if he did. There was the matter of bullion, for instance. Early in the year, when the first rumors of a new coalition began to be heard, with probable subsidies for the Continental states, there was a great boom in the precious metals. Rothschild was the only considerable man on 'Change who was not looking at silver; he was in fact bearing the market. The prophets predicted his ruin. But presently it was learned that the Government had made other arrangements and was not going to ship any cash. That sort of thing happened again and again. Now it was the Funds, and another time it was Continental drafts. He rarely steered with the current, yet almost invariably he touched shore first. He was called a speculator; but he appeared to know, when others merely guessed.

Did he really know? A web of myths began to form about the strange unkempt alien. People talked of the Rothschild instinct, a sort of infallible inner light. Others whispered about a pigeon post, about his brothers in Germany who were reported to be monsters of wisdom, about occult Jewish divinations. No one even gave a thought to the Commissary-in-Chief. For that was a dead official secret, of which no one in the Government itself except the Chancellor of the Exchequer and Mr. Herries's private secretary had the smallest inkling.

Nathan impassively relished the interest he was arousing. His prestige and his credit did not suffer from the legends; they were making him an important man at the same time that his operations made him an enormously wealthy one. As the war progressed he contrived, in fact, to deepen the mystery and to provoke gasps of wonder elsewhere than on the stock market.

Like all exceptional men, Nathan was astonished at the stupidity of the mass of mankind. The Royal Exchange, for instance, was alive with individuals who called themselves speculators. That meant, if it meant anything, that it was their business to read the future, and they really pretended that they were going about it in rational fashion. What they did read in actual fact were the newspapers and the government decrees. That is to say, they tried to make capital from events after they had become common knowledge. It was a case of the halt leaning on the lame; for editors and authorities alike muddled along on general sources of information. Such a thing as exclusive news was unknown in their system. No one seemed to realize the importance of knowing things in advance, not of their occurrence, but of publication. Time after time the Government learned of battles and their outcome from him, hours before the official dispatches arrived, and hours (of course) after he had turned them to account on 'Change. And when they did learn them they either wagged their heads incredulously or gaped admiringly at his cleverness, but seldom knew what to do with their information.

After the Battle of Belle-Alliance, for example, the Government did hear the results before he did; only what they heard was not so. He got word of a victory for the British troops, and when he brought the news to the Treasury, the officials there laughed patronizingly. Oh, yes, Mr. Rothschild was very kind and helpful, to be sure. They appreciated his desire to be of service. As it happened, however, the Government had got a dispatch from its own people on the ground, and unfortunately there had been a defeat. Later the truth came out, and then the most fanciful stories were invented and believed about the sources of Mr. Rothschild's knowledge.

Then came Waterloo. As often before, it was he who first communicated the facts about that epoch-making event to the authorities. This time there was no shoulder shrugging; they had learned to take him seriously at last. But what legends, in the City and everywhere else, were spun out of that scoop of his! He had himself (so it was said) gone to Belgium, witnessed the battle, then rushed back home to make the most of what he had seen. The tale was embroidered with breath-taking circumstantial detail: how just as he had reached Ostend a hurricane had broken out on the Channel; how after much haggling he had hired a fisherman to take him across and had paid two thousand francs in advance for the service; how on arriving on 'Change the next day he had looked so mournful as to cause a violent drop in the British Funds, the while his secret brokers bought up every piece of scrip they could get their hands on at panic prices; and much more of the same sort.

No, he was simply a speculator who used his wits. His notion of looking into the future was to obtain news of significant events before it reached other people. To this end he cultivated high Government functionaries; not so much to learn about policies and decisions as to influence and help form them. The reason he was cool to bullion and sympathetic to Continental drafts in '13 was because the Government plan of transferring the Allied subsidies was of his own making. And to this end, too, he had devised ways of keeping abreast of world happenings, independently of both press and officials. He had, to all practical purposes, set up a private news service away back in his smuggling days. He had found out then that prices and the ups and downs of his business were affected by what Napoleon did on the battlefield and in the council room. Therefore it had seemed to him a very simple thing to instruct the skippers who carried his cotton cloth across the Channel to bring him the latest issues of French, German and Dutch newspapers. Later his Wellington enterprise had made military, naval and financial developments a matter of vital concern to himself and especially to his brothers. Therefore at the first opportunity he had thought it good business to secure a small fleet of his own, so that officers and crews might devote themselves exclusively to his needs. These boats were not common carriers; they were a bridge between the London house of Rothschild and its associates on the mainland. Chiefly used for the conveyance of money, securities and letters, they were in effect one of the earliest foreign news services in the world. For their commanders had orders to hurry back, regardless of wind and weather, whenever any event of outstanding importance had occurred on the Continent. It was thus that Nathan learned of battles and things ahead of the British Government. That was all there was to the mystery.

III

Following the fall of Paris and the first abdication of Napoleon, in the spring of 1814, Mr. Herries was able to show Mr. Rothschild in a larger way than before how greatly he valued his services. The Count of Provence, long a refugee in England, was proclaimed by the Allied victors king of France; the sacred principle of legitimacy had been (for the Austrian chancellor, at any rate) one of the higher aims of the great struggle against the usurper. This, to be sure, did not prevent them from imposing a crushing indemnity upon the restored monarchy. Meanwhile Louis XVIII, after these twenty-five lean years, was in no pecuniary position to undertake the triumphant entry to his capital. He applied for a loan of five million francs ($200,000) to his good hosts, the British Government. The Treasury granted the request, and the Commissary-in-Chief called in Nathan to handle the transfer. As a transaction the affair was not in itself of any especial moment but Nathan saw further than immediate gain. The House of Rothschild, so strong and honored in England, had no standing proportionate to its wealth on the Continent. In France especially it was in fact suspect and obliged to carry on under cover. To hand the new ruler this round sum at such a memorable moment as this, in checks payable at the Paris office of Rothschild Brothers, could not but raise the firm's prestige enormously. It promised even to knit a permanent tie with the court, and give James a position there comparable to that of his brother in London.

That was not all. Though the long Napoleonic nightmare was over, temporarily, the impecunious Allies still required, and were by agreement entitled to receive, the British subsidies. It was not entirely out of friendship for Nathan therefore, that Herries now energetically undertook to convince the ambassadors of the Allied powers in London that it would be to their advantage as well as England's to centralize the payments somewhere on the Continent; he was thinking primarily of the economies that arrangement would effect for the British treasury and of the salutary influence it would have on sterling exchange. Incidentally, however, he proposed that the place be Paris, and without naming Rothschild, that the choice of the agency be left to the English financial authorities, which in this department meant the Commissary-in-Chief. The amiable thought behind the proposal was, as in the advance to King Louis, to smooth the path for young James and the remaining Continental Rothschilds.

But the Allies, particularly Austria and Russia, raised objections. They were conservative powers; they liked to do things as they had always done them; besides, they owed favors to their own money-men. The negotiations, moreover, were now conducted with the principals of the Allied governments in Paris itself, whither Nathan had accompanied Herries; and the Eastern statesmen entertained certain sentiments toward the name, the sectarian affiliations and the social and personal traits of such people as Mr. Rothschild. Prussia, being the neediest of the brethren, was more agreeable; and some little progress was achieved with the others after lengthy discussion. On the whole, the project did not promise to have the success that Herries had anticipated. During the remainder of the year 1814 the major Allies continued realizing their subsidies by drafts on London executed through their own bankers.

Early in 1815, while the victorious statesmen sat haggling over the spoils around a green-baize table in Vienna, the alarming news rang out over Europe that Napoleon had landed near Cannes on the Riviera, had been wildly acclaimed by his old followers, and was rapidly collecting an army and marching on Paris. The intelligence had a sobering effect on the Congress. Irritating differences were suddenly ironed out, and the diplomats who had the day before sat glowering at one another embraced affectionately and became allies once more. In a trice the coalition was reconstituted. The armies, dawdling at their ease in France, shouldered their muskets again, reinforcements set out from every corner of Europe, and England loosened her purse-strings and began pouring out fresh subsidies. Under the stress of renewed war Herries was pleased to note a more accommodating spirit on the part of even Russia and Austria toward the Rothschild plan of handling the remittances. It was the last but probably the greatest in the long series of services which Napoleon unconsciously rendered to the five brothers.

Indeed, the problem for Herries and the Rothschilds was now, not to persuade the Continental governments so much as to find the wherewithal in cash and credits on the spot to satisfy their needs. Once again the British Treasury was obliged to coin French louis-d'or in its own mints and otherwise to resort to extra-legal means. The Prussian command in Belgium was during the Hundred Days as before in the gravest straits, so that at one time Bluecher was driven to the expedient long ago adopted by Wellington of issuing his own drafts on London, while von Buelow, the Prussian finance minister, urged and implored to have at least a hundred thousand pounds advanced without delay.

The pleas remained for a time unanswered because both Herries and Nathan were themselves at the moment busy on the Continent. They returned to London late in April. Thereupon the Commissary-in-Chief referred the entire matter to his associate; and Nathan, perceiving that one of the great opportunities for which he had been waiting had come, dispatched an order to his brother Salomon to deliver in person to the Prussian minister of finance two hundred thousand pounds on behalf of the British treasury. The diplomatist of the Rothschild family did not fail to make the most of this the first direct contact of his house with one of the first-class powers on the Continent. Finding that Buelow was in very great financial difficulties, he offered on his own responsibility to take over a hundred and fifty thousand pounds of the English subsidy obligations, over and above the sum he was instructed to pay out. Considering, however, the low rate of sterling in Berlin and his want of authority and the risks involved, he was regretfully constrained to charge so heavy a discount that Prussia had later to ask Britain to make up the difference. Nevertheless Buelow was delighted. In his letter of thanks to London he commented with enthusiasm upon the energy, the helpfulness and the amiability of the House of Rothschild. He saw to it personally, moreover, that both Herries and Salomon were fittingly rewarded, the British official with a porcelain service from the royal manufactory, the banker with the title of a Prussian Trade Councilor. Best of all, he retained a lasting impression of the evident influence of the firm and never after lost contact with it.

IV

Nathan's delight was at least equal to Buelow's. The immediate profits of the operation, or even of similar business to come, meant little to him. Reading between the lines of the minister's gratitude, he saw that Salomon had made a permanent conquest. Prussia had clearly been won, definitely and unreservedly, for the House of Rothschild. That was matter for congratulation. For Nathan's restless spirit, looking beyond the moment, had begun to be concerned about the future. However it might end, the renewed struggle with Napoleon could not go on forever. And the moment it was over, victors and defeated alike would have to take stock of the damage and set to work rebuilding. Rehabilitation would take money; and as virtually all the governments were bankrupt, the only way money could be raised was by loans. Nor was that all. This quarter century of disorder was not likely to be lost even on the backward-looking men who governed Europe. Therefore standing national armies were here to stay. Troops must be fed and clothed, munitioned and housed. Lastly, one side or the other was going to pay a goodly sum in damages, and that, like all the rest, would have to be borrowed from those who had had the foresight to lay by a bit during the storm. A rich harvest was awaiting the firms with sufficient resources and the right connections. He and his brothers were amply provided with the first item. They must make haste to secure the second as well. That was why the news from Berlin was so heartening.

But Prussia, though splendid for a beginning, was, when all was said, but a rather small patch on the map of Europe. The great prize on the Continent was imperial Austria. Austria was not only the leading state in the German Bund; she was a great power with immense subject lands, and she stood only second to Britain in the councils of the Coalition. The banking house which secured a firm foothold in Vienna would gain something more than prestige and a leverage for future conquests. It would become the first financial institution on the European mainland.

Unfortunately Austria was not to be captured so easily. Her own favored bankers had neither the vitality nor the necessary connections to handle the subsidies with the vigor and dispatch that the situation demanded. Yet, though the good Herries did his utmost and though her forces suffered from inefficient provisioning, it was only with the greatest difficulty that she could be persuaded to accept payment according to the new system even during hostilities. Her big men, unlike the alert Prussians, held aloof away off there in Vienna, and were inaccessible to mere business men; with the consequence that the war ended and no Rothschild had got within earshot of an Austrian minister. After Waterloo she stiffened still more. Her haughty governing clique, accustomed to servility from all who came near them, demanded preferential treatment and made endless difficulties. At the base of their resistance was mistrust toward the still little-known Jewish concern.

But Nathan and his brothers were persistent. Amschel in Frankfort and James in Paris sat on the doorstep of the Austrian envoys, and gave them no peace. Without so much as a hint at the possibility of their standing or credit being questioned by anyone, they played up in glowing colors the services they had rendered and the favor they were enjoying at other courts. Not that it had any bearing on the subject in hand, but it might interest His Viennese Majesty's representatives simply as a fact of common knowledge that the House of Rothschild was delivering the subsidy moneys for Prussia, Wuerttemberg and numerous other German states in so satisfactory a manner as to earn the commendation and the gratitude of their governments. No other firm in all Europe probably possessed the facilities of Rothschilds for the prompt, safe and economical disposal of that business. This was simply a fact which it would be immodest to ascribe to any superiority on their own part but was owing to the complete and extraordinary confidence which the London member of the concern enjoyed at the hands of the gentlemen charged with the administration of the subsidies by the British Treasury.

All these strenuous endeavors, however, seemed to go for naught; and in the end it fell to Herries to bring Austria around. He tried persuasion through his agents on the ground; he addressed communications to the imperial authorities, dwelling upon the savings in time, in money and in the good influence upon the exchange which the improved remittance plan effected, confirming all the boasts of the Paris and Frankfort Rothschilds and adding his own high opinion of their ability, their financial strength and their entire reliability; and when Vienna still hesitated he ended the interminable discussion by summarily taking the matter into his own hands and relieving Austria of responsibility altogether. For while the Allies doubtless had the right to employ what men and means suited their own fancy in converting the subsidies, it was, after all, the British Treasury that held the purse, and so long as the remittee got his money safely, promptly and without loss, he could not reasonably complain as to the manner or the agency. Herries, therefore, quite simply instructed his friend Nathan to pay the monthly instalments to Austria as and when she wanted them and to accept her drafts on the British Government at par. As to costs, commissions and discounts, why, England would take care of them herself! He, Herries, would show the people over him that the arrangement was the cheapest in the end.

This somewhat high-handed procedure had the desired effect. Vienna at last realized that the queer English meant business, and that this suspect Rothschild plan and Rothschild concern were evidently held in some regard by the one European nation to whom finance and business were second nature. And since the islanders were the rich uncles of the Coalition, it might be as well for proud but needy kin to keep on the sheltered side of the tradesmen they favored, even if the terror of Europe was now safely stowed on St. Helena Island. Austria, therefore, did more than submit to Herries's decision. She went a long step further and arranged with the House of Rothschild to handle her share of the French indemnity. Presently, finding that these payments were coming in too slowly to mend her disheveled finances, she approached the concern with the idea of liquidating the outstanding instalments in advance of their maturity. These transactions were not only enormously more profitable than the subsidy affairs, they brought the House into immediate contact with the finance administration in Vienna, and in addition served to raise its prestige in France. Nathan had sized up things correctly: the rapprochement with Austria was to make Rothschilds the first financial institution in the world. Right off it enabled James to establish himself definitely in Paris. In a very short time it was likewise to erect Salomon's house in Vienna and Karl's in Naples.

CHAPTER IX

NOBILITY

ONE good turn deserves another—in the same direction. Having got what they wanted, the brothers now considered that they deserved well of their new clients. True, they reasoned, they had made a good thing of the subsidy transfers to Vienna; but then the bargain had turned out still more advantageously for the Austrians. The imperial treasury had, owing purely to the Rothschild influence in London, saved an enormous amount of money in bankers' commissions and an even larger one in interest on the advances. These sums, to be sure, had not come out of the Rothschild pocket; they had been made good to the last penny by the British Government. The fact remained nevertheless that Austria had got several millions ahead of time without paying the customary charges. Only a house having the influential friends in London that they had could have done such a thing for her, and she knew it; her own bankers had asked one per cent commission and six per cent interest. Was it not legitimate, therefore, for Austria to show some appreciation for their loyal services?

This logic of business, whereby the merchant made the profits and the client emerged as the beneficiary, was no invention of the Rothschilds. It had come to them by inheritance, from their father and from William of Hesse-Cassel. Had not old Meyer earned his Court Factor title as a kind of bonus from the Landgrave for the privilege of letting him buy a batch of trinkets? Had not the Landgrave himself been elevated to the dignity of an Elector in recognition of a loan he had made to the same Emperor of Austria at a good rate of interest? And had not Prussia, upon a gentle hint, recently honored Salomon with a Trade Councilorship in circumstances similar but much less favorable to that state than the present ones were to Austria? How else were men of business to become gentlemen of rank?

It was not vanity altogether; the Rothschilds were painfully in need of lifting up. At least the Continental ones were. Nathan, over there in England, could afford to smile loftily at ribbons and crosses. He was a full-fledged citizen of a country where a comfortable balance at the bank was as good as an earldom, and where race, religion and family descent counted for little in a man's affairs and for not much more in his social position. But in France, and particularly in Germany, a Jewish merchant could not live by bread alone, nor be anybody with mere millions. These incurably aristocratic lands rated people by their antecedents, or at least by the length of the handles attached to their names. The Frankfort patricians could not forgive the Rothschilds their Judengasse origin and their shopkeeping past. Their amazing rise, their incredible financial genius, their fabulous wealth, did not help to advance them socially; Continental Europe took no stock in the self-made man. It was jealous of him and distrusted him. Napoleon, the supreme example of the species, was a fresh and painful memory to ruling families lately returned from exile. The Rothschilds' money, far from exacting respect, only heightened the contrast between their present magnificence and their lowly beginnings, threw into the more striking relief their cultural rawnesses and provided wags and Jew-baiters with handy gibes. While their Gentile competitors, like Bethmann, mingled on easy terms with statesmen and field marshals, they neither received invitations nor could get their own accepted. It hurt, that; also, it made the ladies unhappy; not least, since finance was so much a matter of teacups and small talk behind potted palms, those bolted doors were not good for business.

So it was urgent that something be done. Those minor dignities were not any good. They must get no mere Kommerzienraths and that sort of thing any more, but a spangle so gigantic and lambent as to cast their entire previous history into the shadow. Now the country where the name Rothschild stood in highest repute was England. If Nathan cared, he might possibly obtain a knighthood by way of reward for his aid to the Duke of Wellington and subsequent usefulness. But Nathan was the one brother who did not care, and even if he did, it was hardly likely that the honor would be of any use to his foreign relatives who needed it most. Prussia was very friendly, but the shining things in her gift were not big enough. There remained only Austria. That conservative state, for all its unenlightened treatment of the Jews in general, was not ill-disposed toward deserving individuals of the faith. The present emperor had conferred nothing less than a barony upon one Jewish financier. What he had done once he might be induced to do again. In any event Salomon thought the attempt worth making.

II

As one dynasty to another, the House of Rothschild approached the House of Hapsburg initially through the latter's envoy at Frankfort. This was not just conformity to diplomatic usage; in the absence of more direct channels, it was the only thing to do. In times to come the firm found it quite unnecessary to speak to emperors through mere ambassadors. But this was only 1816, and one must work with the tools at hand. So Salomon, after alluding to the cordial relations that had always existed between the two Houses, passed on to more recent history and begged Schwinner, the financial man in the Frankfort legation, to recall the loyal and unselfish services which he and his brothers had rendered to All-Highest in connection with the English subsidies, as well as of their readiness to be of use in all future undertakings, specifically in the matter of the advances on the French indemnity. Concluding, he begged to be so bold as to suggest that some recognition from His Majesty of their endeavors might not be out of place and would certainly be treasured by himself and brothers now and forever. It was not for him to say what form such recognition was to take. (Why ask for a knighthood? Suppose he should want to make it a dukedom!)

This verbal feeler was in due course transmitted to the minister of finance in Vienna, Count Stadion, who in his turn handed it on to the emperor. Stadion, though he had never laid eyes on any Rothschild, recommended favorable action. The man was nearly frantic with the effort to save the country from bankruptcy, and the opportunity to gain the adherence of this energetic young house with its powerful connections in London looked to him like a god-send. Negotiations for the liquidation of the French indemnity were still in progress with James in Paris. They had come to nothing so far because the brothers, for all their unselfish devotion to His Majesty, were obliged to offer the somewhat low figure of sixty kreutzers to the gulden. Were the emperor to confer upon them some fitting honor, they might perhaps reconsider the question and be content with a twenty-per cent profit on an advance repayable over five years.

The monarch, however, was not to be rushed. Stadion's troubles did not disturb *his* sleep. Besides, a Christian emperor could not just like that hand out distinctions to people who not only were theologically unacceptable, but were tradesmen of doubtful origin and foreigners to boot. So Francis took his time to reflect. Also he consulted his chancellor and one or more of his courtiers. The chief minister, Prince Metternich, was on general principles disposed to cultivate good relations with moneyed people, regardless of race, creed or antecedents. One never knew when they might be needed. Leader and fountain-head of the reaction though he was, he had a singular tenderness for the Jewish people, individually and collectively, and was doing everything in his power to secure the rights of citizenship for them in Frankfort, if not in Austria. So Metternich seconded his colleague's motion.

But in other, no less influential, quarters, the Rothschild proposal encountered severe and ironic opposition. A gentleman about the court, Lederer by name, subjected the petitioners' claims to such close scrutiny that the project seemed in peril of falling to pieces. What, he asked in effect, had they done to merit consideration? As far as those subsidy remittances were concerned, now, it was quite true they had not required Austria to pay any commissions on the matured instalments nor any interest on the advances. Well, they were not entitled to any. England had squared the account with them in full. They had not sacrificed a penny in the whole operation. Did they expect to be paid twice? Similarly, their great to-do about having carried through a complex financial enterprise without disturbing the exchange. So they had. But their cleverness had nothing to do with it. Events over which they had no more control than over the weather, had been favorable; that was all. As for their punctuality and efficient management—good heavens, what were the men thinking of? They were bankers, weren't they? Was it not their simple duty to be punctual and efficient?

Then Lederer gave some attention to Stadion's doctrine of putting the firm under obligation for the sake of future needs. To him the whole notion seemed the veriest innocence. Did the minister of finance suppose that business men governed their conduct by sentiment? It was one thing or the other: either Austria was a client worth having or she was not. If her affairs were profitable they would go to all lengths to get them; if they were not profitable they would not lift a finger, no matter what favors were shown them. The only criterion was profit and loss. This was the first time he had ever heard of the idea of men of the trading class being expected to operate on any other basis.

Lastly, they were Jews. Not that he entertained any prejudice against any people or faith. Still, facts were facts. In Frankfort where the men in question had their home, the Jewish question was just now particularly acute.

A proposal to grant the Jews equal rights with Germans was under discussion before the council of the states sitting in that city, and feeling on both sides was running high. Were His Imperial Majesty to single out a Jewish family of Frankfort for distinction at this time, the impression was certain to go abroad that Austria was taking sides with the Jews and trying to force the issue; which surely was not what All-Highest intended.

However, when all was said, the brothers, or one or two of them anyhow, had certainly given valuable service to the empire. He was not in the slightest degree disposed to minimize that, however much they might have to thank England and the course of events for the result. Nor did he mean to suggest that they were entitled to no consideration at all. Just what form the reward should take, it was not his place to decide. But if his opinion were required, he would suggest that they be given each a gold case with His Majesty's monogram outlined in diamonds!

III

This devastating analysis came very near dashing the brothers' hopes. The emperor hesitated and weighed the pros and contras as if it were a question of war and peace. But Stadion, backed by Metternich, pressed on. No doubt, there was much to be said for Lederer's objections. Still, Austria was in no position to repulse friends with money and influence. Inspired reports from the legation in Frankfort dwelt on the power and the wealth of the House of Rothschild, on its eagerness for social recognition and on its goodwill toward Austria. There would probably never be another opportunity like the present for winning its gratitude. So at last His Majesty assented. Now came the question, What kind of a spangle? Several motions were made and considered. There was Lederer's satirical idea of the gold case. Someone else suggested a sum of money; but Stadion felt that would not do. A mere token of recognition in that form would scarcely interest the Croesuses, and a bounty large enough to impress them might strain the imperial exchequer. In any event they were more likely to appreciate some less tangible honor which would have the advantage, moreover, of costing the government nothing. The police director of the city of Gratz favored their being named Imperial and Royal Councilors, a distinction, however, which was reserved exclusively for deserving state functionaries. An order, again, was not in keeping with the nature of the service rendered, and the Civil Medal was sure to disappoint their expectations. All in all, therefore, a title of nobility seemed best calculated to answer the purpose, even if it did promise to stir up jealousy among Gentile bankers and the squirearchy at home. That, of course, was the solution which the gentlemen in the Frankfort legation had been driving at from the start.

Meantime, before the grave discussion had come to an end, the Rothschilds had made bold to supplement their petition. Originally the plan had contemplated honoring only the two eldest members of the family, Amschel and Salomon. On second thought, it was pointed out that, while they had been particularly active in the subsidy operations, the firm was a solid unit and worked together on each and every undertaking. Consequently it might be both invidious and prejudicial to the solidarity of the family were some of the brothers to be raised above the rest. The logic was clearly sound and incontrovertible, and that point, too, was granted.

Salomon was now asked to convey to the imperial heraldry office his ideas of a coat of arms for his House, and Salomon complied to the best of his ability. Left to himself, he would have taken the opportunity to paint a symbolic history of the family, or at least of those aspects of it which lent themselves to public admiration. Wasn't that what armorial emblems were for? Besides, one was not asked to become a nobleman every day in the year. A natural reserve, however, bade him be moderate. The quartered field, therefore, showed but three colors, red, yellow and blue; figures, all told, a meager seven—two lions, a leopard, a stork, a hound, half an eagle and an arm holding five arrows, the whole surmounted by a crown. Even this was largely in grateful allusion to the honored patrons of the family rather than to its own magnificence. Thus the leopard symbolized England, the eagle Austria, and the lions the Elector of Hesse-Cassel. In the field itself only the arm with the arrows spoke of the unity of the five brothers, while the hound and the stork, which held up the shield, stood for loyalty and piety.

The martinets in the heraldry office, however, were not in the habit of letting things go through just like that, and they blue-penciled Salomon's draft unmercifully. The animal collection was wiped out almost entirely. Why? Tradition! The rules of heraldry forbade the arms of a foreign country, or any reference thereto, to appear on a device granted by Austria. The crown, too, must go; it belonged to a loftier style than was being contemplated for the moment. Even the hound and the stork, those gentle creatures representing the virtues that had made the

House of Rothschild great, were not allowed to remain. The ridiculous slashing went to the length of reducing the number of arrows in the arm from five to four. Sheer stickling! By the time the experts were done there was so little left of the original design that Salomon hardly knew it. Nevertheless the 25th of March, 1817, was a red letter day in the history of the family. For on that day the final document went forth from the imperial palace in Schoenbrunn declaring that henceforth the four continental Rothschilds were members of the Austrian aristocracy. The snobs of Frankfort might now give themselves what airs they liked; the sons of Meyer, the Jewish curio dealer, were by imperial decree as good as any of them. And James in Paris could prefix a significant "de" to the Rothschild Frères on his office sign, and look the proudest courtier of Louis XVIII straight in the face. Only Nathan remained a humble plebeian. But he did not mind.

IV

But though Nathan was inclined to smile at armorial bearings, there was one species of official dignity to which he was not indifferent. Cordial relations with Herries had shown him the value of being on the inside of government. There was more worth-while information to be picked up around the ministries in a day than in all the London drawing rooms in a year. Now that the war was definitely over and subsidies a thing of the past and the British connection safely clinched, it behooved him to spread his nets into new waters. For any number of reasons, but chiefly because of the geographical distribution of his brothers, France and Austria were the most desirable waters in sight.

Paris would take considerable wooing. Vienna, on the other hand, was coming along very nicely. The past performances on behalf of Austria were, however, no more than a good beginning. If the same rate of progress were to be maintained, it was essential to keep the closest kind of watch on developments in her fiscal policies. Her old bankers at home were surely making the most of their proximity to the court; and although Salomon and the others were nobles now, they had no firm footing on the ground. There was no Rothschild office in Vienna,—not yet. By the time news reached Frankfort it was apt to be of little use. Therefore some channel of a more direct kind must be cut to the great capital on the Danube.

It so happened that the Austrian consulate general in London was vacant at the time. It seemed to Nathan that that was the very thing for him. Were he to fill that place he would be in effect the financial attaché of the embassy. Considering that London was the world's money capital and that Austria was bound for a good while to come to borrow, this would mean that the ministry of finance in Vienna would guide its fiscal policy by his, Nathan's, reports and opinions. That is to say, he would not only know far ahead of the court bankers when a loan was being contemplated, he would have a hand in determining when and whether such operations should be undertaken. Incidentally he would, as the accredited representative of a great power, be brought into intimate contact with the official folk of other countries as well, not by way of fox hunting and tea parties, but in their business capacities—the only aspect of fashionable society that mattered to him.

He conveyed his thoughts to his brothers, and Amschel went to work at once. While he was about it, indeed, Amschel discovered that the Austrian consulate general in Paris was likewise in need of a good man, and it occurred to him that he might as well give his little brother James a boost at the same time. So he wrote to Vienna that should the chancellor contemplate filling those two vacancies he knew the very men for him. He was not, he explained, seeking any new honors for members of his family; his brothers and he were much too grateful for the splendid surprise His Majesty had lately seen fit to give them. It was precisely for that reason that he was anxious to make some small return. The members of his House in London and Paris, owing to their prominence in the business and banking of those capitals, were in an excellent position to further the commercial interests of the Empire abroad. They had, moreover, no thought of asking any kind of pay for their services. They merely wished to demonstrate their gratitude and loyalty.

Meantime Nathan himself let no grass grow under his feet, but plied the Austrian ambassador in London to the same effect. Vienna, however, was in no haste this time. It looked to the authorities there as if the Rothschild people had an unhealthy appetite for distinctions which grew by what it fed on. Without exactly refusing their request, the Austrians decided that a little check would be good for them just now. It might spur them on to show their devotion in some more tangible form, such, for instance, as an offer of better terms in the French indemnity matter. For the time being, therefore, nothing much happened. The Rothschilds, however, were not discouraged. They kept on begging and pulling wires. But it took three years before Vienna got around to the appointments.

That was a long time to wait. Fortunately there were

other things to keep Nathan and James occupied in the interval. Early in that eventful year 1817 the royal government of France, upon balancing its books, discovered a rather staggering deficit. Prospective revenues would not only leave nothing over for indemnity payments, they would not even meet current expenses. A loan of some three hundred and fifty million francs was imperative. Such a sum could not at this time be raised within the kingdom, to be sure; but the credit of France, despite the instability of the last quarter of a century, was still good abroad. The ministry therefore set the machinery in motion by calling in, not James Rothschild, but that financial wizard, Napoleon's old banker, J.-G. Ouvrard. Ouvrard, however, though he had made several fortunes in his time, was richer in ideas than in money just now; so that he in turn sought the help (again, not of de Rothschild Frères)' but of the great British financiers Baring Brothers and their associated firm of Hope & Company.

James was frantic to take a hand in this first great operation since the war. It was not so much the profits—he was not doing so badly in his other affairs—but if he could at least participate in the syndicate, his standing in France would be assured. But neither the Englishmen nor the Frenchmen would have anything to do with him. The Rothschilds' exploits in the Peninsular campaign were no secret any longer; but far from being admired for them, they were looked upon as unscrupulous tricksters who had abused the confidence of French bankers, had helped the enemies of France and would very likely do so again if they had the chance. Labouchère, the brother-in-law of Alexander Baring and the head of Hope & Company, conceived an unconquerable aversion, moreover, for young

James personally. He despised the insignificant little man with the marked Semitic features, the deep restless eyes and the curly red hair, who could cringe when he wanted something, became arrogant when he had got it, and was insufferable at all times. Ouvrard more than concurred in this estimate. To him the Rothschilds were "simple money changers, who owed their fortunes more to accident than their own ability."

But James was determined. Unable to gain access by the door, he tried the windows as it were. Associated with Baring and Hope in the preliminary negotiations was the dashing David Parish, a Hamburger of British descent, one of the most picturesque and adventurous figures in the world of finance. James managed to strike up an acquaintance with him. It was a strange fellowship: Parish the bon vivant, the intimate friend of Talleyrand, the beau who was at home in the best circles of London, Paris, Vienna and even Washington, and the rich but crude shopkeeper's son. They were attracted to each other by a mutual need. For Parish, with all his personal charms and high connections, lacked the capital just then to play the kind of part he desired in the syndicate, while James had the funds but lacked the connections. An understanding was therefore reached between the two, whereby Parish was to secure James's admittance to the consortium and share in his part of the winnings. But though Parish did everything in his power to push his partner forward, his efforts went for naught. He succeeded in bringing young Rothschild to the attention of the ministry of finance; and that was as far as he could go. Labouchère and Ouvrard were adamant. For no consideration would they work with the upstart. Indeed, they advised Parish to steer clear of all the Rothschilds. In years to come Parish wished he had taken his friends' warning.

The loan meanwhile was awarded to the two British houses without Rothschild participation. James took the blow hard, and vowed that he would make the snobs rue it. Nathan, on the other hand, did not mind. Precisely because it was the first big international transaction since the peace, it was an enormously risky thing. Let others make the trial flights. There was no telling how the investing public, spoiled by the fat profits of the war years, was going to react to this relatively sober business. The loan might very well be a fiasco, and in that event there would be neither glory nor money in it for the promoters. If, however, it was a success, it would serve to create confidence in state bonds, and the House of Rothschild could then make a more active bid for future loans. This was only the first; there were plenty more coming. For the moment it was just as well for the brothers to go slowly, make friends and build up their fortune. Besides, even though they had failed to be included in the consortium, nobody could stop them from playing as big a part in the loan as they liked and as seemed to them safe. The moment the security had made the grade, they could step in and acquire as much of it as they wanted. They need not even use their own capital in the speculation. Just as once long ago the Hessian Elector's Consols had laid the foundations of their fortune, so now the French indemnity payments to Austria, Prussia and the rest of them, which the House was handling, could be employed to expand it.

As it happened, the French loan was a brilliant success. Baring and Hope—though not Ouvrard—cleared enormous gains. But the Rothschilds were not impoverished by it either. They bought on margin and largely with the untransferred indemnity funds, such great blocks of the securities that they presently controlled the price of them. Ouvrard later calculated that they made a good fifty per cent with the self-loaned Allied moneys in this affair. Ouvrard, however, did not know the half of it. In his bitter hatred and contempt of the Rothschilds he could not believe that they ever thought of anything but gain. As a matter of fact, their interest in mere profits was only a passing phase this time. For a while, indeed, they bulled the market with great energy, much to the joy of Baring and Hope. But the sequel was much more interesting and rather less agreeable to these gentlemen. Of this, in a later chapter.

CHAPTER X

THE FIRST LOANS

NATHAN had sized up the situation more accurately than he knew. Of course, there would be other loans. His brother James was still lamenting his rebuff in Paris, when along came Berlin to cheer him up. True to her promise, Prussia had never forgot the help she had got from the Rothschilds during the critical Hundred Days. What was perhaps even more to the point, her finances were in a desperate state. The British subsidies and the French indemnity, mere stop-gaps at best, were about drying up; a few millions which, thanks to Salomon and Karl's good offices, she had lately borrowed from the Elector of Hesse-Cassel, were gone almost before they had reached her; her own people, burdened with taxes and economically exhausted by the long war, were as poor as their government; and the state treasury was barely able to pay the military and the civil servants their salaries. A foreign loan was the last and only hope.

With Karl virtually residing in Berlin, this state of affairs was no secret to Nathan. Therefore, along about November 1817, he sought out the Prussian consul in London, and after several conversations reached an understanding with him. This gentleman—Barandon was his name—without taking the time to consult his country's ambassador on the spot, communicated what he had learned (or such part of it as seemed to him relevant) direct to Berlin. There were, he said, but three firms in all England equipped to place a loan for Prussia in the London market. Of these the House of Rothschild was held in the greatest esteem both by the investing public and by the British government; so that, were this concern to undertake it, the operation was a foregone success. He then went on to state the factors which might have an adverse influence on the project, lest too sanguine expectations should lead to disappointment later. The British were a clannish lot and loaned their money very reluctantly to foreign governments. When they did it at all they expected a high rate of interest, having been spoiled by the French *rentes* which yielded about eight per cent, while the Prussian loan, as contemplated, would pay only five. Moreover, several recent attempts to launch foreign bond issues in England—Austrian, Spanish, Russian and Neapolitan—had been complete failures. Nevertheless he was hopeful. Prussia's integrity and thrift were much admired beyond the Channel. At the present moment, also, Consols only yielded a little less than four per cent; so that if Berlin could see its way to offer a rebate of ten per cent to the investor and a five per cent commission to the bankers (thus raising the interest rate to seven and a half) he believed success to be assured.

This highly inspired communication no sooner reached the Prussian chancellor than he authorized Barandon to proceed, and negotiations were opened forthwith. It soon transpired, however, that Barandon had misunderstood something. The House of Rothschild was indeed prepared to float twice as big a loan as the royal government desired, only the rebate would have to be not ten but thirty per cent. Why should anyone want to invest in Prussian bonds at ninety when French ones could be had for seventy? This seemed reasonable, and a provisional agreement was drawn up on these terms. But before the final contract could be signed, news reached London of projected flotations by several other countries, with the consequence that money became tight. Thereupon a very curious thing happened. Barandon, namely, made public Nathan's printed plan for the Prussian loan. In that document the amount of the issue was stated at twelve millions, instead of the twenty provisionally agreed upon, and the emission price not seventy but sixty. The purpose of this interesting procedure, as Barandon apparently understood it, was to discourage other prospective borrowers away from the London market. However that might be, it was received in Berlin with raised eyebrows, and Barandon was asked to explain just what the changed figures signified.

Barandon's explanation was so clumsy and tactless that Nathan saw with dismay that the man he had picked was not exactly a Buderus either for financial astuteness or for keeping those over him in the right mood. He blurted out things as they were told him, without stopping to think of their possible effect. Thus he told Berlin straight out that the reduced price had been dictated by the fall of the French *rente* to sixty-five. Sixty was, of course, less than that; but then the British investor preferred the French paper because it represented the recognized national debt of a first-class power whose credit had safely weathered three successive revolutions. As a matter of fact, he added, Austria was offering her five-per cents as low as fifty-two, and Russia was vainly trying to float a loan at seven and one-fifth per cent. So what could Prussia, whose securities were quite unknown to this foreign market, expect! How all this sounded to Chancellor Hardenberg can only be imagined. But Nathan was sufficiently discouraged to drop the rough-and-ready diplomat, and henceforth transferred the negotiations to the embassy. For a space it seemed as if the entire project would go aground. The Berlin authorities were extremely put out with what seemed to them a highly suspicious way of doing business, and efforts were made to secure a loan elsewhere or to manage without one. Ambassador von Humboldt (a brother of the famous scientist) succeeded, however, in calming the air.

Humboldt put the whole blame on the unfortunate consul, and recommended sending over a well-trained man specially for the purpose. As for Rothschild he was not only "easily the most enterprising merchant here now" but an entirely trustworthy man, honest, fair and intelligent. He transacts much business with the British government, and is through his brothers thoroughly familiar with the Prussian situation. To advance his brothers' interests he is disposed to make himself agreeable to "our Court" and it will not be easy to find another house as friendly. What Barandon had said about the difficulty of placing foreign loans over here is quite true, and the success of the French issue must be regarded as a special case; so that it were best to think twice before trying someone else. Rothschild, on the other hand, is not going to be very manageable. He has the independence which comes with wealth and prolonged residence in England, and the ministry of finance must be prepared once the conditions were agreed on, to let him handle the whole thing without interference. His affairs and speculations are so comprehensive and varied that it means very little to him whether he secures this particular enterprise or not.

II

Prussia then sent over her keenest financial intellect, a man named Rother, who having started as a regimental clerk had risen by sheer force of character and ability to the directorship of the treasury. The negotiations now began in earnest. Nathan at once perceived that in Rother he had met his match. Here was another Buderus indeed, but a Buderus who took his responsibility with the utmost seriousness and would represent his royal master's interests as loyally as if they were his own. Nathan not only respected what was to him a quite novel type of official mentality; he found delight in pitting his wits against those of an equal. This was going to be a chess game after his own heart, with no victory assured in advance. Well, he would rather lose against an opponent like Rother, than win with Barandon.

Rother shared this feeling; only he had the advantage of having something like his opponent's measure in advance, whereas he was an unknown quantity to Nathan. Before proceeding to England he had painstakingly prepared his retreat. All in all, he preferred to have the loan launched in England, but only provided the amount and the conditions were at least equal to those that could be obtained elsewhere. To make sure of this he had entered into negotiations with bankers both in Berlin and in Amsterdam. Moreover, he had outlined a plan for a direct government flotation without the aid of bankers. As it happened the Netherland authorities were contemplating a loan themselves and could not permit a foreign one to be offered on their exchanges at this time, but privately a number of capitalists assured Rother that they would be glad to invest in the Prussian securities if they were issued abroad. In Berlin, despite the general depression, a consortium was improvised which was willing to take up fifteen million, possibly twenty, on acceptable terms. Prussia was thus well armed for the fray. The Rothschilds by no means had the field to themselves. They must reckon with strong competition.

Realizing all these initial disadvantages, Nathan called his brother Salomon to his support. This was the first government loan the family had ever been called upon to float, and it must go warily. Salomon had had dealings with Rother before, was closely in touch with developments in Berlin, and might well know something about the rival terms. Nathan, moreover, though he was confident of his own business skill, did not trust himself in delicate manœuvres with diplomats, especially Continental ones. That was Salomon's forte.

The conversations began at noon on the 25th of March and continued for an entire week, sixteen hours a day, frequently till the small hours of the morning. Rother opened by declaring the conditions named in the printed plan unacceptable. To this Nathan replied that he was prepared to listen to any reasonable proposal. However, that plan had been made public, and it would be a breach of faith with prospective investors, as well as compromising to both Prussia and his House, to dishonor it entirely. Prussia was about to make her initial appearance in the London financial market, and such a beginning would injure her

K
W
SALOMON
VON ROTHSCHILD

prestige. While, therefore, he would be glad to consider raising the price somewhat, he would suggest that at least a portion of the loan be offered at the figure originally named. But in any case, he wished to say at once, it would be useless to try to float the issue at over sixty-five on the average. As Herr Rother was aware, even the French bonds were unable to lift themselves above that level, and the Prussian Funds were a new and untried investment over here. Yes, Herr Rother had heard this reasoning before from Consul Barandon. Also, he knew that he could do better than match these conditions much nearer home, and that in all probability Mr. Rothschild would not let it come to that.

Aloud Rother observed that without wishing to make odious comparisons, he regarded his own country's credit as an infinitely sounder risk than that of France, and that this he had reason to believe was also the general view. If the public had any real confidence in the newly restored French monarchy, its securities would command a much higher price. But France, as the last quarter century had amply shown, was a turbulent country. Besides, her national debt was tremendous, and she was at present groaning under the burden of a still unpaid indemnity. Prussia, on the other hand, was a young and vigorous state, with an orderly population devoted to its reigning House and quite proof against revolutionary infection. Her internal debt was trifling, her foreign one almost non-existent. The entire world admired and trusted her honest and efficient government, and her hard-working, pious, intelligent inhabitants. In sum, the low state of the French *rente* had nothing whatever to do with Prussia.

The Rothschilds conceded that there was much to be

said for this reasoning, and requested a counter proposal. Rother replied that Prussia must have five million pounds (thirty million thalers) and was prepared to offer the bonds on a sliding scale of seventy-five, seventy-eight and eighty net, that is, without any deduction for bankers' commissions. This was, of course, merely an asking price. Even so, however, Nathan found it fantastic; and after submitting reasons why it would be useless to undertake the loan at anything like those terms—reasons which commanded even Rother's admiration—he frankly declared that unless his opponent was in the mood for large concessions the conferences might as well be abandoned at once. For a moment the air grew extremely tense. Rother, partly because he felt that he had the inside grip on the situation, partly as a tactical move calculated to force the bankers to name their final figures, said that he feared there was nothing else left. As Humboldt had warned beforehand, Nathan was too independent and prosperous to care. Had he been alone, he would at this stage quite likely have walked out of the room without any further ado. Salomon, however, was anxious that this undertaking should not end in failure; his mind was dwelling on the still exposed position of himself and his brothers on the mainland. So he counseled patience. Both sides, therefore, retired to think it over, and the heated session ended in mutual expressions of friendship.

The next day a succession of compromises was proposed and discussed. Finally Nathan declared himself willing to float the bonds at seventy straight. In view, however, of the condition of the market and the consequent risks involved, he must ask for no less than four per cent commission. Again, the negotiations were in peril of an abrupt termination. Rother was still soaring in the region of eighty, and commissions of four per cent he declared to be unheard of. The discussions continued until long past midnight. Not only the price but the amount of the loan were still in dispute. The Rothschilds argued that to launch five million pounds' worth of an unknown security was to risk both their own fortune and the credit of Prussia unnecessarily. It were far more prudent to start modestly with three millions, and in the event of success to follow it up with a further two, which would then doubtless command a better price. As the hours dragged on with no solution in sight, a spirit of accommodation possessed both sides. Rother agreed to the four per cent commission, Nathan gave in on the five millions. On the price, too, a compromise was reached. The first half was to be issued at seventy, one half the remainder at seventy-two and a half, and the last quarter at seventy-five. The understanding was verbal; papers were to be signed on the morrow.

III

Between supper and breakfast, however, Rother did some sums and observed that at this rate the treasury would realize on the average somewhat less than seventy per cent of the face value of its script. This was no better than the German bankers were prepared to do, and he would have a difficult time explaining his reasons for placing the profitable business with foreigners, in particular as public opinion was strongly opposed already to having the bonds go out of the country. Besides, were he to sign up on these terms he would be exceeding his authority. He disliked very much reopening the discussion—it meant a deadlock now, he feared—and seeming to be going back on his word; but there was nothing else he could do. In the morning he therefore dispatched a letter to Salomon explaining his position.

He began very pleasantly by paying a warm tribute to Nathan. His journey to London, he felt, had been worth while because it had enabled him to become acquainted with Salomon's brother, "for whose intellect and character I have the greatest admiration—*even if our affair comes to nothing.*" Having thus casually introduced the main purpose of his letter, he went on to say that his hands were tied by explicit instructions which prevented him from definitively entering into the provisional agreement of the night before without consulting his government. These instructions he would gladly lay before Salomon—"not as Mr. Rothschild but as my friend"—when they met again. To Berlin he surely enough did write that same day—not, however, to ask for wider powers but to say that the negotiations were progressing favorably! But that he really held Nathan in high esteem he showed in the way he spoke of him to the authorities at home: "The London Rothschild is a very estimable man and has an almost unbelievable influence on all money affairs in the city. It is saying a good deal, yet it is well-nigh true that he controls prices on the exchange here. His strength as a banker is very great."

Salomon was not to be outdone in courtesy; for his gifts as a diplomat were superior to his grammar. If he was put out he did not show it. Writing back promptly, in language which even old Meyer would have been ashamed of, he assured Rother that they wished nothing to be done in haste, that good-fellowship and sincerity were more to them than business, and that they were his cordial and devoted friends.

There followed four more days of fencing and bargaining and threats of rupture. Finally at three o'clock in the morning of March 31 an agreement was secured. It was not this time a compromise; all the concessions came from the bankers, and Rother emerged with flying colors. The flotation figures were unchanged—seventy, seventy-two and a half, and seventy-five—but the commission of four per cent had been eliminated entirely. Immediately upon the signing of the contracts Nathan dispatched a boat to Hamburg with a million thalers in silver, to await Rother's arrival there, and a second million in commercial paper on the same city was handed him on his departure. Humboldt was delighted; Rother's skill had achieved a triumph beyond all expectations. The felicitations, however, were premature; Rother still had a card in his sleeve. He had held it for a climax all along.

When, early in the negotiations, Rother had painted the economic outlook of his country in bright colors, the picture represented his genuine convictions. All that Prussia lacked was a world market for her credit. This loan, now happily arranged, would give her that. He trusted the Rothschilds to handle the exchanges with skill. In these circumstances it would not be long before the bonds would rise in value. Why, then, should not the royal treasury share in the profits? The country did not need the entire five million pounds at once. She could afford to invest a bit in her own securities, now that the pressure was relieved. In a final conversation with Salomon he, therefore, suggested that Prussia would cheerfully take over one million pounds from the loan herself. Considering that the bankers had throughout fought for keeping the total down to a lower figure, they could hardly object now that Rother so obligingly lightened their burden. The brothers graciously consented, and the parting letters exchanged between the negotiators were almost tender. Rother wrote to "my dear Salomon" that he was leaving London happy, and Salomon replied by assuring him that he had done "a divine piece of business. God knows," he added, "that our hearts are with you and that we are moved by no desire for profit. . . . We are heartily, eternally and loyally your friends."

Why should they not be? The new loan was taken energetically in hand by all the five brothers and pushed simultaneously in all the more important exchanges of the Continent as well as in London. Trading in it was so brisk from the start that within six months the price rose to eighty-three. It went back for a little time, without however falling below the level at which it was issued, and then recovering it went on upward till at the end of six years it mounted to par. The Rothschilds thus had reason to be content with their first venture into state financing. They had been generous without exactly sacrificing themselves. Doubtless they could have wrung more favorable terms out of Barandon. But where would have been the glory? They had learned something from the contact with Rother, had triumphed over competitors, and had recaptured the confidence of the Prussian court, which in the first stages of the negotiations they had almost forfeited.

As for Rother he had during a time of depression succeeded in obtaining terms which were the admiration of the experts. His last-minute move had been a stroke of genius. The bonds had scarcely been put on the market when a Paris banking-house offered to take over the million pounds he had reserved, at five per cent above the flotation price. Many people in the government were in favor of accepting, but he held on till the height of the boom, and the state realized a round hundred and fifty thousand pounds on the incidental operation. Moreover he had avoided the risk of a direct loan and had put Prussia definitely on the European financial map.

CHAPTER XI

HONEYMOON

TO return to France and the sequel to James's rebuff. Why the Rothschilds should take the lead in bulling the loan of 1817 puzzled Labouchère and Alexander Baring not a little. It looked to them like the purest benevolence. The brothers, after being not only beaten but snubbed into the bargain, were returning good for evil, like apostolic Christians. It did not sound like them, or even like rational business. What might they be up to? Make a killing? Naturally. But that was too obvious. They could as easily profit by bearing the market. The only plausible explanation seemed to be this: they were currying favor with their rivals by a demonstration of their power on the exchanges. It was a peace offering. Ouvrard and Labouchère lost what little respect they had for men who could resort to such groveling tactics.

The gentlemen were in error, however, and unjust to Nathan's resourcefulness. Not that he was not capable of precisely those tactics; only in this instance he had other objectives in his eye. A corner in the new French *rentes* was desirable on general principles, as well as for two or three specific ones. In view of the firm's manifest destiny, the public ought to have its confidence educated in state securities. A weak response to this initial venture would be a setback for all loans and hurt more people than Baring and Hope. Contrariwise, a brisk absorption of the

French offering would create a thirst for future issues. But public spirit aside, Nathan did purpose a show of strength,—to impress, however, not his rivals, but the financial world in general and the French government in particular. What with her economy disordered by a quarter of century of almost constant war, the Allied armies in occupation of her territory eating her out of house and home, and a sizable part of the indemnity still to be paid, France had only begun to borrow. True, helping the present loan to its feet might merely result in strengthening Baring and Hope. The Rothschild demonstration, instead of showing the authorities where the real money power was, making them regret the error of their past ways and disposing them for a wiser course in the future, was running the risk of leading them to the superficial conclusion that the two British firms were so influential that even disappointed competitors were bound to support them. Well, that might happen. And then again with a bit of caution one might very well induce the French public, if not its government, to ask a few embarrassing questions about this too successful (and too profitable) loan of Baring and Hope. And lastly, control of the market would make the House of Rothschild the arbiter in the next flotation; would not only enable them to dictate the price, but give them in effect the power to veto the project altogether. In given circumstances the exercise of this last would be nearly as sweet as the award of the loan itself.

What followed came close to bearing out Nathan's calculations. Within less than a year the French bond issue of 1817 soared twenty per cent—from fifty-five to sixty-six. The British firms came off so well that the Paris investors and even more the French taxpayers complained loudly at the tribute they were forced to pay the foreign bankers. Even the government was stirred, and brought suit against Ouvrard for profiteering. Nevertheless, when early in 1818 the budget again failed to balance, the ministry of finance turned for help once more to Baring and Hope, and the Rothschilds found themselves as much on the outside as the year before. Neither gratitude for past aid nor veiled threats of future obstruction would make Labouchère overcome his aversion for the brothers. This time, however, Nathan as well as James must be reckoned with. The London Rothschild, fresh from his triumph with Prussia and his victories on both royal exchanges, was determined that no new French loan should be launched without at the very least his participation in the syndicate. If Baring and his friends refused to take warning, then he, Nathan, would have no choice but to use his veto power.

II

Negotiations in Paris began early in the year. By summer a tentative agreement had been concluded with Baring and Hope, whereby the two associated British firms were to raise two hundred and seventy million francs for the final liquidation of the indemnity. By way of a sop to public opinion, the government did for a while give some perfunctory attention to schemes of a direct treasury loan, and listened with one ear to proposals of the native bankers; but nothing came of either alternative. In one respect at least Nathan's fears were thus justified. For the government took the position that it could not risk untried men and methods at a critical time, and that the British houses had more than earned their profits by the great lift they had given French credit at home and abroad through their successful handling of the last loan. Indeed, it was owing to their efforts that the nation was now able to command a much improved figure for its bonds.

For the time being, however, the agreement was provisional. France must first secure the assent of the Allied governments, and that meant a wait of several months. In the autumn a conference of the Powers would meet at Aix-la-Chapelle to consider the evacuation of the French provinces, the payment of the balance of the indemnity and some related matters. Till then, therefore, the precise terms of the loan contract must remain in abeyance. The Rothschilds were going to have their delegate at Aix, and Nathan was still hopeful that Baring would be realist enough to come to terms. The last word at the conference would rest not with France but with the statesmen of England, Russia, Austria and Prussia. With all these countries the Rothschilds were in good standing. At any rate, James and his brother in London went on trading in the French bonds of the previous loan and pushing them up.

Meantime Karl, the fourth son of Meyer, had reached his thirtieth year and felt it was time for him to marry. Choosing a mate for a Rothschild had, by the year 1818, become a serious matter. Amschel and Salomon had taken wives in the dim days when the family were Judengasse shopkeepers; Nathan had wedded Hanna Cohen during the smuggling interlude. But Karl was fifteen years younger than Amschel, and thus the first to attain marriageable age since the House of Rothschild had become a dynasty. They were not only the richest Jews in the world, but nobles to boot. Their former neighbors and business associates were away beneath them; families on their own economic level still hesitated to accept them as equals. Moreover, Karl was the least clever of the brothers. It was therefore a brilliant achievement and another step in the rise of the House when the erstwhile Kalmann won the hand of Adelaide Herz. The young lady was not only beautiful; her family belonged to the small and exclusive circle of cultivated German Jews who had had their money long enough to attain enlightenment and social graces.

The wedding took place on the 16th of September, at the very time when Frankfort was filling up with notables on their way to the Congress at Aix. It was a gorgeous throng. From the four corners of Europe Emperors and kings, statesmen and generals and great ladies were converging upon the ancient capital of Charlemagne. Originally it had been planned that Salomon should be the sole plenipotentiary of the Rothschilds at the big show; diplomacy was his bailiwick. But Adelaide was tempted; and since the young pair must go on a wedding journey somewhere, why not combine pleasure with business and take their honeymoon at Aix amid the gilded pageantry? The notion caught Salomon's fancy. Finance being so largely an affair of the right social contacts, the presence in the delegation of a lady with Adelaide's accomplishments would be a distinct asset. Her beauty, her poise and her family connections might easily turn the scales in the delicate mission ahead of him. By all means let the couple come along.

III

In truth, Adelaide and her people had begun helping out even before the wedding. No one surely who had thus far come into their ken was fated to mean so much in the destiny of the Rothschilds as Friedrich von Gentz, and it was Frau Herz and her sister who provided that introduction. Salomon and his brothers, not being reading men, were unaware that Gentz was the most distinguished publicist in Germany. Nor is it likely that they would have gone out of their way to make his acquaintance on that account if they had been aware of it. Writing men doubtless had their merits. At least princes seemed to think so. The Duke of Weimar, for instance, had made one of them, a Frankforter named Goethe, his chief minister. But what possible use could they be to bankers? What was interesting about Gentz was that he was the secretary, the close friend and adviser, almost the other self of Prince Metternich, the man who in the affairs of Europe had inherited the mantle of Napoleon, who was the power behind the throne of Austria and who would hold the Congress at Aix in the hollow of his hand. That was important, and equally so was the fact that Gentz was a gentleman of expensive tastes and meager income, so that he probably must make ends meet somehow.

The facts in the case were a great deal more interesting than that. In his youth Gentz had shown decided leanings toward the radical ideas of the Revolution. Later, the excesses of the Jacobins and an offer of employment at the court of Prussia had made a wiser and a disillusioned man of him. He read Burke's "Reflections" and swung completely around. A man of rare political insight and literary gifts, he soon attracted notice in influential quarters by his eloquent defense of the old order. Foreign diplomats in Berlin approached him with assignments in behalf of their governments. He sold his pen and his editorial connections to England, to Russia, to whoever was willing to pay for them. At a time when courtiers and even ministers balanced their private budgets with gifts and loans from court merchants, when reigning princes themselves bartered their subjects for money, it was too much to ask of an impecunious young writer to be swayed by ethical scruples. Gentz was anything but ashamed of the "subsidies" he got; he noted each item gleefully in the Journal he kept as "an agreeable transaction" or as "good news." Subsequently, after entering the service of Austria, he discovered that bankers were prepared to make safe investments for him with their own capital in exchange for advance notice of his master's intentions, and he delivered this intelligence as freely and with no more thought of wrong-doing than he had previously shown in merchandising his literary wares.

Gentz preceded Metternich to the congress, and arrived in Frankfort on the 3rd of September. The same evening, his journal records, he saw Moritz Bethmann the banker, by whom he was "very cordially received." (Bethmann's firm, like most financial houses, had irons in the fire at Aix.) On Sunday he lunched at Bethmann's home. But the man with whom he spent most of his time was David Parish, the young Vienna banker who was again operating on the sidelines for Baring and Hope. Parish, however, was no mere check-book to Gentz. "David Parish," he wrote to another friend, "is the matador, the pearl of the business world in all Christendom on both sides of the Atlantic Ocean, one of the most complete men that I have ever seen." They too met and talked every day for as long as Parish remained in Frankfort, which was till the eighth, when he left for Aix, after "important arrangements" with his friend.

It was only after Parish's departure that Gentz found time for the Rothschilds. At ten in the morning of the next day they paid their first call. Three days later there was another visit of an hour, during which Gentz and they had "an interesting conversation about the local Jewish question," then up before the council of the German states sitting in Frankfort. Thus far neither "agreeable transaction" nor "good news." But presently the tempo quickened. Sunday the 20th was a hectic day for Gentz. In the morning he had a conference with the Austrian ambassador, on leaving him he stopped in to see Salomon and his brother at their own place, where "everything was happily disposed of." Then he must rush to Bethmann's for lunch. At nine A. M. on Monday one of the brothers came alone, and the conversation was important enough for Gentz to write his Prince the moment his visitor left. Tuesday evening he dined with "the family," which included beside the Rothschilds, Madame Herz, Madame Frohberg (Adelaide's aunt, an old friend of Gentz), a general and several lesser notables. At daybreak next day he was off to join his master.

Salomon, accompanied by the honeymooners, followed him the same afternoon with a light heart.

IV

At Aix the proceedings got slowly under way. At least the official ones did. How much was being accomplished at the ceaseless round of luncheons, dinners, soirées, balls, the

Rothschilds had no way of knowing for certain, but what they surmised made them uneasy. A score of bankers—Alexander Baring and Labouchère among others—had arrived on the ground before them, with their suites of well-groomed, genteel-mannered lieutenants. They were seen everywhere, riding about in their proud equipages, halting at one palace after another, gold-laced magnificoes and splendid ladies at their side. Parish and Gentz apart, Saloman saw scarcely anyone in that whole brilliant assemblage with whom he was on speaking terms. Hardenberg was there for Prussia, but Rothers was not in the delegation. England had sent Castlereagh but not Herries. Even Barbier was absent. Neither Adelaide's beauty nor Gentz's friendly offices seemed to be of much use. The shimmering pageant rolled past, but the Rothschilds looked on at the windows, wistful spectators.

Gentz was touchingly attentive. The busiest man at the congress, he would tear himself away from a reception at the Nesselrodes', a tête-à-tête with Lady Castlereagh, even Metternich's dinner table, to spend a couple of hours with Adelaide and her husband and brother-in-law. Almost every day he found time to receive Salomon and Karl at his own rooms. And he did his utmost to convince his Prince that the Rothschilds were too rich and powerful to be overlooked, while Parish on his side urged the same logic upon Baring and Hope. But it was all to no purpose. Metternich and the bankers were committed. In those two or three days before Salomon's arrival an understanding had been reached between them, and there was no going back. It was too late for a peaceful solution of the Baring-Rothschild rivalry.

Already in September, while the forehanded guests were

assembling in Aix, some rumblings had been heard on the Paris bourse. They were mere warning signals, however, which soon passed. On the second of October Gentz had a reassuring talk with Parish about "important money affairs in Paris;" on the ninth he received "good news" from the same quarter. On that day, too, the Congress fixed the conditions for the remainder of the French indemnity, Baring and Hope undertaking to float the loan—at a greatly advanced figure, of course, in view of the high standing meanwhile attained by the issue of the previous year. The Duc de Richelieu for France approved the enhanced terms with pleasure. The Allied representatives gave the enterprise their blessing. All the nervousness of the past fortnight had disappeared. Bankers and statesmen told one another confidently there would be no storm, and Aix gave itself up to unrestrained gaiety. The Rothschilds seemed finally and irretrievably beaten. Gentz's visits to "the family" came to an abrupt end, though Salomon and Karl continued to call on him from time to time. He was very, very sorry; he had done his best. But what was the use? The decision was patently irrevocable; they could see that. And he was terrifically busy. He was the secretary not only of the president of the Congress (Prince Metternich) but of the Congress itself, and the protocols of the proceedings devolved upon his shoulders. Well, better luck another time.

Nevertheless the two brothers remained serene and devoted. On the twenty-seventh, after Gentz had about made up his mind that they had at last given up,—they had come only twice since the ninth—Salomon appeared and handed him eight hundred ducats, winnings from a little investment in the English Funds. The busy secretary pocketed the windfall gratefully enough, though he was a little puzzled. The persistence of those people was astounding. What could be their game now? The mystery was to be resolved a week later.

On the fifth of November the thunderbolt fell. While Aix had been enjoying itself, some terrifying things had been happening in Paris. About eight days ago—on October twenty-seventh, to be exact—a mass of 1817 government bonds had suddenly been unloaded on the bourse. The result had been pandemonium. Within five days the state securities had dropped from 74 to 68. Every other paper had followed suit. There was no let-up in sight. It was a panic. From the French capital the movement was spreading to the other Continental markets. Even London was showing the strain.

V

The bad news threw the Congress into confusion. "They all pretty much lost their heads," says an eyewitness; "only Baring kept his." Lucky for him that he did. He had something more tangible to save than his self-control. By the contract which he had signed here at Aix less than a month ago, he had on his hands a trifle over a quarter of a billion new French obligations, which he had bought at an average of seventy, and which therefore meant not only an immediate loss but that they could hardly be offered on the market at all. Unless he held his wits together and found a way out, he was a ruined man. The situation was as desperate as could be imagined; there was no mistake about that; all the greater the need for straight thinking.

"An Englishman the like of whom there are not many," was Gentz's characterization of Baring. He proved himself worthy of the compliment now. No muddling through for him. A glance showed him pretty clearly what had happened, who had made it happen, and why. Patently a couple of gentlemen in London and Paris had decided to show him who was master. Well, they had succeeded. It was useless to deny that. But they were mistaken if they thought they had got his scalp. One way or another he was going to squeeze out of that contract. That was all, and that was enough satisfaction for any rival surely. There would be no new French loan just now; but the House of Baring Brothers would go on standing for yet awhile.

The proposal, however, to break the engagement could hardly come from the banker. It would be not only undignified but useless. He would be read a stern lecture about the sacredness of contracts, and be held to his pound of flesh. As it happened, a number of the leading Allied statesmen had an interest in the ill-starred loan, other than official. Hardenberg of Prussia, Nesselrode of Russia, Prince Metternich, not to mention Gentz and other smaller fry, each had signed up for a parcel of the as yet unissued bonds. They had not actually put up any money of course. If all had gone well, they would have clipped the coupons every six months or so, and eventually have collected the full value of the matured paper, without the bankers being too petty about the accounts.

But things were not going well, alas! not well at all. So Baring via Parish via Gentz begged for an audience with Prince Metternich and the other chiefs of the Congress;

which was grudgingly granted. The statesmen would rather have avoided the meeting; it did not promise to be pleasant. The unlucky financier would probably whimper and crawl and appeal for mercy. But no! surprisingly. The thoroughbred was taking misfortune like a man. He did not so much as hint at release. A contract was a contract; he meant to stand by his guns, whatever the cost. What could be finer! However, there was something more—another surprise, not so agreeable. He expected the good gentlemen to honor their commitments also, and thus distribute the burden! In view of the fact that the operation was to be a loss from the outset, he must respectfully and regretfully suggest that all subscribers pay up in advance, trading on margin being feasible only on a rising market. And so on . . .

This was unheard of, fantastic. Metternich was thoroughly outraged. No banker had ever made any such proposition to him before. He had no money for investments of any kind, least of all for flivvers. Rather than do what Baring wanted, he would throw the loan out altogether. And that was what happened. At the session of November 19, the chair informed the French delegation that, mindful of the deplorable news from Paris and having the credit of France at heart, the Congress was obliged to reopen the matter of indemnity payments. A canvass of the assembled powers revealed that the representatives of Russia, Austria and Prussia favored postponing the question to some future conference. The Duc de Richelieu had no choice but to agree. The houses of Baring Brothers and Hope & Company were saved, but they left Aix with their glory dimmed. Metternich never forgave them. Their primacy in world finance was gone forever.

VI

Meanwhile, between the fifth and the nineteenth, while the wearisome bargaining was going on, Metternich managed to spare a little time for Salomon and Karl. On the twelfth he asked Parish, Gentz, the two brothers and one or two other people to take lunch at his table. As an earnest of friendship and goodwill, the busy Gentz dropped everything the next day to prepare a memorandum on the Jewish question for the Council at Frankfort. That was on the thirteenth of November. On the fourteenth Salomon, considering his task done, quit Aix-la-Chapelle, together with the honeymoon couple and David Parish. The Congress continued for a fortnight longer. Journeying home to Vienna, Gentz stopped off again in Frankfort for a week, and while there saw the brothers daily. Prince Metternich arrived in the Main city on the evening of the fourth and left the next morning, but Salomon and Karl could not let those fourteen hours pass without paying their respects, whereupon Gentz noted briefly in his journal: "arrangements with the Rothschilds." Finally Gentz himself was off for Vienna right after lunch on December sixth; but though he had many friends in Frankfort, and though he had taken leave of the Rothschilds at their home the evening before, he ran in again for a last handshake while his coachman waited whip in hand.

His next halt was Munich, where he was received by the Bavarian king and treated on all hands as a personage. He felt himself that he had acquitted himself more than creditably at Aix. As he added up the proceeds of those two months' work he must admit that he had not done so badly: two orders (the Red Eagle from Prussia and the Anna

Order from the Emperor of Austria) besides six thousand ducats in cash, thus: France eight hundred; ditto from Prussia and Russia; seven hundred pounds from England, and from a Herr Bentheim on behalf of "the mediatized" nobles one thousand ducats. Nothing at all, of course, from Baring, but to make up for it, another eight hundred from the Rothschilds, with much more in prospect. And his total expenses, including gifts for loved ones in Vienna, barely more than a quarter of the total.

Money, however, is not everything. Aix had been a turning point in his career. Writing to a friend from Munich, he let himself go in exultation: "Never, I can truthfully say," he declared, "have the laurels been heaped so thick on my head; every day I was flatteringly assured that without me it was no longer possible to have a congress. . . . It was proposed I regard this period as the culmination of my life . . . that I be forced to marry, so that my stock at least might not die out. . . . Partly for official reasons, but also because I felt I could make no better or more interesting use of my spare time, I have had the most instructive conversations with the most powerful figures in the commercial world—Baring, Labouchère, Parish, Rothschild, etc.; and it was no small advantage to hear the innermost secrets of the greatest money affairs that have ever been carried on among men, negotiated in my little house."

Exciting and delightful as all this was, it did not prevent him from observing the financial gods with a twinkle in his eye and making thumbnail sketches of them. Parish, "the matador, the pearl," was a boon companion after his own heart. He admired the intelligence and the broad training of Baring. But the phenomena, the marvels, of the entire assemblage were the Rothschilds. As men they could not compare with the others, and he frankly despised them: "They are common, ignorant Jews, outwardly presentable, in their trade the sheerest materialists, without the remotest inkling of any higher relationship in the world." But they are "endowed with an admirable instinct which always makes them take the right course and between two right ones the best. Their enormous wealth (they are the biggest in Europe) is entirely the product of this instinct, which the vulgar call luck." It must not be imagined, however, that all the Rothschilds are equally gifted. Of the five one is only so-so, (Amschel) and another (Karl) is wholly negligible. Finally, the moral of the financial drama he had witnessed:

"The profoundest reasonings of Baring, now that I have seen everything at close range, inspire me with less confidence than a single healthy glance from one of the more intelligent Rothschilds. If ever Baring and Hope go wrong, it will be because they think themselves wiser than Rothschild and do not follow his advice."

But there was little danger; Baring had learned his lesson, and he had no thought of defying his rivals again. In the years to come the two houses coöperated often and amicably.

PART III

GRANDEUR

CHAPTER XII

IN THE SADDLE

AIX was a turning point. It was another milestone, like Nathan's fateful journey to Manchester, like the banishment of the Elector William, like the gold purchase from the East India Company. No, it was more momentous than all these. Everything that had gone before had been but a preparation; this was the harvest, that magical time when dreams and scarcely articulated hopes take solid shape. With Gentz, like a very genie, unlocking fairy palaces; with Metternich, the portentous, the all-powerful, safely in tow; with the majestic Hapsburg himself waving a genial scepter, the whole past had grown dim, shadowy, far-away. Buderus, the Elector, Rother, even Herries, shrank and faded and became unreal like the characters in some tale read long ago. With Parish a devoted associate, with every major financial house in Vienna reduced to a state of virtual vassalage, with the proud Baring himself making overtures of peace, friendship and alliance, how remote and insignificant seemed the foes and rivals of another day—Feidel David, Michel Simon and his son-in-law Levy, Rueppell & Harnier, even the Bethmanns, even Van Notten! Had all those people, indeed, ever existed? Had they actually ventured to put themselves in the path of the mighty, irresistible juggernaut? They were such vague, insubstantial shapes. And, most incredible of all, could it be true that only yesterday Salomon Rothschild and his brother Karl had been slinking about on the twilight edge of Aix-la-Chapelle, patronized by Gentz and Parish, snubbed by Labouchère and Baring, outsiders in the grand show? How strange and sudden were the ways of destiny!

But now,—now came the sky-rocket years,—the glamorous, golden harvest years. Fortresses so long besieged that they had almost appeared impregnable suddenly surrendered without resistance, with hardly a blow, unconditionally. The whole battered front gave way, wilted, and collapsed. The conquering five, with flags flying and drums rolling,—the strangest host in all history—marched on to victory. So swiftly that it made their heads dizzy, everything that they had ever aspired to, things that they had hardly dared breathe of even to themselves, dropped into their hands, all in the space of three brief years. The Austrian Consulate Generalships in Paris and London went to James and Nathan; a new house rose up in Vienna with Salomon in command; Naples, at the extreme tip of the Continent, was taken, and Karl, too, reigned in sovereign grandeur; and then came the splendid climax: all the brothers were raised to the baronate, with their children and their children's children to perpetuity.

It was Austria, the one country that had taken such long and arduous courting, which, having once yielded, gave herself so unreservedly and so whole-heartedly. Scarcely had the *agenda* of the Aix Congress been finally disposed of when Salomon emerged as His Imperial Majesty's chief banker. The haughtiest and most fastidious court in Europe opened its proud doors wide to welcome Salomon and Karoline (née Stern) Rothschild. With the mighty Chancellor securely bound to the golden chariot, the rest of the cabinet were drawn into the procession as a matter of course. Where the political power of Austria was ascendant, there also the financial power of Rothschild swayed. Salomon had but to whisper that he desired honors for a man in his employ or privileges for a relative, and the Imperial Hapsburg thought twice before he declined. Invitations poured in upon the banker and his wife; hardly a state function passed without them; archdukes and ministers dined and danced at their home. On the bourse he was supreme. He made and destroyed men and fortunes with a nod. To be in his good graces was better than credit; to incur his displeasure was ruin. Former rivals and competitors submitted to his dictation and prayed fervently for his continued success; for, in the words of Moritz Bethmann, the very prosperity of Austria was inextricably bound up with the fortunes of the House of Rothschild, "and the fall of such a colossus would be terrible."

But not alone in Vienna was the sun shining. In France also a new king had arisen, or at least a new minister of finance. Count Joseph de Villèle, like Metternich, was an ultra-monarchist Christian gentleman and thus had a natural aversion for the people of Jesus; but, even as the Austrian Chancellor, he was drawn toward the Rothschilds, and—so it was rumored and insinuated—by the same irresistible lodestone. So James acquired an ancient palace on the Rue Laffitte and filled it with masterpieces of painting, sculpture and such things, hired a box at the opera, and became a patron of the arts. The last of the sons of Meyer to be born, he was still a bachelor; but his position in society, the multitude of his friends and retainers, and his elaborate entertainments, made a wife indispensable. Therefore he bethought himself of marriage presently. The latitude of choice, however, had since the last Rothschild wedding become still more restricted. What with being Austrian barons and all the rest of it, even families like the Herzes could now hardly aspire to family alliances with them. They were, like royalty, a subspecies apart. Only a Rothschild was fit to breed Rothschilds; and surely none but a Rothschild could provide the dowry fit for a Rothschild. The consequence of all of which was that in the summer of 1824 James was wedded to Betty, the youthful daughter of his own brother Salomon.

II

Imperial Austria, as distinguished from its imperial Chancellor and his efficient secretary, took Salomon to her bosom for pressing reasons of her own. The "good news" and the "pleasant surprises" which came to Gentz; the loans and gifts and holiday remembrances which Metternich received, the mediation and expert advice of David Parish, certainly removed obstacles; but the ministry of finance was in no position and in no mood to be choosy anyhow. The state exchequer had been suffering from distempers and violent attacks of vertigo for decades; the wars with Revolutionary and Napoleonic France had aggravated the malaise immeasurably; and no amount of subsidies, indemnities and kindred doses had sufficed to effect a cure. The Vienna bankers administered temporary relief from time to time; but their resources were limited, they lacked the necessary connections abroad, and, the authorities having once or more suspended cash payments and defaulted on the interest, they entertained serious doubts about the solvency of the fatherland. It thus fell out that the monarchy was chronically hard up, that its securities found few buyers on the home markets and none at all on the foreign ones, and that the publication of bids for a new loan seldom occasioned bloody strife amongst the competing financial houses. It had been years, if the truth must be told, since more than one bidder had shown any interest in the nation's fiscal affairs; and even that was commonly such a lukewarm one that it must be bolstered with extravagant concessions to make it stick. Meanwhile the state's responsibilities were enormous and growing. The monarchical establishment, with its "Roman" traditions, its pretensions, its battalions of archdukes and courtesans, was the most expensive in Europe; the government departments were fantastically over-manned and putrid with incompetence and corruption; and the aftermath of the Napoleonic business had brought in its train a whole series of local combustions which, in view of Metternich's self-imposed duty as the guardian of law and order and legitimacy, was involving Austria in one costly military adventure after another.

In these circumstances the financial alliance effected at the Congress of Aix was as gratifying to the distracted Minister of finance as it was to Gentz, Metternich and Salomon. Here was a concern with unlimited means, with youth, energy and ambition, and with powerful roots in Frankfort, Paris and the world's money capital, London. Most happy augury of all, the Rothschilds were making the advances; they were clearly taking a sanguine view of the Austrian economy. Count Stadion, the then head of the treasury, was not disposed to play the blushing maiden: he met the bankers more than half way. At the first opportunity he displayed his goodwill by putting business into Salomon's hands. Not many months after the dissolution of the Congress several trial operations of the already familiar type were entered into,—indemnity transfers and the like—and cordial feelings developed between the minister and the banker. A shrewd official without any nonsense about him, Stadion took the measure of his man at once, and having satisfied himself that the connection was promising, went to work with all his might to clinch it. Rothschild craved decorations, social advancement and an improved status for the Jews of his home city; he, Stadion, was prepared to labor with the Emperor, with the council deliberating in Frankfort, with Metternich, to secure them for him. It was an article of his faith that men placed under obligation made loyal servants; Austria, heaven knew, had little enough to offer; and if this useful house could be bought with such counters, why, he was willing to pay the price.

The next year business began in earnest, and Salomon justified Stadion's trust in human gratitude. There being as yet no Rothschild office in Vienna, and the nature of the enterprise being new to the firm, David Parish conducted the preliminary negotiations and shared subsequently in the result. Early in April the Emperor authorized the associated houses of M. A. Rothschild & Sons and Fries & Company (the Parish concern) to float a lottery loan of half a hundred million florins. Salomon, however, had ideas of his own about ways and means. With Stadion's approval he proceeded to throw open to the public only a fraction of the issue. He calculated, and rightly, that an undeveloped market like Vienna and an untrained investment community like the Austrian would be swamped with such a mass of securities released all at once. Therefore, naturally, not a word was whispered about the next step, not for three months at any rate. With the help of Gentz, meanwhile, and with the aid, also, of a Baron Meseritz, who represented in Frankfort the *Augsburger Allgemeine Zeitung* and a syndicate of lesser journals in other German cities, a brilliant publicity campaign on behalf of the loan was launched in the press —not paid advertising, but a regular modern public education fanfare, with advice to investors, and short, snappy, popular disquisitions on finance and thrift and the like. Nor was the effort wasted. In a few weeks the scrip rose from barely over fifty to eighty, ninety and par; and long before the time the bankers had planned to let out the secret about the remainder of the loan, the first twenty millions were selling at three times the flotation figure. The loan was a riotous success.

Salomon's objective had been something more than a comfortable margin of profit; he was expecting a storm, and the ballyhoo with its effect on the market was to serve as a screen. Surely enough, the moment the remaining thirty-five millions were announced, there was a violent and agonized outcry from the purchasers of the earlier issue. It did no good for the bankers to point to the splendid results of the manœuvre and the high price at which the security was quoted. The public suddenly remembered that the culprit was a Jew, that the state (which meant the Austrian Christian taxpayers) would have to pay back almost two guldens for every one the loan had netted, and—worst of all—that they discovered, too, that owing largely to the release of the new scrip the old was tumbling furiously and disastrously. There were open charges of manipulation and Jewish trickery (the participation and the correct church affiliations of Parish being overlooked) and whispered insinuations that Metternich, Gentz and many other high officials, including even Count Stadion, had had their palms greased. However that might be, the market gradually rallied, and thereupon the popular indignation subsided.

Salomon subsequently declared that his firm alone had cleared six million florins; but that must have been the gross. Extraordinary charges, such as the newspaper campaign and other expenses, were borne by the Rothschild part of the combine alone; and unless Parish lied on the night of his tragic death six years later, he did not even know of them. At least, he said then that he knew nothing of the other expenses, which included one or two items recorded by Gentz in that outspoken journal he kept. Under date of June 7 (1821) Gentz noted a conversation with Rothschild, in the course of which the secretary conveyed "remarkable and flattering comments" of his master on the banker, which "produced favorable results" from the latter. Neither the nature of the comments nor in whose favor the results were had is indicated; but an entry of some weeks later is more explicit: "He (Salomon)," says Gentz, "gave me an accounting of my share in the last few financial operations, and it turned out that, contrary to my highest expectations, I was five thousand florins to the good."

III

Parish performed his part of the contract efficiently and loyally, and it does not appear that Rothschild was in any way dissatisfied or that any differences had come up between the two firms in all the months of their coöperation. Yet Parish was left completely in the dark about the friendly support given the common enterprise from the office of the Chancellor, and about its cost. It could not have been reticence on the part of Salomon; for Parish and Gentz were old comrades and men of the world, and he knew it. It seemed to have been something else. Parish, in the letter which he wrote Salomon on his last day on earth, accused him roundly of having deliberately and systematically worked around Metternich so as to set him against himself, and he repeated the charge to Metternich also. No doubt a despairing man on the brink of death may say wild and bitter things. This much is certain: the first important venture of Rothschild in Austria was carried out in intimate association with Parish's firm; but the first was also the last time the two concerns worked together. There were many and greater transactions in the years to come; but Parish had no part in them. The friendship between Salomon and Gentz and Gentz's master ripened into close companionship, and in proportion as it did so, Parish (whom Gentz had on his way home from Aix described as the pearl and the matador) faded from Gentz's diary and from Metternich's favor. His elimination may, of course, have been merely coincidental with Salomon's advancement. Statesmen are notoriously fickle friends.

As far as the Rothschilds were concerned, their consciences were easy. Where was the bad faith in the matter? A year ago Parish filled a need, and they used him. No one could say that they had failed in their obligations toward him, that they had not lived up to the letter of their contract. Now his usefulness was finished, and they had let him go. It was the way of business, of progress, of the world. He had ceased to be useful because Salomon having set up headquarters of his own in Vienna, the firm was now directly represented in the empire. Naturally he had done what he could to strengthen his position at court. If Parish with his personal attractiveness and his prior connection did not do the same he was simply neglecting his opportunities and had only himself to blame. Naturally, too, Salomon did not hesitate to inform the proper authorities that the association was off. Why should he? He was the House of Rothschild in Austria, and it was his right and duty to conduct his business as he saw fit. It would have been intolerable to let the government dictate to him. Therefore when the following year the Naples affair came up he very broadly intimated to Stadion that the concern was quite strong enough to handle it alone, and he had his way too. As a matter of fact, Parish did not weakly accept the situation; he tried, poor man, to assert himself. Only his judgment was faulty; he lacked the gift of sizing up men. When he found himself shelved in the Naples operation, he attempted the next time a loan came up to exert pressure on the finance minister; but Stadion was merely the workhorse and the figure-head of his department; the power was in the Chancellor's hands, and the way to the Chancellor's ear was through Gentz. What happened? The kindly treasury chief made an honest effort to have Parish participate; in a mild way he even insisted. Thereupon Salomon paid a visit to Gentz, and complained (says Gentz's diary) "with many tears about the inconsiderate manner in which various people were behaving towards him in connection with the new loan project." And within the week Gentz, to his "no small astonishment," received three thousand ducats on the Naples account and a day or so later two thousand more. Parish, in the meantime, went on shooting and drinking parties with Gentz—the jolliest pair of boon companions in the gayest capital in Europe. What could the unsocialized product of the Frankfort Ghetto do to match that?

IV

Any other piece of business would not have mattered greatly. But Naples was not commerce; it was conquest, empire. A banking firm might share risks and profits, without injury to its standing. Sovereignty was quite another thing. You either held it in solitary grandeur or you did not have it at all. And it so fell out, to Parish's misfortune, that the Neapolitan adventure followed hard upon the lottery loan.

The beginnings of the affair went back, like everything else in European politics since 1815, to Napoleon. Under the empire the Kingdom of Naples and Sicily had been governed by His Majesty Joachim Murat. After Waterloo the legitimate monarchy was, of course, restored by the holy alliance of the victors and for a space Ferdinand I ruled the land autocratically and more or less tranquilly. The embers of 1789, however, which Napoleon had unwittingly carried to all the ends of the Continent, went on smouldering, and it was only a question of time when they would burst into flame. What actually occurred was not a conflagration but a smudge. The liberal elements, that is to say, did not assault the strongholds of absolutism; nor did they guillotine the monarch; they only surrounded the palace with cannon and bayonets, deposited a constitution after the French Rights-of-Man mode, under his beard, and suggested that he sign on the dotted line. He very much disliked complying, but he was a prudent man with a good memory, and he did as he was told; after which the rebels departed and left him to reign though not to govern. Ferdinand, however, was not half so irritated by the high-handed proceedings of his subjects as was Prince Metternich in far-away Vienna. This sort of thing was getting altogether too fashionable. Only yesterday it had been Spain,—another of the Corsican's late satrapies; now it was Naples; where was it all going to end? And if the unspeakable liberal ideas went on spreading what, in heaven's name, was to become of the sacred principle of legitimacy? Well, it just must not spread. Metternich buckled on his shining armor; that is, he issued a call to the threatened monarchs of the Holy Alliance bidding them assemble in solemn conclave to deliberate on the menace. The Congress of Laibach summoned the spineless compromiser from Naples and ordered him to explain what he thought he was doing. He vowed that he had not meant to surrender, that nothing in the world was dearer to him than the doctrine of absolutism, but that he had not had much choice. The upshot of the discussion was that Austria was authorized to dispatch an army to the disaffected realm, tear up the newly granted constitution, and restore the monarchy to its ancient and rightful glory.

In Vienna, meantime, Stadion was breaking his heart in the endeavor to keep the leaky treasury from drying up. The news from Laibach did not fill him with rejoicing. He had not enough money to pay his clerks their salaries. And now he was to clothe, feed and equip an army! But Metternich reassured him. Austria would indeed furnish the troops, but the bill would be paid by the people of Naples. In the interval the funds would have to be raised somehow. In all probability Herr von Rothschild would be delighted to advance the initial million or so. Salomon's feelings, however, upon being sounded, were found to be divided. He wished profoundly to be agreeable to Metternich, to strike out into new territory, to get the profitable business. But the situation was fearfully involved. The British and the French governments were opposed to the whole adventure, and if the House of Rothschild gave it its financial backing there might be unpleasantness for Nathan and James in London and Paris. Nearer home, too, there were complications. It was the time of the violent agitation against the lottery loan, the market (owing in part to the intimations leaking out of Laibach) was depressed, and the name Rothschild was in the worst possible odor. All in all, therefore, it would be rather imprudent for the firm to identify itself openly at this unfavorable moment with a project which already was causing uneasy stirrings in various quarters.

There was no thought, of course, on Salomon's part of keeping out of the enterprise. The needed advances, indeed, he furnished forthwith, so that the expedition might be set marching without delay. He only begged Metternich not to insist on his personal presence in Laibach at this time. Instead, he would send him down his younger brother Karl. Karl was still floating about vaguely in the old way, running errands, keeping up contacts, filling in, the last of the five brothers to find a local habitation. Who knew? Perhaps his chance had come at last.

So the weakest of the Rothschilds—as Gentz had long ago described him—showed up at the Congress, and after receiving the final instructions from Metternich, proceeded southward on his great adventure. For a moment, just before he started, panic seized him. The Piedmontese, taking heart from the happenings in Spain and Naples, rose up against King Victor Emmanuel and demanded not only a constitution but an end of the monarchy. The explosion threatened to engulf Austria's own Italian possessions in Northern Italy, the Lombard and Venetian crown lands through which Karl must journey. As it happened, however, Metternich's forehandedness saved the day. Before the movement in Alessandria (Piedmont) could get fairly under way, the Austrian troops had pushed forward without appreciable resistance, had taken Naples and restored order, with the consequence that the revolutionary stirrings throughout the peninsula subsided. Gentz, who was in Laibach with his master, and who a few days before was nearly out of his head with fright himself, now assured Karl that there was no further danger and that he could start with an easy mind. In Florence, where King Ferdinand and his ministers had interrupted their progress till the Austrian commander gave the all clear signal, Karl discovered that he would have to reckon with competition. Not only was an Italian syndicate prepared to float the loan at better terms, the Neapolitan

KARL
VON ROTHSCHILD

authorities were disposed for political reasons to arrange the affair with people whom they knew and whom they could control. Ferdinand felt it in his bones that if he signed up with the Rothschilds, the proceeds would go in the main to Vienna while his own part in the transaction would be limited to paying the interest. As it turned out, the royal anticipations were, if anything, over-sanguine. For upon His Majesty's arrival in Naples, the Austrian envoy gave him to understand that it was indicated from headquarters that no other banking house was to be considered; and although the diplomat exerted himself at the same time to keep the Rothschild terms within reason, Karl, knowing that he had the field to himself now, could not be budged. Naples must guarantee repayment by hypothecating the state domains, she must pay three per cent commission, for three years she must not borrow another ducat, and after that time the preference in future loans must be given the House of Rothschild. The Austrian troops stayed on for four years, faithfully guarding the country against revolution, and the bookkeepers in Vienna regularly sent in a bill for their upkeep, which Karl (as a sort of treasurer extraordinary) promptly paid. Pretty soon the first sixteen million ducats had dried out, and then His Majesty signed for another bit and still another. For awhile the difficulty was to dispose of the royal obligations. The country being poor and the government eyed askance, the natives did not invest very heavily. Then Nathan conceived the idea of having the interest made payable in sterling and in London, so that the British market was won over. Meanwhile Karl and Adelaide grew fond of the lovely southern city, and though the conquering army marched away again the conqueror lingered. He and his descendants lingered on till Italy became a nation, more than forty years later. At last, after years of wandering and waiting on his brothers, the last of the sons of Meyer had found an anchorage.

V

Six years before, for a mere little job of transferring, the good Emperor Francis II had seen fit to raise four of the brothers to the nobility. As he thought of it now, Salomon felt that His Majesty had behaved rather handsomely. In comparison with the services the House had rendered since, that subsidy affair had been the veriest trifle. The lottery loan had, on the other hand, done nothing short of putting the state's credit on its feet. The business in Naples, moreover, had saved the world from liberalism and republican chaos. Was not the time, therefore, ripe for another bit of an honor? He put the rhetorical question to Gentz; Gentz put it to his master; and Metternich repeated it to All-Highest. Looking before and after, the chancellor, the monarch and not least the minister of finance, agreed that the time surely was ripe. Stadion was not only grateful for past favors; he was thinking anxiously of his flat exchequer and the weary days ahead. Metternich, for his part, was actively preparing to do for Spain what had just been so brilliantly accomplished for Naples. It so happened, besides, that his personal finances were in somewhat of a muddle just at the moment, and he was intending to obtain a loan of a million or thereabouts from Salomon himself. By all means the obliging fellow should have anything he reasonably wanted.

Fortunately there was no need to ponder this time what would please Herr Rothschild. He was right on the ground now, and he was not making any mystery of his aspirations. For five years he had been hankering after those fabled beasts that a martinet in the heraldry department had cut out of the coat of arms he had submitted. He wanted them back, and he wanted a title that sounded like something. Well, he should certainly have them. No officious meddling by experts now, no irony and no captious criticism. On the 29th of September 1822 all the five brothers were by imperial letters patent admitted to the hereditary aristocracy with the dignity of barons. Amschel, Salomon, Karl and James rejoiced and celebrated. Nathan eyed the sheepskin sardonically, dropped it into a desk drawer and forgot it.

CHAPTER XIII

IN QUEST OF A HALO

THEY should have been happy; they were not. They had the world at their feet in a way that Napoleon had never had it. Yet there was an emptiness at their hearts, a void that craved to be filled. Shimmering with orders, with stars and jeweled crosses; caparisoned with the ribbons and decorations of a score of states, from France to Russia and from the Mediterranean to the North Sea; courted and fêted by emperors; richer probably than any five men had ever been in history before; dwelling in palaces like princes, surrounded by hosts of servants, subordinates and retainers; flattered and envied and their supremacy acknowledged by the financial potentates of the whole world; in the prime of vigorous youth, loaded down with achievement, confident of the future, lacking nothing that money or power could give—what more could men want on earth? Cynics railed and called them unappeasable; courtiers shrugged their shoulders at their ceaseless pursuit of honors; their foes hated them for their covetousness. It was true; their ambition was boundless. It gave them no peace. It drove them on relentlessly, as if against their will, without bringing them to their goal. They grasped at ever more wealth, more power, more recognition; and when they got it they saw it was not what they wanted.

For they felt, without knowing it, that they were out

of their element, creatures torn from their background and their native surroundings. Their very splendor oppressed them, and in their simplicity they strove on, vaguely hoping that somehow a little more magnificence would ease the discomfort. Their uneasiness, their restlessness, sprang from an unavowed sense of having failed to make themselves over. They did not fit. No wealth, no power, no grandeur, had changed them. They were still the sons of the "Little Bauer," of the unassuming Guetele, of the shop and the Ghetto. Far from sensitive, they none the less were conscious of an incompatibility in the air. They sat at the tables of statesmen and kings, and tried to pretend they were in bliss; but the dainty morsels stuck in their throats. They were not used to them, and they suffered in their consciences at eating forbidden food. The court tailors sewed their garments; but no skill on earth could make them wear them as they should be worn. They danced with archduchesses and princesses, and the gracious creatures listened to their talk and laughed at their wit; but the next moment they floated away in the arms of a guard officer, and even an Amschel or a Karl was not so obtuse as not to note a difference.

There was something far more painful than all this. Monarchs, chancellors, ministers, aristocrats and their ladies made one feel at his ease. Lesser men were not so considerate. In Austria and throughout the German lands, a strange, confused wave had suddenly arisen against the "kings of Jews and Jews of kings." The most incredible assortment of people and passions were stirred against them. Liberals who abhorred Metternich and all his works; functionaries and petty nobles resenting invasion of their privileges and dilution of their rank; staunch yeomen of the old régime suspicious of all change and innovation; philosophical race purists and sectarian obscurantists; impoverished scions of decayed old families who scorned the trader class; and at the base of the whole, the motley horde of the disinherited mistrustful of wealth on principle. Nor was this curious army leaderless or without a tongue. Their sentiments were given voice in nearly the entire press and made graphic by scores of caricaturists. A flood of scurrilous articles and cartoons poured forth, retailing the doings and lives of the financiers, casting aspersions on their past, ridiculing their persons, and asking embarrassing questions about the source of their wealth, bases of their power, and the reasons for their favor in high quarters. The Rothschilds endeavored to stem the nuisance. They threatened; they paid hush-money to individual writers; they invoked the aid of their friends to silence newspapers or to suppress them; they got other friends to reply or to exert a counter-influence. Whereupon new journals and new authors stepped into the breach and enlightened the public about the reasons why the silenced had ceased to speak. It was most annoying and disturbing.

II

The great trouble was that Salomon and his brothers lent themselves so aptly to this sort of thing. Humorists with pen and brush found them a god-send. They were not only fabulously wealthy; not only parvenus of obscure and doubtful origin, and the favorites of the mighty of the land, and members of a hitherto despised race and religious sect; other people were all these things, yet it occurred to no one to make sport of them. The Rothschilds, as even the devoted Gentz had observed, were a species apart. They hobnobbed on terms of equality with distinguished and cultivated men, with the flower of breeding and learning; and all the while they remained the crudest ignoramuses. They spoke the harsh, guttural jargon of the Ghetto; they could not write a presentable letter; their manners were offensive, their persons unattractive, their voices rasping, their gestures irritating, their minds commonplace. Advancement had no effect on them; contacts did not develop them; they seemed incapable of growth; their brains were impervious to ideas; their souls resisted refinement. The brilliance in which they moved only heightened their ludicrousness.

Where had they come from and how had they got there? It was known only that they hailed from Frankfort. The rest was a mystery; and they did nothing to dissipate it. Their father was a merchant—vague word. Merchants, even Jewish ones, educated their sons. These astonishing monarchs of finance were all but illiterate; they had risen to their commanding position with less learning than their humblest clerk; it was reported that they were not at home even in the lore and traditions of their own people. Surely any merchant, however lowly, could scrape enough income to bring up his children respectably. And it was hardly imaginable that the shadowy Meyer was a poor man. He must have given his sons some kind of a start. Such fortunes as the Rothschilds' do not grow from nothing in a single generation. And they were still young men. The oddest, and certainly not the most reassuring part of it was the consistent silence—one could almost call it secrecy—in which they wrapped their antecedents and their beginnings. They seemed to be ashamed of them.

The more scandalous sheets harped on the racial and religious aspect, rehashing the age-old imbecilities which have not even yet quite lost their currency, conveniently forgetting that there had been great banking establishments and great fortunes before the Rothschilds, that the mass of Jews then, as now, were poor, and that this particular Jewish family were only a little more skilful in exploiting situations which they had had no part in creating than were their rivals of other creeds. More intelligent critics in the absence of data concerning the origin of the Rothschild wealth gave attention to the methods by which it was growing. And on this latter subject there was considerable light. While thousands of small people had been ruined by the lottery loan, Herr Rothschild had had the hardihood to boast that he had cleared six million florins on the transaction! And he had done it by a shameless trick, by sharp practices, by deceiving the public. The best that even such a learned and judicious authority as the Bavarian state councilor Von Goenner was able to say on the topic was that he was quite convinced "that these manœuvres could not be laid at the door of the very estimable Herr von Rothschild. They were the work of subordinates, brokers, and dealers in this wretched speculation." Perhaps so; but the wretched speculation would never have afflicted the nation at all if the very estimable Herr Rothschild had not backed the authorities into a corner and ordered them to deliver. Fifty-two kreutzers for a florin! More than a hundred millions to pay back for fifty-five borrowed! Was ever a people so mulcted in all history? And who was to sweat and starve so that the Jewish baron and his brothers abroad might pocket the difference? (The excited economists naturally omitted to mention that the insolvent state was unable to induce the Christian bankers to take the business even at that figure.) How had Herr von Rothschild succeeded in misleading and betraying the populace? By spreading lies in a press that was either too dull to see through his game or something worse. By giving away whole parcels of the securities to people whose names need not be mentioned because everybody knew them. By driving up prices on the exchanges which he held in the hollow of his hand. By withholding the truth. In short, by subterfuges to which no gentleman with honest Teuton blood in his veins and the teachings of Holy Church to guide his footsteps would ever have stooped.

Then the liberals took up the lament. An edifying spectacle: the Prince of the reaction and the king of coin cooperating to extinguish the freedom of Europe. In Naples, in Piedmont, in Spain, oppressed peoples arise to demand their rights; they exact constitutions from their tyrants; liberty and justice triumph; a new era of democracy and progress is about to dawn; when, lo! the unholy alliance descends upon the helpless lands with steel and with gold and restores the cowardly assassins to their thrones. The artists performed their part with devastating effect. One cartoon showed a gentleman with marked Semitic features, attired in slovenly Ghetto garb and an aristocratic lace shirt-front, standing in a chariot made out of a strong-box and propelled by the two-headed imperial Austrian eagle, careering over Europe. In another, entitled "The Pump," Rothschild, obese and coarse, stood knee deep in a pool of gold and with both arms acting as suction levers poured the world's wealth into the pockets of monarchs.

III

This was cruel enough; but what cut Salomon and Amschel to the quick were the everlasting insinuations about their un-German blood and their antecedents. The wags never wearied of the grotesquerie of the Jewish tradesmen airily whirling in the charmed circle. Hapsburg, Metternich and Meyer's boys! Gold lace, diplomacy, courtly etiquette, the destinies of Europe, willowy archduchesses, and Yiddish! It was too rich, and the humorists squeezed the last drop of succulence out of it. They celebrated it in word and song, in black and white and in color. And the public relished each bit with gusto. The lampooned bankers writhed in agony; but what could they do? Devoutly religious from childhood and pillars of the synagogue, it was unthinkable for them to change their faith. They would not, even if they could, deny their race. And in any event that would hardly mend matters. The only real way to raise the standing of Jews in the community was after all to improve the lot of the race as a whole. In Frankfort the council of the German states was still sitting on the question, despite Gentz's memorandum of six years ago. Would not the good Chancellor exert a little pressure on the chairman of the body, possibly on a few picked delegates also, and have the business over with? That was one thing. Then, as to the family history, why not let the public have a sympathetic and dignified account of the Rothschild antecedents, before some unfriendly individual got out a malicious one?

Some such step as this had become particularly urgent of late. So long as mere newspapermen nibbled at the matter, the risk of any serious divulgence was slight. The enemy, however, had some little time ago been reinforced by a formidable ally. The new adversary, a personage by name of Hormayr zu Hartenburg, was not only powerfully connected; he possessed, in addition, the inconvenient qualifications of being a trained investigator and a trenchant writer. He had, as a matter of fact, till recently held the post of curator of the imperial archives. Thus far he had been only annoying. He had quarreled violently with the Emperor and Metternich over some court intrigue, and among other things he had openly charged the Chancellor with having held up the diplomatic mails arriving from Constantinople for a day or two just outside Vienna so as to enable his friends the Rothschilds to effect a coup on the exchange. Incidentally it had been he who had first used the phrase "Kings of the Jews and the Jews of kings"—an alarming hint of what the fellow could do when he got a pen into his hand. Suppose that this individual now, with his nose for documents, his virulent style and his connections, should take it into his head to get a line on the parentage, the boyhood and the early activities of the Rothschilds? Heaven alone knew what court tittle-tattle he might be already having in his possession. Gentz was a boon companion and no little of a gossip, as who should know better than his friend Salomon? Was it altogether impossible that certain affairs between the banker and the courtier had been confided to third parties? And if there *were* leaks, there was no telling what else had trickled out by this time. Nothing could be more innocent than the tributes of respect, for instance, which Salomon now and then sent to Frau Metternich and the children—a costly bonbonnière, a live American deer for Christmas, a trifle of some sort for a birthday—and surely no transaction was straighter business than the loan to His Highness himself. Yet it could only too easily be imagined the interpretation that a scurrilous press and an evil-minded public would put on them.

And that was only the beginning. Once a gentleman like Hormayr commenced prying, what lengths might he not go to? The Elector William was dead, and so was Buderus; but their correspondence files were not buried with them. And the Jewish community of Frankfort still had its tax records. And the police archives of Dunkirk, Gravelines, Paris. And London. What a tale it would all make! Salomon shuddered at the thought.

IV

The protracted deliberations of the council in Frankfort came to a sudden head. For years the Jewish question had been bandied about, while a determined clique with the presiding officer at its head blocked its final liquidation. Metternich had been friendly all along; but he was a very busy man, and the rights and liberties of a few thousand Jews in a single city were rather a small patch on the map to a statesman who carried the world on his shoulders. When, however, Baron Rothschild intimated that his good offices would be gratefully remembered, the thing began to look very different, and word went out to the Austrian delegation as well as to a few lesser ones in the Chancellor's sphere of influence urging speedy action. The obstructionist chairman, as it happened, was himself a Metternich subaltern. He was given to understand that his tactics were unpleasant, and that he had better change them. He resisted; whereupon the axe descended upon his head. His successor received explicit instructions from the outset, so that there was no further trouble. In the summer of 1824 the Jews of the free city of Frankfort were at long last citizens.

It was not as brilliant a victory as had been hoped. If the new citizens expected to find themselves on the same footing with their German neighbors, they were disappointed. They were free to reside in all quarters, and the Ghetto passed into history; but the marriage limitations remained, and so did the restrictions on trade and property ownership. Still, even this niggardly compromise was something, and there was much rejoicing in the now obsolete Judengasse. Amschel let himself go completely and somewhat tactlessly. He gave a great dinner party in honor of the delegates; but so bitter was the feeling in the city that even the friendliest members of the council deemed it wiser to stay away. In Frankfort first, and presently throughout Germany, it was openly declared that the whole thing was but another triumph of Rothschild money—and (sotto voce) of Rothschild methods. Subtle persons adverted to the curious phenomenon of the imperial Chancellor giving his ardent support to liberty, equality and fraternity. For, to begin with, in Austria itself the status of the Jews was no better than medieval; and, besides, that the man whose very name had become a sort of symbol of reaction should take to his heart one of the pet doctrines of the French Revolution was, to say the least, remarkable. So tongues continued to wag and eyebrows went on shrugging.

But Salomon was unrebuffed and proceeded with his program. The next year he and Gentz set earnestly to work to appease the public curiosity. Early in 1826 the product of the extraordinary collaboration was given to the world; it was entitled "A Biographical Account of the House of Rothschild." Gentz in a private letter to a friend boasted that it came from his "workshop"; but though he considered it "well done," he modestly withheld his signature. In reality, several hands contributed to the final result. The material was collected and winnowed by Salomon; Gentz then whipped it into shape and handed the first version around to a few select journals. It was thought desirable, however, that the story should receive as wide publicity as possible. It was therefore sent on to Amschel. He, after suggesting a number of additions, passed it over to Baron Meseritz for revision. Lastly, Meseritz not only syndicated it broadcast but persuaded his friends on the staff of the great Brockhaus Encyclopedia to include a slightly condensed form of it in their edition of 1827. Subsequently the story found its way into popular collections of hero-tales, such as the "Sprichwoerter der Deutschen." For the better part of a hundred years it remained the sole authentic history of the Rothschild family.

V

The modern personality magazines could do worse than go to school to Gentz and Meseritz; for it is very much to be doubted whether these early nineteenth-century publicists have yet been surpassed as writers of success stories. They were certainly past masters in the art of omission. (Or perhaps that was where Salomon's skill entered; it is always difficult to apportion credit in collaborations.) Gentz's "Biographical Account," being mainly concerned with background, devotes little space to the activities of the five sons. A general phrase thrown in here and there about "extraordinary circumstances," "fortunate conjunctures," and "world-shattering events" is about the only allusion to the contraband episode, the Peninsular War, the Wellington drafts, Herries, and the dramatic happenings at Aix-la-Chapelle. On the other hand, old Meyer emerges as an overshadowing figure, as the founder not only of the family but of its fortune. The shop and the Judengasse days do not come in for treatment. Meyer is from the start a banker, a man of substantial resources, a personality in affairs. "His capacity, his untiring energy and his well-tried integrity" win him the confidence of important people, and presently he comes in contact with the man who is destined to be the "great influence in his gigantic rise,—the then Landgrave, later Elector, of Hesse." Beyond an appointment as court factor, however, nothing much happens apparently till the year of William's flight. Then the distracted prince, in a panic over his menaced millions, bethinks himself at the last moment of his faithful Jewish agent. Meyer reluctantly but obediently consents to guard and administer the entire fortune, and Serenity goes into exile with an easy mind. But, alas! the predatory French descend upon the Rothschild premises, seize every penny that the good Meyer has been able to lay by in a life of untiring energy and well-tried integrity; and it is only by the sacrifice of his own property that the wealth entrusted to him by the Elector is saved from the clutches of the invader.

Then follows the dramatic climax. There being no such person as Buderus in the cast, the exiled William and his trusted banker are wholly out of touch with one another during the seven years of the captivity. Only a distant rumor reaches the Elector of the bad behavior of the French toward Meyer; whereupon he resignedly concludes that his own fortune has been seized along with the Jew's. What, therefore, is his surprise and delight when, returning home in 1813, he learns that not only is every kreutzer of it safe and intact but that the House, having kept it active, is prepared to return the capital with accrued interest. Naturally no prince, least of all William of Hesse, would think of considering such a generous proposal. William, indeed, is so overwhelmed with astonishment and gratitude that he entreats the family to carry on with his money, and only with the greatest difficulty is he induced to accept a nominal rate of interest for the future. The Rothschilds, then, continue working with his millions for several years more, and providence blesses them with prosperity. And the Elector, mindful of their "honesty and right conduct," shows his appreciation by commending their services and their virtues to other princes.

Meyer, in the meantime, has passed away, but his soul lives on in his sons to guide and direct them. When about to die he calls them to his bedside and adjures them to keep the torch of high principle aglow, to love one another and work in harmony; and so deep is the young men's piety and veneration toward their saint-like parent that they never forget or depart from his will. "Herein lies the answer to the question which so many people have puzzled over; namely, how it has been possible for the House of Rothschild to achieve its unprecedented and miraculous success in this short time." Every project, no matter from what quarter it may issue, becomes the subject of common counsel; each operation, be it even of relatively slight importance, is carried through in accordance with a previously elaborated plan, which all have had a share in devising, and with united effort; and all the brothers share alike in the result. Another of the basic principles bequeathed to them by their father is to move with the times, though all the while keeping a reverent eye on the hallowed past. Should there on some rare occasion be a difference of opinion between the brothers, the difficulty is at once overcome and harmony restored by the simple device of each one asking himself how father would have acted in the given circumstances. "Finally, it must never be overlooked, that in addition to the reasonableness of their terms, the punctuality of their services, the simplicity and clarity of their methods and the intelligence with which they are carried through, it is the personal moral character of the five brothers that has had the greatest influence upon the success of their undertakings."

With the example of the Rothschilds before us, concludes Gentz in a brilliant philosophical peroration, it is idle for people to talk about luck. "In particular instances good or adverse fortune may, indeed, determine a man's destiny in life, though even then not exclusively. But enduring success, like persistent ill-fortune, is always and to a far greater extent than is commonly supposed, the fruit of personal merit or personal inefficiency and wrong-doing."

VI

Gentz looked upon his handiwork and found it good. Salomon was pleased enough with it to pay for it. Amschel only wished there were more of it. And what editors thought of it, from the *Augsburger Allgemeine Zeitung* to the Brockhaus *Konversations-Lexikon*, can fairly be inferred from their readiness to publish it. One man's judgment alone has, unhappily, not come down to us. Back in Cassel, the Elector William II was reigning in his late lamented father's stead. A man of thirty-six in 1813, he had witnessed one or two of the post-exile passages between his parent and the heirs of Meyer not recorded in the "Biographical Account"; and if he read the Gentz idyl, his comments must have been worth hearing; but his literary interests appear to have been limited, and he may never have laid eyes upon it.

There was, for instance, the irritating affair about wine. During the occupation Marshall Kellermann, commanding the army of the Elbe, made his headquarters just outside Hanau. He fancied the liquids in the palace cellars, and when he was obliged to move on he ordered them taken along. They were later offered for sale in Frankfort. Someone notified the rightful owner, at the moment languishing in Prague, and William, after sampling them, sent word to Meyer that he buy them back and store them in his warehouse against a happier day. There the barrels, fourteen in number, remained till 1814. On their being delivered to Cassel, it was found that the numbers did not tally and that the quality of the contents did not measure up to the price. There followed a lengthy and acrimonious correspondence, the court demanding that one of the bankers present himself at Cassel to "straighten out the difference." The Rothschilds, at the moment occupied with more important matters, politely declined the invitation. Serenity's letters becoming from this point on a little too hortatory, the Rothschilds did not answer at all. Thereupon an ultimatum from All-Highest reached the offices of the Bornheimerstrasse, which elicited the following reply:

"As we have most humbly explained already, our only motive in this transaction has been to give satisfaction to Your Royal (!) Highness. The wines were brought to us by the late Councilor Winzingerode. We have faithfully stored them; but we can hardly be held accountable for the invasion of our cellars by foreign troops, for the outbreak therein of a conflagration and for the consequent breaking in of all sorts of people. . . . It is impossible for us to know what has happened to the wines in the course of these catastrophes. We are nevertheless willing, though we cannot justly be compelled, to stand the loss to this extent: We will on our part waive the very considerable traveling expenses to Prague which are still due us, as well as the equally substantial and likewise unpaid advances on account of courier and mail charges; providing that Your All-Highest will at the same time agree to regard the mine matter as closed."

Whether or not it was has not transpired. But William could in this instance hardly be blamed for being a little suspicious. It so happened that some time earlier another incident had set him wondering. He had asked for those boxes of documents which at the time of his departure had been taken to the Rothschild cellar in the Judengasse. He had needed only to glance at them to perceive that they had been tampered with. One may imagine his consternation when, upon their being opened, it was found that not only had his own papers been grievously disturbed but that a number of bond certificates belonging to the departed Meyer had been stuffed in among them! The young Rothschilds had offered a curious explanation: Originally the boxes had been placed in the house cellar. On the night preceding the raid by the French police, it had been deemed wise to remove them to the secret space under the courtyard. The boxes were large, and the connecting passage was narrow. At the last moment it had, therefore, become necessary to break the things apart and after effecting the transfer nail them up again. It was dark and damp, and the time was short; effects of the family's own were being brought to safety at the same time; so that some confusion was inevitable. Why had no word been said about the matter at the time? To that the only reply they could make was that they did not know; it had happened so many, many years ago.

But William II had no wish to reopen old sores, and if the Gentz-Meseritz version of the Rothschild relations to his father did come to his attention, he kept silent. Other people, on the other hand, were less discreet. If, said the cynics, Meyer really was the noble soul he was represented to be, why then there had been a distinct reversion. His successors had certainly inherited his energy, his punctuality, and his capacity; but whether he had also bequeathed to them some of his other shining virtues seemed open to doubt. On the whole, therefore, the immediate effect of the "Biographical Account" was somewhat disappointing; and in the years to follow, Salomon and his brothers found that Gentz's extravagant pæan had done more to make them suspected and ridiculous than all the libels and calumnies of their enemies put together.

CHAPTER XIV

LEADEN SKIES

DEEP was Salomon's disappointment, and bitter were his reflections upon human incredulity. A callous and cynical world declined to take him at his own valuation; his toilsome effort to set opinion straight had been useless, worse than useless. But the rush of events did not let him mourn long. Over in the West forces shifted suddenly and terrifyingly. Rumblings from above and below, at first faint and far-away, but swiftly coming nearer and gaining in intensity, brought the five brothers up with a start. The very year of the misfired "Biographical Account" witnessed developments in Paris and London that made the most insulting caricature in the German press look trivial; and presently there followed a crisis so grave and menacing that the Rothschilds were forced to give thought to the foundations of their House, without worrying over its outward glory. Uninterrupted progress, a rapid and continuous rise marred by never a reverse, had almost made them believe in their own star. Now for the first time in over two decades the question they must ponder was not how to make their light shine more brilliantly but how to prevent its being extinguished altogether.

The ominous part of it was that, each time, the upheaval occurred in the territory of the family's titans, Nathan and James. Salomon's imperium in Vienna, though younger by many years than the Western seats, grew daily more solid; the home base in Frankfort and the newest outposts in Naples held firm, for all the mediocrity of their command; while the very men whom the rest tacitly acknowledged as the brains of the whole combination contrived, not once but twice, to get themselves into the most breath-taking perils. And "get themselves" precisely described it. Certainly the "conjunctures" of Gentz's glib phrase were not as fortunate as usual; "extraordinary circumstances" did on these occasions the reverse of playing into their hands; but what were great financial minds for if not to turn accidents and eventualities unforeseen by common clay to account? In reality it was worse than that. Twice within four years James, teamed with Nathan, plunged headlong and with his eyes shut to the edge of an abyss. They plainly did not see what was at the end of their noses. Closer than any other moneymen to the governing powers in their respective capitals, they ventured into undertakings that staked the family's whole fortune, preposterously over-confident, misinformed, grossly out of touch with the forces at work. And of all places, in France!—in that fluid, mercurial, unstable country, which had violently changed its constitution a dozen times in four decades and where a rejected and discredited dynasty was being maintained by foreign dictation in the teeth of an awakened national will. Shortsightedness, political miscalculation, insufficient understanding of economic factors and—inexcusable in a Rothschild!—failure to get inside information, were the elements of the threatening ruin. Was the time at last come when horse sense and empiricism were not enough, when the Rothschilds, unschooled, instinctive and (as

Gentz had long ago said of them) "without the remotest inkling of any higher relationship in the world," must go down before rivals with culture and education? It looked very much like it. Their enemies, believing what they hoped, were convinced of it. But providence had other plans.

II

The series of operations with the French monarchy, when they were begun three years before, had held out every promise of being the most productive, as they were the boldest, stroke the House had yet attempted. Patterned on a gigantic scale, executed by James under the immediate and constant direction of Nathan himself, assured of the government's adherence by the complaisant and powerful Villèle, (who was now chief minister) they had seemed a foregone success. They were to be one more turning point in the sweeping Rothschild advance. With their limitless resources in capital, influence, connections, nothing could possibly go wrong; yet, as it turned out, nearly everything did go wrong. No danger, no accident was overlooked or unprepared for—none, except those that actually came along. When, by 1830, the great muddle was cleared away, the firm emerged shaken and sobered, its standards very much bedraggled, its losses in prestige, friendships, confidence and money so vast that any other organization would have collapsed under them.

The preliminary step was taken in 1823; and although the transaction—involving a capital of over four hundred million francs—was far and away the most ambitious in its line since Waterloo, it was only a step. Government loans, however large and lucrative, had begun to pall on Nathan. He had had them now for half a dozen years, with nearly every state in Europe, and his restless spirit was reaching out for something fresh and different. His whole reputation and fortune had been made by short-cuts, by daring ventures, by doing things that others were afraid of or did not see. Now Rothschild's was in a rut; leadership it had certainly, but not originality; it was plodding along at the head of the herd; but the whole financial brotherhood was keeping timidly to the beaten path. And there was no particular reason why it should. One instance: England, and to a smaller degree the Continent, was wallowing in money. An era of prosperity, of capitalistic expansion, such as the world had not witnessed since the time of the Lombards, had followed the Napoleonic nightmare. Investors were frantically tossing their surpluses into everything and anything that promised a dividend. Mushroom corporations, literally by the hundred, were springing up everywhere—in England alone over six hundred of them were organized in a single year—bubbles and schemes of the wildest species were being launched. Across the South Atlantic the Spanish colonies were breaking away from the mother-country, and Europe had suddenly discovered Latin America with its undeveloped resources. Business was booming; speculation was going mad. Yet all the while government credit remained stationary. England alone excepted, the rate of interest on state securities had not changed by a fraction since the wars. It was preposterous. Even Neapolitan and Papal annuities were safer than mining stock in the Andes.

Lack of imagination and old-world inertia alone were responsible for the burden of usury under which the nations were groaning.

The idea of converting the whole accumulated debt of Europe to a lower-interest basis seized upon Nathan's mind. He began with France; that is to say, he put that country at the top of his list; but before he even broached the scheme to Villèle he gave it a try-out at home. The advantages of such a move were obvious. Twenty-five years of disorder, instability and foreign wars ending with the débâcle of 1815 had made the French national debt the biggest on the Continent. For all that, her economy and her finances were probably as sound as any in the world. She was thus an excellent risk; but she, like every other European state, looked across the Channel for guidance and leadership in all fiscal matters. Should the English conversion, therefore, come up to expectations, it would have an encouraging effect on Villèle and furnish him with a weapon with which to silence opposition. The trial operation, moreover, need not be large, whereas in France the game would run into the billions. As it fell out, the British investor did not respond to the plan with as much warmth as could have been desired; for a year later Nathan still had close to three million pounds' worth of three-per cent converted Consols for which no buyers had applied. This, however, did not prevent him from going ahead, nor Villèle from being impressed by the example of his English colleague. If Chancellor of the Exchequer Vansittart believed in conversion—so Villèle, prompted by Nathan, reasoned,—the scheme could not but be sound. He did not pause to reflect—and Nathan apparently quite overlooked—that France, with her hundreds of thousands of small investors represented in the chamber of deputies, was another kettle of fish. He grasped at the proposal with enthusiasm, partly because the annual interest charge had become an intolerable drag on the budget, and partly (if Ouvrard's insinuations are to be believed) on more human grounds.

And so the preliminary loan of four hundred millions was floated. This preparatory manœuvre had a twofold purpose. It was to provide an opportunity for forcing up the price of all the previous issues of French government securities, and it was to furnish Nathan and James with quantities of cheap capital for the great operation that was to come. Clearly, it was not much use asking bondholders to accept a three-per cent paper in lieu of one yielding five per cent until the state was in a position to redeem its obligations; that is, until the older issues had reached par. Whichever the investor did: whether he converted his holdings or cashed in, a hundred francs must be worth a hundred francs; otherwise the royal treasury would be losing capital instead of saving interest. It so happened, however, that the *rente* was at the moment fluctuating between ninety and ninety-two. That, then, was one thing. The other was this: Considering that the loan was designed as an aid to the government and the national credit, Nathan argued, would it not be just common humanity if the treasury were to issue the securities to him now and wait for payment till the bull market for which both were hoping had been realized? Villèle apparently thought the suggestion reasonable, and agreed.

Having got that far, Nathan proceeded to set up his consortium. The preliminary loan was a family affair, none but the Rothschilds participating. But, daring as he was, he hesitated to plunge into a four-billion franc operation single-handed. So for the conversion scheme he called Baring in London and Laffitte in Paris to his side. The tables had turned somewhat since the Congress of Aix-la-Chapelle; and the distinguished British house made no difficulties. The three firms then made up a pool of a billion francs, in the event that they should have to take over a sizable part of the three-per cent *rente* solid, and lined up the smaller banks in their respective spheres. How Baring and Laffitte raised their part of the outlay the story does not tell; but a circumstantial account of the trouble that Nathan went to is given by Ouvrard in his Memoirs. Ouvrard's feelings toward the Rothschilds make him normally a prejudiced witness. In this instance, however, his testimony is largely corroborated by another, more credible, contemporary. What the Rothschild brothers did, it seems, was this:

Nathan, it must be remembered, still had his mass of unsold Consols from the English conversion deal. It occurred to him that by withdrawing them from the market at this time, he might kill several birds with one stone. First of all, the impression would go abroad that the securities had found buyers, thus enhancing their price. Secondly, the same idea would just at this moment have a salutary influence on French financial opinion. Lastly, the Bank of England, eager on its own account to bull Consols, would do whatever it could to lend color to the above-named impression. The Bank, in fact, took Nathan's unsold bonds as collateral, and advanced him bullion at a nominal rate of interest. The gold was now shipped across to James, who deposited it with the Bank of France against fluid capital. This complex operation, however, only netted a matter of seventy million francs, while the pool required a third of a billion. There was, to be sure, the deferred payment arrangement in connection with the four hundred million loan; but from that source only about a quarter had thus far been realized. Total: a bare two hundred million. Then Villèle came to the rescue with a hundred and twenty millions' worth of treasury certificates (*bons royaux*), which James took over against future payment and at a rate of interest far in excess of the current market.

In the meantime the bull movement was coming on at high speed. Within a few months the old French *rentes* had touched par; by the beginning of spring, 1824, they had soared to 110—away beyond what was needed for the purpose of conversion. Even for the promised but as yet unissued three per cents, investors were offering over 80, which was several points above the quotation at which the government was prepared to float them. The Rothschilds looked on with delight at the strange spectacle of their old rival stocking up on French bonds, so that a loan of their own might be boomed. It was the performance of Aix over again, with the rôles reversed and the motivation slightly revised.

III

"Looked on" is hardly an accurate description; for James was enormously active. The moment 110 was reached Baring and Laffitte advised the head of the consortium that in their opinion it was time to start selling. Well, it certainly was. James had thought so long ago. He had been unloading for weeks past, not only the five per cents destined for retirement but the as yet non-existent threes. Without putting too fine a point on it, this quiet lone-hand work was nothing but bear tactics against the converted security and something not to be distinguished from a betrayal of associates. At any rate that was how Baring and Laffitte viewed it, when they found out what had been happening. Baring, indeed, took the matter so hard that he never again coöperated with the Rothschilds, though James protested he had only been throwing off his last year's loan in which the consortium had no share.

The worst was yet to come, however. While the bankers were busy tuning up the market, Villèle was making ready to have the scheme approved by the nation. Early in April he laid his bill before the Deputies. It was in this lower house that the mass of large and small rentiers were concentrated, but the minister had assiduously oiled the machinery in advance and he was confident of the result. An agonized outcry, to be sure, did go up. Charges of manipulation, exploitation and dishonesty were hurled at the government, and Villèle was accused of robbing the country to enrich the bankers—a thrust which, considering that the syndicate was to receive the entire proceeds of the difference between the old and the new rate of interest for one year, was not as wild as it might sound. But the shouting soon died down, and the measure was carried with a comfortable majority. It now went to the Peers—a mere piece of ceremonial mummery, as every-one knew, the great nobles and landowners having no preponderant economic interest in the *rentes* and always loyally working in unison with His Majesty's advisers. What, therefore, was Villèle's surprise and disgust when the upper house suddenly developed a profound concern over finance! Led by the Viscount de Chateaubriand, a member of the cabinet but a violent personal enemy of the chief minister, the opposition carried the day and the measure was beaten.

The consternation among the bankers may be imagined. Here for months Baring and Laffitte had been raking in all the old French bonds they could get their hands on, and driving up the price beyond all reason, on the assurance of Rothschild and Villèle that the chambers were as good as in their pocket; and now, with hundreds of millions of the paper in their possession, these two bunglers let the game slip through their fingers when it was all but landed. Nor was that all. The head of the syndicate himself, clearly knowing something more than he imparted to his associates, had been playing with his left hand against a storm, and crawled out from under just as the clouds burst over the heads of those whom he misled. On the day of the Peers' vote the old *rentes* stood at 106—having gone back several points during the debate—on the morrow they dived to 98. It was small comfort that the king dismissed Chateaubriand; there was, indeed, a flicker of hope upon the announcement, but it could hardly last. To begin with, a powerful syndicate headed by Ouvrard had been bearing the conversion scheme from the start, and it now applied all its might to halt any upward tendency. Moreover, with ruin staring them in the face, Baring and Laffitte as well as the scores of minor houses associated with them lost their heads and took the brief respite to help the depression along. The result of this combination of forces was to send the *rente* back to 98 within a few days, where it stuck for a long time.

Ouvrard and his friends cleared several millions, while the Rothschild consortium (minus Rothschild) barely scrambled out alive.

A year later Villèle returned to the charge. He had learned something by experience, it seemed; for this time both houses of parliament docilely approved his measure without delay and almost without discussion. The Rothschilds, however, had likewise profited by the past, and committed themselves to nothing outright. Their precaution was justified by the event. Out of four billions in outstanding bonds hardly thirty millions were turned in for conversion. The unlucky scheme was doomed. And then in the course of the summer the shadows of the approaching crisis—the greatest that the world had seen in a century—began to lengthen over every bourse in Europe. The wild era of speculation had come to its disastrous and inevitable end. In England alone there were in the ensuing year more than three thousand bankruptcies—two and a half times the normal number. Nathan Rothschild, looking out over the havoc, could only be grateful to the Viscount de Chateaubriand for having balked him in his ambition. He often said that had the French conversion operation succeeded, it would almost certainly have dragged his house down to ruin.

IV

To one of the Rothschilds' former friends and associates, fortune proved less indulgent. In Vienna, among the first victims of the great crisis was the ancient firm of Fries & Company with David Parish at its head. Driven out of the lucrative state affairs, in which it had played a leading rôle since the time of Maria Theresa, its position during the past three years had been precarious enough. Still, so long as fair weather prevailed, it managed to keep up a brave front. In a storm such as was now raging it was bound to be blown down. Signs of its impending doom became visible early in the year 1826. There followed a desperate and pathetic struggle, while Parish fought to save his fortune and his name. He sought aid among his hosts of friends in London, in Paris and at home; but the weakness of his house was an open secret, and his urgent pleas hardly tended to restore confidence. Those, moreover, who might have been moved to help him were themselves in difficulties. Meanwhile obligations were falling due, protested bills were being returned in floods, credit was tightening on the panic-stricken bourse, and the anterooms of the bank were filling up with impatient creditors. Then Parish was seized with terror. In a mood verging on derangement he presented himself at Metternich's office. Years ago he had advanced the Chancellor a hundred thousand florins. It was one of those familiar transactions between bankers and statesmen which, while duly executed with promissory note and interest clause for form's sake, are really honoraria for value received. In prosperous times Parish, the man of the world, would have been the first to declare anyone expecting them to be redeemed a lunatic. It was exactly what Metternich thought now. He protested that the obligation had been canceled by mutual agreement way back in 1818. But the despairing man, though he had no illusions about saving his firm with this bit of small change, insisted that it was a proper debt. At least it would silence one or two of his most nagging creditors, and give him a breathing spell. Rather than have a scene, Metternich handed him part of the money and signed a fresh note for the rest. Now came Gentz's turn. Poor Parish had not the heart to go in person to his old companion, and he handed over *his* note to a third party. Gentz, however, did not mix money matters with sentiment. He declined absolutely to recognize this "utterly rimeless, crazy, antiquated obligation."

All along Parish knew that only one man in Vienna could save him—Salomon Rothschild. Indeed, he not only could but would. He was a rough diamond. Had not Moritz Bethmann said that "no person ever left him uncomforted?" But he hesitated in his present plight to appeal to the man whom he had once helped, patronized and perhaps slightly despised. He went finally when every other hope had vanished. Was it the distracted mood, the too proud tone, the dignified manner as if he were asking his due when he ought to have humbly begged a favor? It might have been any of these or all; or possibly, because Parish simply could not bring himself to say what was in his heart, Salomon did not fully realize the desperateness of the situation. Only this is sure. Parish did leave Salomon uncomforted. And the next day—it was April 27—his body was found in the Danube. In his rooms were several letters. One of them was for Prince Metternich. It began:

"Before I leave the world I must write a few words to you, my Prince, to tell you that I am going to my grave without malice but with the conviction that you have treated me very unjustly and have sacrificed me to the greed of a family who have known better than I how to attach you to their side. It is unnecessary to go into the early history and development of our acquaintance with the Rothschilds. That these people are with all their riches heartless men, with no feelings other than for their cash-box, the world has long known; and how ungratefully they have acted toward me under your special patronage cannot after my death remain a secret either."

After telling him what arrangements he had made for the collection of the residual note, Parish concluded the letter thus:

"Farewell, my Prince. Should you ever think of an unfortunate who was sincerely devoted to you, I hope that the recollection may cause you no remorse."

To Salomon he wrote with even greater bitterness: "I am leaving the world because I have been most shamefully betrayed on the one hand and rewarded with the blackest ingratitude for very real kindnesses on the other. If you have any conscience it cannot but tell you that you and your brothers richly deserve my last reproach, and that by your recent heartless conduct you have caused the ruin of one of the best friends your house ever had. When I drew you in 1817 into the French and Austrian affairs, against the wish of my oldest and most intimate friend, I was warned on all sides that you would leave no stone unturned to force me out of them. How well and by what means you have succeeded, under the patronage of Prince Metternich, to grab for yourself alone a variety of transactions in which I was by the laws of God and man entitled to have a share, I have known for some little time . . . Although my house is pretty badly shaken, I could still have managed, with the help of friends and family, to meet all our obligations—had you only found it in your heart to restitute a fraction of the money which would never have become yours if I had during our association stood upon my rights and demanded my just share in the business with the Austrian and Neapolitan governments. You, however, have found it more convenient and more profitable to come to an understanding with the Prince in the matter of the old bond operation and by this means to get him entirely on your side. The moment I found myself on the outside of this combination, I knew that it was impossible to save the firm, and I decided not to live through the disgrace. Now I must close. I hope for your sake that you will but rarely think of a friend whose memory can only be painful to you."

There were echoes in that letter that reminded Salomon as he read it of other days and other controversies. Where was it and when that a rival, beginning as a friend and associate, had pitted himself against the House of Rothschild and lost? Why, of course, Rueppell and Bethmann, the innocents who, away back in 1801, made the then young Amschel and Salomon their brokers to the court of Cassel! Oh, but this was really sad. Poor, poor Parish! Such a proud, brilliant fellow, to end like this! Yet, what could one say? Or do? It was the way of the world, of business, of destiny. The giant wheel turns, one basket goes up, another down. It is no good to sit and lament. For some must perish while others triumph. But life must go on.

V

The giant wheel gave another lurch, and for one breathless moment it seemed that the turn of the great colossus itself had come. Two years after the unlucky conversion adventure King Charles X had weakly submitted to the popular will by throwing over Villèle and his cabinet. The last of the Bourbons refused to believe that the nation's mistrust was directed less against his minions than against the monarchy. At first he had even toyed with the idea of resisting altogether; but despite his family's reputation to the contrary, he had not quite forgotten the miseries of '89 and their sequel. He had therefore compromised to the extent of appointing a somewhat less intransigeant ministry. No sooner, however, had public feeling calmed down a little than he regretted his moderation, and disregarding parliamentary majorities, he called his ultra-royalist friends back to power. The new cabinet, composed of such fire-eaters as Polignac and Peyronnet, was, if possible, more reactionary than the Villèle group, and constituted a direct provocation to the disaffected country. The climax soon followed. In the general election of the spring of 1830 the voters, instead of ratifying the monarch's choice, as he had rather hoped, returned a chamber of precisely the same coloring as its dissolved predecessor. The government now resolved upon a showdown. In Paris the most exciting rumors circulated. It was asserted that Polignac was mobilizing troops to prevent the people's representatives from taking their seats, that the king had already signed an order declaring the city under martial law and that revolutionary bands in the suburbs were preparing to resist.

Just prior to these developments, meanwhile, the House of Rothschild had secured a contract, in open competition, for a large new French loan. What with the market artificially boomed up by the conversion manœuvres of a few years back, and the brisk bidding, the new issue had been taken over at an extremely high figure—above par. If the gossip was even partly true and there was to be a coup d'état, then riots were sure to follow, there might be a revolution and not impossibly a general war. What in these circumstances would become of French credit and of the expensive new bonds? From London Nathan reported that a group of bankers and brokers headed by the ubiquitous Ouvrard were busy unloading French securities at panic prices, and he urged his brother to stop the avalanche by a bull manœuvre and to get to the bottom of the persistent rumors about the government's plans. James could hardly believe that Ouvrard was acting on inside information unknown to himself; but the situation appeared so ominous that he went to Polignac and asked him point-blank what his intentions were. The minister smiled at him blandly and assured him that all the talk about a coup d'état was idle tittle-tattle, that if any important action were contemplated he (James) would be the first to know about it, and that as a matter of fact the government was on the point of convening the new chamber.

This was on the evening of July 24. The next morning, before he went to mass, Charles X signed the Polignac decrees, and of the following day they were published. Among other things, the recently elected chamber was declared dissolved, fresh elections upon a more restricted suffrage were ordered, and the press was gagged. Paris immediately took up the challenge. Overnight barricades made their appearance in the streets, and there followed bloody encounters with the military. On the bourse pandemonium reigned, with the *rente* falling thirty points in a single day. Old inhabitants said it was 1789 all over again. The king and the ministers, terrified by the storm they had let loose and deserted by their supporters, fled the capital. Then unexpectedly a savior appeared. Louis Philippe, Duke of Orleans and a cousin of Charles X, was known for the liberal proclivities he had inherited from his popular father, the famous Philippe Egalité of the first revolution; and when he now gallantly rode out among the embattled mobs, he was acclaimed with enthusiasm. France had a new king and a more or less new dynasty; the Bourbons were dethroned for ever; and the July Revolution was over as suddenly as it had begun.

That was all very fine, but it hardly comforted James and his brothers. The compromise was a great victory for the commercial middle classes, and that was all to the good. As James, who was, moreover, personally very close to the new monarch, wrote to Salomon a little later: "Business will certainly be safer here in France now than it was under Polignac." The situation, however, was not just local. There were apt to be European complications. Within a few weeks, indeed, the conflagration, though it had been so miraculously got under control at home, leaped across the frontiers to devastate the innocent bystanders. In numerous places in Germany, including the district around Frankfort, there were peasant uprisings, castles were attacked and burned and their noble occupants driven out. The exiled liberals of Spain and Italy, emboldened by events, became active again. In the United Netherlands a revolution broke out which not only deposed the king but ripped the country across the middle and made Belgium an independent state. Grave rumblings were heard as far east as Poland. Naturally the Tsar was disquieted, and refused to speak to Louis Philippe, whom he somewhat illogically saw as the source of all the mischief. Metternich, it goes without saying, was thoroughly scandalized at this destruction of his life-work for absolutism and legitimacy. War and peace hung in the balance.

James, Nathan and Salomon went to work with all their might and energy and influence to save the world from catastrophe. It was not an easy task. Luckily for them, Louis Philippe was reasonable and conciliatory, and England saw no menace to her interests in the Continental realignment. The powder magazine lay over in the East with Metternich holding the match. If Vienna was determined on hostilities, the Holy Alliance would follow its leader and even pacific London might be persuaded to overcome her indifference. Then the fat would be in the fire. The Rothschilds concentrated their efforts upon their great friend and patron, the Chancellor of Austria. Their French loan commitments were merely the largest single stake in the pot; and although they were the responsible underwriters of the issue, the loss, if loss it must be, would be fairly distributed among their satellites. Doubtless the little fellows would yell; that could not be helped; they must take their chances of loss as well as profit. The House was directly involved with some twenty millions of the ill-starred operation; distressing enough, in all conscience; but France was only one item. All Europe's credit was in their strongbox. Their entire might and greatness stood and fell with the solvency or bankruptcy of the governments. The House of Rothschild was literally a paper house; and war, whose first casualty was invariably in the financial sector, would dissolve it in smoke.

And so the Rothschild couriers kept the roads hot between Paris and London and between both these places and Vienna. With arguments, with solemn warnings, with exhortations almost religious in their earnestness, they labored over Metternich to preserve mankind from the frightful shambles. Louis Philippe, they assured him, far from having started the miserable conflagration, was in reality the one man who had checked it. Had he not intervened in the nick of time, no one could tell what might have happened. There might even have been a republic in France today, heaven save us. A democrat, a bourgeois monarch, a citizen king to the general populace, he was among those who knew him at close range a ruler of the old school, the most determined foe of liberalism, a disciple and a sincere admirer of Prince Metternich. He was the last hope of the Metternichean principle in France. One had but to shut his ears to his proclamations (designed for home consumption) and look for a moment at his deeds. The subverters at home and abroad were mercilessly hounded by his agents; revolutionary placards and newspapers were prohibited; he was suppressing riots and every kind of public meeting with a strong hand. Why, to make war on him was to attack the staunchest upholder of the old régime that Western Europe still had. And did His Serene Highness stop to think of the effect war would have on the laboriously erected and still precarious structure of Austria's own credit, of the injury to commerce and industry, of the tragic cost in human life? "And, my dear brother Salomon, . . . everything depends on the Prince . . . we have on our hands eighteen millions' worth of active French bonds, and if it's peace they go to 75 and if it's war they drop to 45 . . . I can tell you it's enough to lose your mind . . . For common sense is all for peace, yet the idea of war is gaining favor on all hands."

The idea might gain; but war, after all, did not come. England held firm; the king of France, assiduously coached by James, conciliated the ruffled feelings of his brother monarchs; even Metternich, after a year of bristling and sword-rattling, listened to the wisdom of Salomon. Providence in its inscrutable way, after having raised up the House of Rothschild upon a foundation of war, now chose to make it its instrument of peace. Surely, it is not for blind, weak man to question or to mock.

CHAPTER XV

PASSING OF A TITAN

THE terrible days of 1830–31 were survived and forgotten. Five years later the House was shaken by a crisis of quite another kind. It was midsummer 1836, and from every corner of Europe Rothschilds, Schnappers, Cohens, Montefiores had assembled at the ancient family seat. Lionel, eldest son of Nathan and heir-apparent of the London domain, was to be united with Charlotte, a daughter of his uncle Karl of Frankfort. At the climax of the festivities—at the very height of the most brilliant spectacle that the city had seen since the coronation of the last Holy Roman Emperor—the blow fell. Nathan had left home in ill-health. For some time he had been troubled with a carbuncle, but neither he nor his physician had made much of it. On the day of the wedding he suddenly developed grave symptoms. The family were alarmed; he, however, insisted that he was all right and refused to do anything that would upset the nuptial program. That night he became delirious. His condition had taken such a bad turn that his London doctor was hurriedly sent for. It was too late. For several days he lingered on. General poisoning had set in, and on July 28 he died.

He was not yet sixty years old. In the ordinary course he might have lived to a ripe old age. The Rothschilds came, on both sides of their ancestry, of long-lived stock.

Meyer had been nearly seventy when he died; Guetele, the bereaved mother, survived her great son by thirteen years; and of Nathan's four brothers three lived to be over seventy-five. Was it the hardships and exertions and perils of his youth that had undermined his resistance? He seemed to thrive on hard work; and surely Amschel and Salomon, both of whom were born before him and survived him by a score of years, had had it no easier. He was wont to say that he paid the price of wealth, success and recognition in universal jealousy, envy, and perennial threats of death; and though he was anything but a sensitive man, unpopularity and insecurity doubtless affected his nerves. Yet, living in England, he was very much safer and more respected than his brothers on the Continent.

Twenty-four years before, the death of his father, the titular founder of the House, was scarcely remarked beyond the Judengasse of his native city, and even the newspapers of Frankfort did not mention it. The passing of Nathan stirred every capital of Europe; a tremor went through the bourses and the chancelleries from St. Petersburg to London; hardly a journal of importance but noted the event and sketched his career. To England, if the tale is to be believed, the news was brought by his own pigeon post. Several days later his body arrived in a coffin so magnificent, "so handsomely carved and decorated with large silver handles at both sides and ends that it appeared more like a cabinet than a receptacle for the dead." Jewish funerals are distinguished for their austerity, for a kind of Oriental gloom; flowers, music, processions are rigidly excluded. The corpse is wrapped in hastily sewn muslin garments, placed in the crudest pine casket, and carried silently to its last destination. Nathan was all his life long a member of the Orthodox congregation, and he was buried in the Jewish East-End Cemetery. But he was after all one of the greatest of his race and time, and so "he was placed in his last resting place with a gorgeous pomp and display that seemed hardly appropriate to the solemnity of the occasion. . . . A procession of carriages nearly a mile in length followed it. Among those who were present . . . were the Austrian, Prussian, Neapolitan and Portuguese ambassadors, besides the Lord Mayor, the sheriffs, aldermen and a crowd of minor dignitaries."

Whether credit for these arrangements belongs to Nathan himself or to his family cannot be determined; for his complete will was not made public. Because of that, also, it has remained a dead secret to this day just what fortune he left behind. Even to his executors the details were not revealed. The skeleton testament which was given out confined itself to the conduct of the business and the marriage of his daughters. The management of the House in St. Swithin's Lane was entrusted to his four sons, and they were to work in harmony with their uncles' Houses on the Continent. Each of his daughters received a legacy of £100,000. They, like the daughters of Meyer, before them, were to have no part or lot in their father's, now their brothers', affairs. To charitable institutions, employees or other dependents, no bequests were made.

II

While the official press and official personages were busy repeating the legends made familiar by Gentz, and vying with one another in hyperbole, here and there critical-minded people did not hesitate to present a slightly different picture of the man and the methods by which he had risen. A mass of anecdotes gained currency—some malicious, some sympathetic, most of them doubtless apocryphal, but each, as is often the case with such stories, seizing upon some central truth of character. The most prolific of these narrators was Nathan's old friend, the famous anti-slavery apostle, Sir T. Fowell Buxton; and though his intention was certainly kindly in every instance, it may be doubted whether outspoken enemies like Ouvrard have done quite so much to strip the greatest of the Rothschilds of his halo. Thus by way of illustrating Nathan's industry and solidity, Buxton reported a dinner-table remark of his which is at least open to less flattering interpretation.

"I hope," said another guest to the banker, "that your children are not too fond of money and business to the exclusion of more important things. I am sure you would not wish that?"

"I am sure," Nathan replied with emphasis, "that I *should* wish that. I wish them to give mind, soul, heart and body—everything—to business. That is the way to be happy. It requires a great deal of boldness and a great deal of caution to make a great fortune; but when you have got it, it requires ten times as much wit to keep it."

And that Nathan meant what he said is confirmed by an incident related by Spohr, the German violinist and composer, who sought him out in London with a letter of introduction from Amschel. Nathan gave the musician a limp hand to shake, which he promptly returned to his pocket. "Music?" he queried without interest. "I understand nothing of music. This," as he rattled the change in his pocket, "this is my music."

But he found little joy even in his wealth, despite his own formula. When Buxton, impressed by the comforts and luxuries of the Rothschild mansion, said to him, "You must be a happy man in such a home as this," the disillusioned magnate replied, "What? Happy! I happy, when just as I am going to dine a letter is placed in my hand saying: 'If you do not send £500 I will blow your brains out.' Happy, indeed!"

To show that the great man was not a mere money-bag but had a vein of humanity and even wit in his make-up, Buxton reports him as saying, "Sometimes to amuse myself I give a beggar a guinea. He thinks it is a mistake, and for fear I should find it out off he runs as hard as he can. I advise you to give a beggar a guinea sometimes. It is very amusing."

So much for the Rothschild sense of humor. Equally self-revealing are Nathan's observations on success in general and his own in particular:

"I have seen many clever men, very clever men, who had not shoes to their feet. I never do business with them. Their advice sounds very well, but fate is against them. They cannot get on themselves, and if they cannot do good to themselves, how can they do good to me?"

Besides there were what he called his principles: "I always said to myself, what another man can do I can do too. I have always been an offhand man. I never lost any time. I came prepared for everything and closed bargains on the spot."

More detached observers believed to have discovered the sources of his greatness in a variety of other principles. "One cause of his success," said a contemporary, "was the secrecy with which he shrouded all his transactions, and the tortuous policy with which he misled those who watched him the keenest. If he possessed news calculated to make the Funds rise, he would commission the broker who acted in his behalf to sell half a million. The shoals of men who usually follow the movements of others sold with him. The news soon passed through Chapel Court that Rothschild was bearing the market, and the Funds fell. Men looked doubtingly at one another; a general panic spread; bad news was looked for; and these united agencies sank the price two or three per cent. This was the result expected, and other brokers, not usually employed by him, bought all they could at the reduced rate. By the time this was accomplished, the good news had arrived; the pressure ceased; and Mr. Rothschild reaped his reward."

An acquaintance of a more sympathetic temper declared: "This is the key to an understanding of Rothschild's character. His ambition tended to the accomplishment of elaborate financial operations—of making money, if you like. But in this phrase the emphasis must be placed on the making; for he did not value either money in itself or the things that could be procured by it. He had no taste or inclination for what every Englishman seeks as soon as he has money enough to buy it—comfort in every respect. His ambition was to arrive at his aim more quickly and more effectually than others, and to steer toward it with all his energy. When his end was reached it had lost all its charm for him, and he turned his never wearying mind to something else."

The inspired Gentz had something akin in mind when he wrote of the family generally that one of their leading principles was "to look for no exaggerated profits in any undertaking, to set definite limits to each operation. . . . In this maxim—servare modum finemque tenere—lies one of the chief secrets of their strength. There can be no kind of doubt that with the means at their command they might have obtained far greater advantages in one or another particular operation. Yet, even though the safety of the enterprise might not have suffered by their so doing, in the end they would nevertheless have profited less than they did by giving their resources the widest scope and thus having a greater variety of business constantly returning to them." All of which is a high-flown way of saying: Not all the eggs in one basket. Quick sales and fast overturn; for low profits never yet ruined merchant.

III

A shrewd and vivid, if not wholly appreciative portrait of Nathan as he appeared on the Royal Exchange has been drawn by a fellow-speculator:

"There is a rigidity and a tension in his features that would make you fancy, if you did not see that it was not so, that someone was pinching him behind, and that he was either afraid or ashamed to say so. Eyes are usually denominated the windows of the soul; but there you would conclude that the windows are false ones, or that there was no soul to look out of them. There comes not one pencil of light from the interior, neither is there one scintillation of that which comes from without reflected in any direction. The whole puts you in mind of a skin to let, and you wonder why it stands upright without at least something in it. By and by another figure comes up to it. It then steps two paces aside, and the most inquisitive glance that you ever saw, and a glance more inquisitive than you would ever have thought of, is drawn out of the erewhile fixed and leaden eye, as if one were drawing a sword from a scabbard. The visiting figure, which has the appearance of coming by accident and not by design, stops but a second or two, in the course of which looks are exchanged which, though you cannot translate, you feel must be of most important meaning. After these the eyes are sheathed up again, and the figure resumes its stony posture.

"During the morning numbers of visitors come, all of whom meet with a similar reception and vanish in a similar manner. And last of all the figure itself vanishes, leaving you utterly at a loss as to what can be its nature and functions.

"The name of this gentleman, the entertainments given by him, the charities to which he occasionally subscribed, and the amount of his transactions in the money market were blazoned abroad. Peers and the princes of the blood sat at his table; clergymen and laymen bowed before him; and they who preached loudest against mammon, bent lowest before the mammon-worshipper. Gorgeous plate, fine furniture, an establishment such as many a noble of Norman descent would envy, graced his entertainments. Without social refinement, with manners which, offensive in the million, were but brusque in the millionaire, he collected around him the most fastidious members of the most fastidious aristocracy in the world. He saw the representatives of all the states in Europe proud of his friendship. By the democratic envoy of the New World, by the ambassador of the imperial Russ, was his hospitality alike accepted; while the man who warred with slavery in all its forms and phases was himself slave to the golden reputation of the Hebrew. The language which Mr. Rothschild could use when his anger overbalanced his discretion was a licence allowed to his wealth; and he who, when placed in a position which compelled him to subscribe to a pressing charity, could exclaim, 'Here! write a check, I have made one —— fool of myself!' was courted and caressed by the clergy, was fêted and flattered by the poor, was treated as an equal by the first minister of the Crown, and more than worshipped by those whose names stood foremost on the roll of the commercial aristocracy. His mode of dictating letters was characteristic of a mind entirely absorbed in money-making; and his ravings when he found a bill unexpectedly protested were translated into mercantile language ere they were fit to meet a correspondent's eye."

Patently the anonymous author of these lines did not admire Nathan Rothschild. Yet the portrait is not malicious or overdrawn. Many men who thought well of Nathan—among them Rother, Wilhelm von Humboldt, Herries and even his own brother-in-law Moses Montefiore—testified to the same effect either explicitly or tacitly. The warmest admirers of his truly great gifts thought it prudent to pass over in silence or to allude in veiled words to his arrogance, his utter lack of refinement and civilized manners, his indifference to the amenities of decent society. Perhaps Humboldt summed up the man, when in a private letter to his wife, he said: "Rothschild is a quite raw and quite uneducated man, but he has much understanding and for money real genius." His trouble, like Napoleon's, was that his rare and special talents lifted him far above the social station for which his birth and his youthful environment had prepared him. Like Napoleon he was in his human relations an "ogre"; and the two had this characteristic further in common that their consciousness of social inferiority was turned by their eminence in another field and by the instinct of self-defense into deliberate insolence. Nathan's brothers rendered him a poor service when they flung a halo round their origin, though he himself played a sufficient part in the silly performance. Long before Gentz had dreamed of composing his "Biography" it was Nathan who, in his memorable after-dinner reminiscence concocted the fantasy about the Hessian Landgrave's six-hundred-thousand pound remittance. And among the credulous English, if not in Austria, the tale seemed to have been taken at something like par. His evident desire to make himself out a scion of "good family" betrayed both his sense that he was passing for something less and his dissatisfaction with his social status. But the effect of the invention was the reverse of what he had expected. The English would have humored a man of genius who had risen from poverty and simple surroundings; and under gentle ministrations his angularities might slowly have polished round to a degree at least. But he was taken at his word; and when he found, since he was not a dullard, that he could not live up to the standards expected of him, he turned round and flaunted his barbarities as the bluff virtues of an honest and gifted soul; and in England, where even shopkeepers and stock-gamblers strive to be gentlemen, this line did not go at all. It was a vicious circle. Nathan sneered at courtesy as so much sham and insincerity; he mocked at his brothers' pathetic endeavors to crawl in among the élite; he loftily refused to wear the baronial title they had wrung from Austria; he appeared on 'Change in even more slovenly garb than was natural for him; he gloried in his Ghetto accent. Cultivated people who could afford the luxury snubbed him; and the more they did so the more contemptuous he grew.

What had he to do with such superficialities? He was an original, a great man. He had trampled on the conventions of business, he had broken all the precedents of the Royal Exchange, and the world applauded him. The weaklings who had got hurt might scream and call names, but in the seats of the mighty he was received with acclaim. Let silly, pretentious idlers with nothing else to distinguish them worry over such trifles; he had bigger things to think about. The world did not expect conformity from such as him. The proof of it was that the strong, the highly placed, even the well-bred opened their homes and their arms to him. He was a doer, a natural aristocrat, one of the chosen of earth. With great wealth, with achievement, there was no need of submitting to the ordinary rules of courtesy; he was judged by standards of his own.

But he found out presently that he was mistaken. He caught people taking him in with raised eyebrows; there were suppressed grins behind well-kept hands. Oh, well; he would make some small concession. His wife and his children had a right to their social position, and he would do nothing to jeopardize it. There was so little to it all anyhow—an affair of externals. A man who had done the big things he had done would hardly be fazed by such trivialities once he cared to attend to them. He would surpass the snobs in display. So he filled his premises with pictures and plate and upholstery. He dressed up. He bought a house in Piccadilly and a princely estate in the country. He even rode and played the country gentleman. It was Napoleon reviving the glories of the Bourbons all over again, and it succeeded even less. Nathan Rothschild being himself was at least dignified; but the up-start of the Judengasse aping the toffs and the squirearchy was ridiculous.

He felt it, and he resented it. He took to making a virtue of his shortcomings, to revel in his enormities. But he found no peace. The older he grew, the more powerful he became, the more the world of rank and fashion fawned upon him—the deeper he raged within, the more hopeless appeared the prospect of his ever belonging on the plane where an ironic destiny had flung him, and the more savage became his behavior. He did not mellow; he soured. The high-spirited boy who flung out at the Manchester traveler grew into an irritable, misanthropic, violent old man. He underpaid and ill-treated his clerks because their grammatical speech, their neat dress, their good manners annoyed him. Most of all he delighted in being rude toward those who by rank and ancestry were his superiors but who must come to him for favors. "I am as good as you," he snapped at the Duke of Montmorenci, while a salon-full of aristocrats and ladies tried not to hear. "You style yourself the first Christian baron; well, I am the first Jewish one." Princes applying for loans were by his orders kept waiting in ante-rooms for hours. One such personage was, after lengthy delay, at last admitted to the presence. He introduced himself and named the object of his visit. Nathan did not so much as glance up; he was busy over a pile of documents on his desk; but he did ask a caller to take a chair. Considerable time passed, and the highness became impatient. "Did you hear who I am," he asked. "I am——," and he named his full title. "Very well," said Nathan from among his papers, "take two chairs."

But he was not alone in his misery. With the possible exception of Karl, all the Rothschilds of the first generation were haunted by the mocking ghosts of their past. The Judengasse and the shop threw a gray shadow across their path; to no matter what heights they rose it followed them and dulled the luster of their achievements. It was the price they paid for success.

PART IV

DECLINE

CHAPTER XVI

LONDON

THE death of Nathan was not only in itself an occurrence of the greatest moment, it was coincident with a profound change in the fortunes of the family. An era had come to its close. In England the young generation was at the wheel, with a background, a tone, an outlook only distantly related to the past; and though on the Continent Nathan's brothers continued to rule for many years, a new spirit was manifest in all the branches. The House of Rothschild, after thirty years and more of storm and stress, had at last entered the tranquil harbor of security and worldwide recognition. Incalculable as the loss of its most gifted member was, it was in a sense only after his disappearance that the family shone forth in all its splendor. Rothschild's became an institution and a household word, like sterling, like the British empire itself. Old rivals were reduced either to impotence or servitude; finance ministers in every state of Europe—of Europe and of America, too—when their treasuries needed replenishment, turned to New Court or the Rue Laffitte before they even thought of lesser firms. In official circles and in the popular mind there was but one world financial establishment, just as there was only one Bank of England and one pope.

Not that within the banking fraternity this monopoly went unquestioned. Far from it. The history of the House for the next fifty years is a continuous series of challenges, with ever-new combinations rising up to attack its supremacy. But it is the Rothschilds who are in possession, while others are on the outside engaged in offensive campaigns to dislodge them. Nor do they lie back on their achievements. So long as the first generation survives—and to a degree even afterwards—there is a ceaseless readjustment to changing times and new conditions. They are among the first and biggest railroad magnates in Europe. They finance and control vast mining enterprises—mercury, diamonds, copper, nitrates, petroleum. For a long time their immense properties in the Baku field make them the principal competitors of Standard Oil. Rothschild money is the power behind Cecil Rhodes and the South African diamond development; they dictate to, and almost annihilate, Mr. Barnato. An interlude comes when it appears as if they would extend their empire to North America; they have the lion's share in the funding of the United States national debt; they play an important, but losing, hand in the financial history of the Southern Confederacy. One Rothschild branch is the exclusive financial agent of the Russian empire, another guards the papal treasury. The firm extends its sway across the South Atlantic to become the dominant influence in the fiscal—and, inevitably, the political—affairs of the major states in Latin America. The death of Nathan was beyond doubt a staggering blow, but the family is far from moribund in consequence.

And yet it is difficult to escape the feeling that all this varied and far-reaching activity, immense and significant as it would look in the hands of a rising young concern, is—against the dazzling background of the age just past—

something of an anti-climax. There is expansion, even conquest; but it comes easily, almost unsolicited, without the fierce clashes, the resounding turmoil of other days. The big moment of the drama with its breathless suspense, its color and its intensity, is past; and the action takes on a slower and more stately measure as it declines to its inevitable dénouement. After 1836 the House of Rothschild, though apparently growing, merely holds its own. It cannot be said—not at any rate for yet a long time—that its vitality has departed; but having climbed to its zenith, it can henceforth do no more than either stand still or descend. Actually its seeming gains are but the harvest of its youth. Everything comes to it in virtue of the past, and its greatest triumphs are only repetitions.

Nor can the historian of the family avoid an inversely corresponding change of tempo. To relate the remainder of the story with anything like the fulness given to the earlier period would be to want in a sense of proportion. The epic rise of the Rothschilds has merited an elaborate narration; but the remaining years are a gaudy and largely prosaic procession of the rewards of success. The very conclusion lacks spirit. There is no crash at the end, no catastrophic débâcle such as has marked the exit of other dynasties.

II

But the end is still a long way off. It is, rather, the entry into the promised land. The promised land, certainly, for Lionel and his brothers; but to Nathan, had he been able to see it, it would have seemed the vale of disillusion. His heirs, alas! did not all fulfil the tender and pious dreams he had dreamed for them. Perhaps in the arrogance of youth and sudden liberation they considered themselves ten times as clever as their father. From infancy he had preached to them the maxim that it takes ten times as much wit to keep a fortune as to make one. They had come to believe it, and having entered into their inheritance, they practiced it. To preserve the parental legacy; to administer it wisely and diligently; to increase it, even, within the limits consistent with the family's high traditions and their own varied and exacting avocations—that surely was their duty to the founder and to their own interests; but as to giving "mind and soul, heart and body, everything, to business," it was not their idea of "the way to be happy," whatever their father's convictions on the subject might have been.

So it has always been, and so most likely it will always be. The self-made man, coarse, greedy, ignorant, capable, ambitious, not too seriously irked by scruples, unaware of the world's disapproval and of life's greater prizes or indifferent to them, a little brutal and more than a little ridiculous, strives for wealth, for power. He attains them; and, not illogically perhaps, he tells himself that if he, in spite of his handicaps (he does not know it is because of them), could get so far, what might not his children, with their knowledge, their refinement, their well-groomed persons, their friendships and their head-start, accomplish? He is not guided by reason or even by affection as much as he thinks, of course. In his children he sees himself again, reincarnated, possessing all his abilities, lacking all his crudities. In them he shall recapture what he missed in youth. They shall have the advantage their father could not have and be the equals of every exalted one who ever snubbed their father, and at the same time they shall have the driving force, and the narrow single-mindedness, and the rude, all-conquering, reckless cupidity with which his own uncouth beginnings equipped him.

And so Nathan the financial genius, being human after all, bungled sadly when it came to bringing up his successors. If he really wanted them to follow in his tracks, he should have given them the same kind of surroundings as he had himself had in boyhood. They should have been reared in the slums of Whitechapel—the nearest equivalent London could offer to the Frankfort Judengasse—and sent to the Jewish communal classes called *Talmud-Torah* till they were confirmed at thirteen, and thrown upon their own resources from then on. There is every indication that Lionel at least, if not his brothers, was as intelligent, as hard-working, as gifted as his father; but he suffered from his advantages. The trouble was that his parent's desires were divided and confused. Nathan strove to make his son a combination of two incompatible ideals. He wanted Lionel to be what he himself was and also what he himself had failed to become. In pursuit of one latter objective he placed him at an exclusive English school and later at the University of Goettingen, lavished luxuries upon him and surrounded him with refined and distinguished companions. Lionel, being a bright and adaptable boy, took to the strange and agreeable environment with avidity. He was growing up a young gentleman. But just then his father remembered with a start his other goal. He snatched the youth away from his college and put him through a rigorous course of training in the business. It did not work out very well: Lionel labored earnestly under his father, under the department chiefs, under the clerks; he was getting a thorough grasp of affairs; but as for this régime exerting a counter-influence, as for its producing another Nathan, devoted mind and soul, heart and body to business, it was disappointing. Nathan had not been trained by any indulgent and obsequious staff of experts in a world banking house. He had learned finance by buying muslins in Manchester. It made an enormous difference.

There were other differences between founder and heir. Lionel was not only a young man of education and culture. He had been born to fortune and to a high destiny. He had inherited a name, a tradition, even a social position. Nathan, too, had rubbed elbows with the great and the fashionable; it was another kind of relationship, a phase of business on both sides. But aristocrats and statesmen, men of letters, distinguished generals, famous and important people of every sort, were Lionel's natural circle. They were his school friends, his fellow-members in clubs, his equals. For he was himself a native Englishman of the upper class. This last was perhaps the most significant departure from the previous generation. He had roots in a country that it was possible to love—which was not the case with Frankfort, not for a Jew at least—and he did love it. Moreover, the intimate association with the upper class gave him a point of view that would have pained his father. He developed a conscience, public spirit, a sense of social responsibility. He discovered the nation, and the poor—and art; his younger brothers simultaneously discovered sport. There were, it seemed, other things in heaven and earth than business and moneymaking. Art, for instance, was something more than an invention for the rich to display their wealth; philanthropy was the duty of a gentleman; and sport, as young Meyer learned, was not only vastly more interesting and exciting than floating foreign loans, it made one a hero with the British populace, while finance did the reverse.

And so there was a sharp break with the past. No more was a Rothschild seen standing with his back against a pillar of the Royal Exchange like an empty flour-sack. Speculation, manipulation, the clamor and dust of the market-place, which were the breath of life to Nathan's nostrils, had no charm whatever for his sons. Shiftless, improvident states and princes, with whom the founder had loved to do business because they paid fat commissions and did as they were told, were dropped from the books without a qualm. New Court became the most dignified, the solidest and most conservative financial institution in the City of London. The Royal Exchange never saw Lionel or his brothers; if it needed them, it could come to New Court, in St. Swithin's Lane. It came willingly and often. Every morning the great procession of brokers, promoters, speculators, merchants, filed by Lionel's desk, each man whispering his mission, none pausing unless commanded to, and under no circumstances longer than two minutes. And as the years sped by the quiet grandeur of the new day shed its mellow luster over the past, the outlines softened, dubious episodes were forgotten, and Nathan was remembered as the legendary hero of a romance.

III

As emblematic of the new order as the toning up of the firm was the spreading out of the younger Rothschilds into the fashionable portion of London and their migration into the country. During all but Nathan's entire lifetime the home remained beside the business in St. Swithin's Lane. In 1835 he had, indeed, yielded to family pressure by purchasing the historic Gunnersbury House and Park, once the estate of a royal princess. He had died, however, before the alterations and refurnishing had been completed, and his eldest son was the one to take possession. But this was only a beginning. Presently Lionel built a magnificent town mansion on a plot adjoining Apsley House, in Piccadilly, and following him his brothers and other relatives flocked to the same district, until that quarter of Mayfair became known as Rothschild Row. In the neighboring counties ancient manors and vast hunting preserves came into the family. Anthony, the second son of Nathan, who was subsequently created a baronet by Queen Victoria, bought a château and a forest not far from Gunnersbury; his youngest brother Meyer set up his stud at Mentmore, in Buckinghamshire, and made it a favorite rendezvous of sportsmen and aristocrats. Meyer, though his rôle at New Court was that of a subaltern to Lionel, was the worldliest and best-known of his name. Eupeptic, pleasure-loving, popular, he was a typical Englishman of the racing, fox-hunting tradition. A lavish entertainer both in town and country, a breeder of fine horses (with one of them he won the Derby), it was he who was Baron Rothschild to the classes as well as the masses of the British public. All the brothers were passionate collectors and patrons of art; but Lionel and Sir Anthony took a more sedate view of their position and their responsibility. Lionel in particular, was circumspect and took pains to consort with the graver strata of society.

He rode to hounds not so much for pleasure as because a gentleman must. His dinners in London and his week-end parties at Gunnersbury were as splendid as those of his younger brother; but it was a splendor tempered with dignity as became the head of a great House and an eminent family.

An excited but anonymous guest at one of these entertainments has left us her somewhat overwhelmed impressions of what she witnessed, the occasion being a dinner to Lord and Lady Lyndhurst, the political god-parents of young Disraeli. "Silver and gold plate shone on the table and buffets; exquisite flowers delighted the eye; while the retinue of servants in full dress, so well trained that not a footfall told of their presence, and the ease and repose that prevailed, the result of perfect training, were forgotten in the distinction of the company." But even that apparently was thrown into the shade by the namesake of the old court-factor of the Frankfort Judengasse. "Another still more splendid and prolonged *fête* in Lord Lyndhurst's honor, to which we were also bidden, was given by the Baroness Meyer Rothschild at her Venetian villa at Mentmore—rather palace than villa, however. The Baroness had sent early in the week to have the house and grounds put in perfect order. Such pictures, such furniture, such park scenery, racehorses and hounds! Such a breakfast and lunch *al fresco* . . . as words cannot describe."

That was all very fine; but Lionel was conscious of duties and a mission in life. That colossus at New Court must be governed and must be reconciled at once with the spirit of the new age as well as with the doings of his relatives on the Continent, those amazing survivors of another world. Just as he was succeeding in drawing the veil over the past, along would come Uncle Salomon in Vienna or more likely Uncle James in Paris and start a stench that wafted itself across the Channel. It was very trying and made him wish sometimes that his father had not insisted on coöperation with the old fellows over there. Nor was that all. Earnestly as he was devoting himself to the management of the business, there were things in the world which claimed his attention and which as a great figure in the community and as a cultivated and educated man he could not disregard, even if he had wanted to. The public side of his life even had a way of getting mixed up with the financial. He was, for instance, a Whig by party affiliation, that is, a liberal. Liberalism was, among other things, opposed to imperialism, his best friends detested the oppressive, medieval Russian monarchy. But Russia was one of his most profitable clients, she was in the market for a big loan, and she was going to use the money to fasten her yoke on Poland. He was loath to forego the operation, yet if he undertook it he would be going counter to his declared principles and lay himself open to charges of hypocrisy. Complex situations like this came up constantly; they were very awkward and embarrassing. How much luckier his simple, unsophisticated parent had been!

Moreover, he was a Jew. Nathan had been content to attend services on the Sabbath and on the High Holidays, to pay his temple dues, and observe the traditional rites and practices. More than likely he would put down his successors as something not far removed from renegades. Nevertheless Lionel and Sir Anthony were, for all their French chefs and their compromises with the dietary laws, devoted to the race and the faith. For the greater part of their lives they were the presidents of their respective synagogues, and the Jewish community of London regarded them as their natural leaders. They erected hospitals, they headed charities, they gave generously of their time and money for Jewish education. In the international field Lionel, as the head of the House, worked indefatigably to improve the status of his people abroad. He backed his maternal uncle, Sir Moses Montefiore, in the latter's efforts on behalf of the Jews in Russia and Poland; and when the Congress of Berlin, after the Russo-Turkish war, met to readjust the jangled balance of power in Europe, it was Lionel's letter to the assembled potentates that, more than any single factor, forced the emerging kingdom of Rumania to promise a civilized solution of its Jewish question.

IV

Undoubtedly, the most notable event in Lionel's career was an outgrowth of his deep interest in the status of his race. English Jewry in general and the Rothschild family in particular had, it is true, little to complain of. Compared with their brethren on the Continent, and more especially with those of them who dwelt in the Eastern parts of it, their position was enviable. They enjoyed economic equality with Christians, socially they were restricted only by income and personal fitness, even politically the British Constitution protected them. Yet one distinction remained—a survival from the ages of prejudice, which set Jews apart as citizens of the second class. No professing Jew could sit in either house of Parliament. Catholics, non-conformists and infidels were all represented. There was, in fact, no explicit law against the Jews either; only the oath of office was so worded as to exclude them in practice. It concluded with the words "on the true faith of a Christian." Reform politicians had repeatedly sought to change the formula, but so long as the Tories were in power all such endeavors were foredoomed to failure. In 1847 Lionel Rothschild began his long, spectacular fight to end the discrimination. His determination to do so was brought about, curiously enough, through the influence of a man who was himself both a Tory member of the House of Commons and an apostate to the Mosaic faith.

Benjamin Disraeli had for many years past been Lionel's most intimate friend. The two men, so different in their backgrounds, their temperaments and their fortunes, had nevertheless many interests in common. "Dizzy," loaded down with debts, dandified, dreaming of literary eminence and the Premiership, converted to the Established creed by the whim of a queer parent, was irresistibly drawn toward the great capitalist. When he came to write his Novel "Coningsby" he took Lionel as the model for *Sidonia,* the ideal young public man. As far as he was concerned, his abandonment of the synagogue had not altered the blood in his body or the heritage of his soul. Certainly it had not by one jot diminished his deep concern over the welfare of the Jewish people. Why, but for a fortuitous incident in his boyhood, he might himself have been kept out of Parliament and his ambition nipped at the start! It was stupid and unfair and dangerous for the nation's own interests to exclude an entire group of useful and intelligent citizens on no other ground than that they differed from the rest of the population about the hereafter. Some day when he became Prime Minister he would change all that. But then the thought came to him, why wait till then? Lionel Rothschild was the man to take up the cudgels against the musty prejudice, and at once. With his wealth, his personal qualities, his powerful connections and his family's long record of patriotic service, he was the natural standard bearer for the cause and no opposition could withstand his leadership.

In truth Dizzy's anticipations were somewhat too sanguine. The fight as it turned out was a very long and bitter one. Lionel, urged on to the enterprise by the leaders of the Jewish community, offered himself as the Whig candidate for one of the two divisions of the City of London. He was easily elected; and his colleague, who happened to be Lord John Russell, the Premier, made a motion in the House of Commons in favor of the "removal of the civil and political disabilities now affecting Her Majesty's Jewish subjects." Later he introduced a bill to the same effect, which being warmly supported by the oratorical gifts of both Disraeli and Gladstone, was after much discussion adopted. When, however, it reached the Lords, the reactionaries would have nothing to do with it. Lionel thereupon resigned, and at the first opportunity stood again. Six times he was reëlected, six times he appeared before the bar of the House demanding to be sworn on the Old Testament, ten times Lord John introduced his bill for the revision of the Oath of Abjuration, and every time it was accepted by the lower house and rejected by the upper one. The electorate protested; the refusal to seat their chosen representative was tantamount to disfranchising the constituency. Finally one of those compromises which have made the British constitution so unique an entity was patched up. A committee was appointed with Rothschild as one of its members, to draw up reasons for disagreeing with the Lords; and upon its handing in its findings, a resolution was offered in the House of Lords whereby each of the branches of Parliament was to have the right to determine the wording of the oath for its own members. This was adopted, and Lionel, after eleven years of controversy, was permitted to take his seat. He was the first professing Jew to gain admittance to that august body, but he was not the last Rothschild to do so. Once the doors had been forced open, they never closed again. Lionel continued to represent the London financial district for fifteen years. He did not, as some of the Tories in the House of Lords had dreaded, disrupt the Imperial legislature either by his forensic talents or by the extraordinary measures he introduced. He was in fact a silent, passive and wholly innocuous member. He had fought his way in to establish a precedent, and having achieved that purpose he was content to relapse into obscurity. But his victory was not a sterile one entirely. From that time to this Westminster has with but rare interruptions always counted at least one Rothschild among its members. Lionel's brother Meyer and his son-in-law Ferdinand held seats in the Commons during his own lifetime, and not long after his death his son Nathan pushed the victory further by becoming the first Jewish peer to sit in the House of Lords.

V

A less spectacular but equally significant result of Lionel's intimacy with Disraeli followed later when the

House of Rothschild became instrumental in giving Great Britain control of the Suez Canal. Under the administration of Lord Palmerston England had had the opportunity of making that enterprise, so important to the trade and the very life of the empire, her own. That jaunty statesman, however, would have nothing to do with it. He characterized the project as a fantasy, and De Lesseps as either a swindler or a lunatic. Even after the waterway was completed and in operation, he could not be brought to see its value. The consequence of that incredible blindness is well-known: the Canal became virtually a French possession. But the gods watch over babes and innocents; wherefore, not many years afterwards, France had to have a war with Prussia and be so badly defeated as to all but destroy her prestige in the concert of Europe and reduce her to the status of a second-class power. It so happened, furthermore, that the Khedive (at that time more or less under the suzerainty of Turkey), in granting the concession, had reserved for himself a large block of the operating company's stock—177,642 shares to be exact, for which he was to pay, and did pay, over a period of years the sum of eighty-nine million francs. These details have a bearing on what ensued, as do also the following: Although by the contract with De Lesseps's company the Khedive was entitled to receive a minimum dividend of five per cent on his stock, he as a matter of fact lost precisely that much in interest on it. That was, to be sure, nobody's fault but his own. His Egyptian Majesty was a victim of the extravagance and improvidence common to Oriental potentates. He never had the money to pay in when instalments fell due, and when he applied to the French financiers for a loan they required ten per cent interest, exactly twice the amount the shares brought him. Moreover, they demanded security, and thus it came about that the Khedive was separated from his dividend coupons for a period of no less than twenty-five years to come. He consoled himself for this loss with the thought that he was still going to come out ahead, since by another clause of the contract he was to receive fifteen per cent of all profits made by the Canal. Unhappily for him, however, the Company was not making any profits. It was, in fact, facing bankruptcy.

In these very unsatisfactory circumstances, the directors conceived the idea of pulling out of a scrape by selling the Canal to the Powers. The Khedive, greatly alarmed at the prospect of an international board of control settling down on his front-door step, tried to protest; but he was a minority stockholder, and his objection was overruled. Thereupon he quietly sent for the British Consul-General on the spot, a certain General Stanton, and begged him to urge his government to buy the Canal alone. In addition, he persuaded his overlord, the Sultan of Turkey, to make a bid for the property, in order to dispose of it later to England. Finally, De Lesseps himself, though he greatly disliked selling out, went over to London and engaged in conversations with the authorities there, in the hope that their offer to buy might stimulate the other maritime powers to compete. The English rulers, however, even though Lord Palmerston had in the interval been superseded by Mr. Gladstone, were not interested, and lent a cool ear to all three proposals. They would not buy themselves, and they gave the Porte to understand that they would not tolerate any other purchaser.

De Lesseps was desperate, but he still had a shot in his

locker. The Canal, as he saw it, was his property and he could administer it as he saw fit. He raised the tolls one franc per ton, and when that did not suffice he resorted to an ingenious scheme of revising the definition of "ton of capacity" in such a way as to yield an additional thirty-three per cent of revenue. The maritime nations protested violently. In France itself the Messageries Maritimes, a shipping concern doing a big carrying trade to the Orient, carried the controversy to the courts. Britain, acting through the Porte, demanded that the whole question be referred to an international commission. It was, and the commission ruled that the old English system of measuring tonnage was the only correct one and ordered the Canal company to refrain from collecting the revised tolls. But De Lesseps balked. He threatened to close the waterway altogether, and he notified the British admiralty and Board of Trade that if they refused to pay the passage dues fixed by his company their ships would "have to take the old route around the Cape." It was not till the Khedive mobilized a force of ten thousand men with orders to evict him that De Lesseps yielded.

De Lesseps's protest against the Commission's ruling reached London on the 12th of February, 1874. Nine days later the Gladstone Government was defeated and Disraeli became, for the second time, Her Majesty's Prime Minister. With characteristic energy he at once went to work and made a thorough study of the whole controversy. Having concluded that his predecessors in office had badly bungled matters and that control of Suez was of vital importance to England, he sought the help of his friend Lionel Rothschild to undo the mischief. The firm had already on its own initiative made several attempts to obtain the Khedive's holdings; but owing to their conservative policy of having no dealings with irresponsible and financially incompetent princes, their connections in Cairo and Constantinople were nil, and they had failed. Lionel now explained to the Premier how things stood. Disraeli, however, was not thinking of the Khedive; he was for reopening the negotiations with De Lesseps of three years ago. The day following this conversation Lionel's brother, Nathaniel, crossed the Channel to Paris and got into communication with De Lesseps. It so happened that in the meanwhile France had paid—thanks to the coöperation of the Paris House of Rothschild—the last billion of her indemnity to Germany, and her foreign policy had in consequence materially stiffened. Lesseps therefore told Nathaniel that he most emphatically was not contemplating any sale. Why should he? His country was making the Canal a national issue, and Russia was backing France on the international commission, so that he was in a position to threaten the Khedive with putting his company under his government's protection.

The prospects for Britain were dubious in the extreme. Then suddenly help came from an unexpected quarter. On October 7, 1875, the government of Turkey went bankrupt. In view of Egypt's connection with the Porte, a financial panic speedily seized Alexandria, the consequence of which was to threaten the solvency of the Khedive. Interest on the Egyptian debt was due before the end of the calendar year. In these circumstances the finance minister bethought himself of his master's Canal shares, and he opened negotiations with two French syndicates. Nominally the stock was to be mortgaged, but the bankers took care to impose terms so usurious as to make it practically certain that the Khedive would default on the payments and thus forfeit his interest in the Canal. Somehow the British government got wind of what was toward and dispatched a protest to Cairo, which produced an assurance that the sale of the securities was not being considered.

In the end the rivalry of the two banking combinations prevented the French authorities from lending their support to either. The Crédit Foncier syndicate, moreover, came to the conclusion that only outright purchase would meet the Khedive's needs. But the government of France hesitated to approve such a step for fear of diplomatic complications with Great Britain. A feeler was, therefore, reached out toward London, which brought an emphatic note from Lord Derby (Disraeli's Foreign Minister) declaring that Her Majesty's Government would regard the "making of the Canal any more French than it already "was" as an unfriendly act. But the Khedive anxiously saw the days rolling by and no money in sight with which to meet the interest payments on his debt. There was no alternative but to send for General Stanton again. On November 23, 1875, Stanton telegraphed that Egypt was prepared to relinquish her entire holdings for one hundred million francs. As it happened Parliament was not in session just then, so that it was impossible to obtain the necessary appropriation in the usual constitutional way. But that did not deter Disraeli from acting swiftly. He called Derby and Salisbury into conference, and having assured himself of the support of these two members of his Cabinet, he sent round to Lionel Rothschild to tell him that the transaction was coming through and to be prepared with the money—a matter of four million pounds. He could not guarantee that the House would make good, but if Lionel was willing to take the risk, he (Disraeli) would warmly appreciate the favor. The risk was not very grave, considering that the valuable stock was to be transferred into the hands of the banker. At any rate, Lionel did not hesitate. There was a two-and-a-half-per cent commission—a hundred thousand pounds—involved. The Khedive gave up not only his hundred and seventy-odd thousand ordinary shares but threw in also fifteen hundred founders' shares as well as his fifteen-per cent interest in the revenues of the Canal; and all this, together with the small batch of shares already held in England, gave the Queen the predominant voice in the enterprise. At least Disraeli told her that it was she who was the sole gainer. "It is just settled; you have it, Madam. Four millions sterling! and almost immediately. There was only one firm that could do it—Rothschilds. They behaved admirably; advanced the money at a low rate, and the entire interest of the Khedive is now yours, Madam."

VI

Less than four years later Lionel died suddenly, and the governance of the London House of Rothschild passed to his eldest son. Even better educated than his father, Nathan (or Nathaniel) was almost exclusively a public man. From his uncle Anthony he had inherited the baronetcy, and his close friendship with the Prince of Wales, whom he had come to know at Cambridge, presently brought him a peerage. The daily morning procession at New Court continued; government loans, particularly with

Brazil and Chile, kept on coming to the House; but it was purely and simply inheritance. Already in the third generation, the descendants of Nathan began showing the tendency, which has since become general among the Rothschilds, of converting their banking houses into mere administrative offices for the investment of their capital. Society, art, politics and Jewish affairs absorbed Lord Nathan almost wholly, and his brothers, like their uncles before them, went in for sport and fashion.

Unmistakably, also, the bonds of family tradition began weakening in the second half of the century. While a majority of the first Nathan's grandchildren married Rothschilds, no fewer than four of them went for their mates beyond the limits not only of their own clan but of the race itself. The strayers from the fold are reputed, it is true, to have remained Jews in faith and have even continued to interest themselves in Jewish charities and public questions; but the same cannot be said of their descendants.

Among the present, the fourth, generation, both these manifestations have become stronger. One of the latter-day Rothschilds has gone to the length of giving up his very name. He has changed it to Pascal, and the street in Paris which bears that designation is named not after the French philosopher but after one of the scions of old Meyer of Frankfort. So also with the firm. Though St. Swithin's Lane continues to be something of a power in British finance, and though its investments in South American loans, in railroads, mines and industrial enterprises are enormous, the significance of the House lies purely in its command of huge capital and not in the least in its skill or enterprise. The initiative, the force, the brilliant originality, the fierce vitality of the days of the first Nathan have passed to younger and more determined men with other names who still have their reputations and their fortunes to make. In so far as Rothschilds in England can be said to have survived, it has done so wholly on the momentum, one could almost say on the inertia, of the past. And the London House is the least moribund of its name.

CHAPTER XVII

JAMES AND HIS HEIRS

THE drift of events in Paris followed lines roughly parallel to the development in London. There was one important difference, however: While beyond the Channel the heirs came into possession early, the first generation continued to control in France for half a lifetime longer. James was but forty-four when Nathan died, and he lived to be seventy-six. In the prime of life, by far the most brilliant of his remaining brothers and so by them acknowledged, strategically located, rich in experience, he readily stepped into the captaincy left vacant by Nathan. More even than by personal endowment, he was equipped for leadership by favoring circumstances. The Revolution of July—that very overturn which had come so near bringing ruin upon his House—once it had survived the crisis and consolidated its gains, fulfilled all his expectations. He emerged from it sobered and immeasurably strengthened. His German birth, his Jewish accent, his obscure and questionable beginnings, his social inferiority, his past failures, were all forgotten and forgiven; and he attained a power in government and a dominance over the national economy which Nathan himself in his best days had never equaled.

Nothing like the July Monarchy had ever been known in the whole predatory history of French royalty. For eighteen years big business was supreme. It governed with an insouciance, a blatancy, a callous disregard of public decency and national well-being that would have made Louis XV blush with shame. The citizen king, mindful of the classes to whom he owed his throne, turned the country unreservedly over to the haute bourgeoisie. Painfully conscious of the precariousness of thrones in general and of his own in particular, he was determined that whatever came he and his family should never be exposed to want. And so there followed an era of stock-jobbing, speculation and corruption in which Majesty, court, parliament, anybody and everybody with a paw in the trough of power shared freely and richly. Above all, Louis Philippe was too loyal to forget his debt to James and his House. It was James's generosity that had enabled him to survive patiently and in comfort the days preceding his accession, and but for the combined support of the Rothschilds he might—he almost certainly would—have been annihilated by Metternich and the Holy Alliance. Well, James should now have his reward. He had been snubbed by the haughty Bourbons; therefore he should never now be absent from palace functions, and his own parties should always be graced by royal presences. The chauvinists held it against him that he was a foreign baron; they should be silenced and James should wear the grand cross of the Legion of Honor. More tangible recognition, also, was to be his. He should have a monopoly of government loans as a matter of course. Privileges, contracts, concessions should be granted him regardless of public policy and public opinion. And incidentally he should handle the royal investment account and hatch Majesty's nest-egg against the evil days that one could only hope would never come.

K
W
JAMES
VON ROTHSCHILD

Squeamish people, at home and abroad, were scandalized by the spectacle—or made a note of it with sardonic humor. Metternich, the high-minded puritan, saw the disgraceful alliance between monarch and plutocrat as the inevitable result of democracy. It caused him to shake his head with pained resignation. "The House of Rothschild," he said, "plays a much bigger rôle in France than any foreign government, with the possible exception of England. There are of course reasons for it, which to me naturally appear neither good nor morally gratifying: Money is the great motive force in France, and corruption—which is in practice the most important factor in our modern system of representative government—is quite openly reckoned with." But he took comfort in the thought that in Austria at least filthy lucre was scorned by all right-thinking men. "Among us the traffic in this commodity finds but few friends."

Heine, on the other hand, who dined in the Rue Laffitte often and had ample opportunity to observe what was going on, reveled in the delicious situation. He declined to grieve over it at any rate; or possibly, like the Barber of Seville, he laughed to hold the tears back. "A few hundred years ago," he wrote, "the king would quite simply have pulled Monsieur Rothschild's teeth out by way of inducing him to consent to a loan. Ah well, the naïve ethic of the middle ages has happily been carried downstream by the Revolution, and now Rothschild the baron and Knight of the Order of Isabella can calmly go for a walk in the Tuileries whenever he is so disposed, without fearing that the hard-pressed monarch will touch a single one of his teeth."

What gave him particular joy, however, was to sit in a quiet corner at the counting house and watch the daily procession of hopeful speculators doing homage. "Best I like to call on him at his office in the bank, where as a philosopher I can look on at the people—not merely God's chosen, but those of all races—kneeling and abasing themselves before him. Such a doubling and contortioning of backbones as you would hardly expect acrobats to achieve! Some I have seen who on catching a glimpse of the great baron are seized with a nervous twitching as if they had unawares stepped on an electric cable. Others have but to approach the door to succumb to a tremor of awe, such as Moses must have felt when he suddenly realized on Mount Horeb that he was standing on holy ground. . . . This inner office is in truth a remarkable place. . . . It impresses one with the insignificance of man and the greatness of the Lord. For money is the god of our age and Rothschild is his prophet."

Another German-Jewish writer was less amused. Ludwig Boerne had known the Rothschild boys in Frankfort before their days of glory. It was after him and not after them that the city fathers later named the metamorphosed Judengasse. In spite of common origin, however—or it may have been because of it—Boerne took little pride in the magnificence that had come to his fellow-townsmen. Gifted with a sardonic pen, he rarely missed an occasion for lampooning their activities. As early as 1832 he reported to his paper: "Louis-Philippe, if he is still king next year, will have himself crowned—not, however, in the church of St. Remi at Rheims but in Paris in Notre Dame de la Bourse and Rothschild will officiate as archbishop."

II

But in truth Boerne was doing James an injustice. For James had no ambition to be a king-maker. The monarch was safely where he wanted him to be, and he turned his attention to seats of power which, for all that they came in smaller containers, were none the less worth subduing. Railroads were a bigger thing than loans now, and to his chagrin France had gone in for a policy of state construction and operation. Louis-Philippe was well-disposed; but in this matter the decision rested not so much with the king as with the people's representatives in parliament and in the press. In 1845, therefore, when plans were in the making for the great new line to link Paris with the industrial regions of the North, James set to work systematically to secure the concession. With a suddenness which took Frenchmen off their feet, the staunchest advocates of public ownership all at once perceived the error of their ways. Ministers, deputies and journalists alike agreed that in the interests of economy, of efficiency and of the public weal the *Chemin de Fer du Nord* ought to be built and run by the banking firm of de Rothschild Frères. Only one newspaper, the *National*, stuck by its guns, and it subsequently explained how its colleagues as well as the gentlemen in parliament were converted.

The company launched the enterprise with a capital stock issue of one hundred and fifty millions, divided into three hundred thousand shares nominally worth five hundred francs each. According to the recalcitrant journal one-tenth of the securities were distributed freely and gratis among the membership of the chambers and the press, in all seven and one-half millions' worth, to each according to his merit and the weight of his support. The *National* itself was not slighted; it duly received its proportionate parcel; only, so it boasted, it preferred the distinction of a clear conscience and the pleasure of enlightening the world. The materialists, on the other hand, had nothing to complain of. With nearly the entire press behind him, James now proceeded to make the shares worth having. By a series of alternate bulling and bearing operations they gradually rose from 500 to nearly 850. Repeatedly he unloaded his holdings so as to depress prices and secure the outstanding parcels. In the end he emerged as the majority stockholder. He retained the presidency of the road till his death, and the property continues in the hands of his descendants to this day.

The line was opened with appropriate ceremonies at Amiens on June 15, 1846, and Monsieur Rothschild was hailed by representatives of the crown and the chambers as a public benefactor. Not many weeks later the public rejoicings were overshadowed by a deplorable accident in which a score or so of travelers were killed and many more injured. A terrific storm broke about the public benefactor's head, who was now denounced as a monster sacrificing human flesh to the golden calf. Old resentments, hatreds, jealousies, long pent-up, took advantage of the occasion to vent themselves in violent tirades. A flood of pamphlets poured forth from the press, with echoes of the Viennese polemists from whom poor Salomon had suffered so long. A disappointed journalist who had been overlooked in the stock distribution of the year before unearthed old Hormayr's venomous phrase and addressed James pseudonymously as "Rothschild I, King of the Jews." The doggerel artists did their share. Ancient *canards* about the unaristocratic antecedents and the early performances of the family, and the malodorous origin of its fortune, were revived and spread before an eager public. The uproar mortified James and made him nervous. This sort of thing was something quite new in his experience, and he was at a loss how to handle it. He appealed to his newspaper and literary friends to help him, and a pamphlet entitled "The Reply of Rothschild I to Satan the Last" was hastily gotten out, in the evident hope that it would end the discussion. But it had, of course, the opposite effect; the scurrilous broadsides swelled in volume and in intensity. Then James redoubled his endeavors on behalf of the poor and outdid himself in good works; whereupon his adversaries warned the public that the cheap bread issuing from the Rothschild bakeries was made of adulterated flour mixed with poison, and called upon the authorities to stop its distribution. There seemed to be no limit to the malice of the wicked.

But James soon found something vastly more disturbing to occupy him. Within little more than a year after the accident on the Nord railroad, signs of the most alarming variety began to appear everywhere in the country. Republicanism, which was believed exorcised forever, suddenly raised its menacing head once more. The apparently solid edifice of monarchy creaked, swayed and displayed symptoms of breaking up. On the second of February it fell in a heap. The Citizen King, scorned, discredited and abandoned by his supporters, fled the country in terror of his life. For a little time James refused to recognize the gravity of the situation, certain that the fury would spend itself, or that some savior would arise to divert it into reasonable channels. It was not long, however, before he realized that this was not 1830. When a mob descended upon his suburban château at Suresnes, pillaged it and only by a miracle was prevented from setting it on fire, and when the following day his eldest son Meyer Alphonse was seized by the Republican Guard, ordered into a uniform and with a musket on his shoulder detailed to stand sentinel on the ramparts, James reluctantly came to the conclusion that this time it was Revolution in real earnest.

III

It was more serious than he could bring himself to admit. The Second Republic, it speedily developed, was animated by a temper hostile not only to the old European political order; it had a social and economic lining. Strange, disreputable, wholly preposterous ideas of the state, of property, of the nature of wealth, of the relative worth of classes and services, distilled out of the destructive preachments of a band of wild-eyed doctrinaires in France and abroad—Louis Blanc, Engels, Marx, Fourier, St. Simon—had taken possession of the new rulers. They did not stop there, however. The upheaval sent out waves, which spread with lightning speed to all the ends of the Continent. East, North and South crowns were rolling off monarchical heads, and the pillars of civilization toppled into the dust. Here in France it looked as if the Revolution were largely a device for hacking away the bases upon which the House of Rothschild had risen and grown strong. One of the first reforms of the republicans addressed itself to the matter of state financing. The good old system was consigned bodily to limbo. Loans were no longer to be handled through any single firm or syndicate. For capital, according to the revolutionary philosophers, was a national resource; and that being the case, the nation could just as well act as its own contractor. Therefore the amount to be borrowed, the price at which the securities were to be floated, and the commissions of the agents and brokers, must be fixed by the state beforehand. The bankers could participate to whatever extent they desired, each house according to its ability, but all on the same footing. The vicious innovation, originating in France, presently gained converts among all the governments of Europe. A curtain descended upon the brilliant scene in which Rothschild's had for so long played a leading rôle.

Nor did it lift again when the Second Republic, after a brief and agitated existence lasting barely three years, turned into the Second Empire. Louis Napoleon was a totally different breed from Louis Philippe. A free-lance and a playboy prior to 1848, flying from one fantastic adventure after another, half the time an exile or a prisoner, he had been scarcely more than a name in France. James had thus had no opportunity to form any sort of ties with him, even if the notion had ever occurred to him that this obscure heir of a buried tradition would some day wear the crown of France. But there he was lording it in the Tuileries. And James, indelibly tarred with the Louis Philippe brush, found himself out in the cold.

What made this depressing state of affairs all the harder to bear was that the imperial court, by no means unfriendly to men of money—not even to Jewish ones—had thrown its favor to the rising young firm of the brothers Péreire, and Emil Péreire was a product and a whilom protégé of Rothschild's. It was enough to make one lose faith in humanity. Heine, it seemed, had spoken truer than he knew. "This remarkable man," he said of James, "has the rare gift of discovering men with extraordinary capacities and attaching them to himself . . . in contrast to his colleagues who prefer to surround themselves with nonentities." Yes, but the difficulty was that he was too good at it. Péreire was only one instance of the danger of encouraging excessively clever men: there were others, as will be seen presently. Péreire at least did not betray his protector's confidence. He learned what he could from him about the usefulness of friends at court, and then went ahead to apply the instruction. Young, alert, ambitious, and enjoying the friendship of influential people in the new régime, he had early made it his business to gain the confidence of the emperor. Within a few months of the coup d'état he had contrived to secure a charter from Napoleon III for the erection of a new kind of financial institution. It was called the *Crédit Mobilier,* and was the first bank in France organized on a joint-stock basis.

Then he went energetically toward his goal, which was nothing less than to supplant his former employer. There ensued a violent and bitter struggle, with no quarter given or taken. For a time the odds weighed heavily on the side of the challenger. Péreire pushed his influence into the provinces, and in a remarkably short time he had the nucleus of a powerful syndicate all his own. When Russia began building her network of railways, it was he who snatched off the concession, though James brought to bear all the pressure of his own and his nephew Lionel's prestige. Presently he carried the war into Austria and came within an ace of annexing the domain of Salomon's heirs. For fifteen years the furious contest raged. In the end, it is true, Péreire was beaten, but the victory cost the Rothschilds more than it was worth.

In the interval James experienced an even more grievous disappointment in his faith in mankind. For ten years he had entrusted the post of chief cashier on the Nord Railroad to one of his favorite understudies, a Frenchman named Carpentier. Few of his employees were so close to him or enjoyed so much of his confidence. He took Carpentier with him when he traveled, he invited him to the less brilliant entertainments in the Rue Laffitte; he even spoke to him freely about his operations and his winnings. Doubtless, that was his mistake; he overdid things somewhat. It did not occur to him that a gifted and modestly-incomed young man was apt to have temptations which the friendship and confidence of his enormously wealthy employer, coupled with tantalizing opportunities, might tease beyond resistance. Early in September 1856, James was on a journey with Carpentier, and in the course of conversation mentioned to him that he had just made a coup on the exchange which had netted him a gain of five million francs. Some hint of the relationship between magnate and subordinate may be gathered from the detail that Carpentier, upon hearing the good news, inquired what share of the proceeds the president of the road intended to bestow upon the chief cashier. James, so the newspapers afterwards reported, took the hint good-naturedly, and replied: "No, I cannot give you any of my five millions, but, here, take my chain, as a souvenir of this day which has brought me so much pleasure and profit." Carpentier pocketed the gift, and requested a leave of absence for several days. It was the last that was seen of him.

At first no particular notice was taken of the man's extended absence. When, however, pay-day came round, and a queue of employees lined up in front of the company's wicket without anyone appearing to hand them their wages, the officials suddenly recalled that Carpentier had not been seen for some little time. It became necessary to notify the president; for Carpentier had taken with him the keys of the safes, and James alone had duplicates. But when the safes were opened, they were found to be empty. An indeterminate quantity of cash, as well as mass of records, had been removed. James was not long in coming to the conclusion as to what had happened; but his first order was characteristic: beyond a bare statement that a robbery had occurred, all details were to be withheld from the public. There was the effect on the company's stock to be thought of. The French press readily acquiesced to hush up the affair. The foreign correspondents, however, were less obliging; and it is due to them that something like the real magnitude of the crime became known.

Carpentier, it developed, had had accomplices—one Grellet, a young man "of very good family," in addition to a number of clerks in the company's employ. In cash alone the sum abstracted amounted to six million francs. So much the directors were, after considerable questioning, induced to admit. That, however, was a small item of the total. Counting in the shares, the entire loss was estimated at the immense figure of "between thirty and thirty-two millions." The thieves had planned and executed the job with a skill and cunning worthy of the booty. Stock certificates deposited with the company being kept in packets of one thousand, the gang withdrew from each parcel two or three hundred shares, tied up the remainder and replaced them in their containers. In this way they had succeeded in carrying on their operations for a long time, without discovery. Six months before their disappearance they had bought a steamer in England for about two million francs, and some time later they acquired a house in New York. Early in September they decided they had enough. Thereupon Carpentier, having obtained his leave of absence, proceeded to Liverpool, where the boat was anchored, had her got ready, and steamed out to keep tryst with his companions. The president and directors were so put out by the faithlessness of their trusted subordinates that they offered to spend ten millions for the capture of Carpentier. But he had got such a good head-start that he was never caught.

IV

For its part the Nord Railroad survived the incident, and James continued to preside over its destinies to the day of his death. Had he been a mere king of France, such a display of bad judgment might have cost him his throne; but stockholders are more forgiving. Nevertheless, the disappointment over Carpentier and the weary struggle with Péreire did their part toward hastening his end. He died the year after the crash of the Crédit Mobilier. The Grand Rabbi of France, the Chief Rabbi of Paris, the head of the Jewish charities, and one or two officials of the Railroad, made moving speeches at the grave in the Père Lachaise cemetery; all the leading newspapers of the capital printed long editorials on his extraordinary career, his generosity to the poor and his devotion to the best interests of the country. A notable procession of diplomats and members of parliament followed the bier, and among the mourners were several hundred uniformed employes of the railway company. In deference to Jewish tradition, no military escort was provided by the government, though the deceased, as a commander of the Legion of Honor, was entitled to it. He was survived by his wife, a daughter and four sons. Three of the sons, Alphonse Meyer, Gustave and Edmond, took over the direction of their father's affairs.

The young men had barely had time to get their bearings when a series of political, financial and social crises in the affairs of France gave them ample opportunity to show their mettle. Less than two years after James's death the country embarked upon its disastrous war with Prussia. There followed in quick succession the capture and abdication of the Emperor, the siege of Paris, the Commune, and the huge indemnity imposed by the victor. Alphonse and his brothers acquitted themselves creditably, even brilliantly, in every instance. The invaders made their headquarters in the Rothschild estate at Ferrières; but as Bismarck was an old friend of the family, strict orders were given that the château and grounds were in no way to be treated as enemy property; the hungry soldiery were not to kill so much as a single partridge in the park; and it was in Ferrières that Jules Favre met the Iron Chancellor to receive the terms of peace. The departure of Napoleon III was accepted by the banking House with resignation if not with relief; Rothschild's had had better friends among the nation's rulers. As for the five billions demanded by the foe, Gambetta felt about it as Disraeli had felt about the purchase of the Khedive's shares: "there was only one firm could do it—Rothschild's." The raising and transfer of the fabulous sum was left to Alphonse, though his cousins in Frankfort and notably Lionel in London gave valuable assistance in carrying out the firm's guarantee that the exchanges should be maintained.

Even the terrible siege was somehow endured. Most Parisians were so hungry that they killed rats for food; but though proper edibles were costly and hard to get, people with the necessary price need not starve. It was the unspeakable mobs within the walls that almost made life unbearable. The Communards, like their brethren of 'forty-eight, rioted, seized wealthy men's homes, and under threat of violence, forced their owners to stand guard on the ramparts. Happily, the fury was short-lived. The decent and orderly elements of the city presently asserted themselves, and the subversive movement was drowned in blood.

With the establishment of the Third Republic James's heirs breathed freely again. The old system of loans, which had made their father the real power in the government as well as in the commercial life of the country, never returned, it is true; nor did the young men possess either the single-minded concentration of purpose or the healthy detachment from local concerns and local opinion, to bend parliament to their will, as their father had done in the matter of the Nord Railroad. No amount of parental solicitude to endow them with an international outlook could quite contrive to neutralize the influences of environment; born and reared and educated in France, they belonged. With all their intermarriages within the family and their complex ties abroad, they could not help thinking and feeling as Frenchmen. Like their cousins in England, also, they were conscious of a deterrent responsibility and dignity which, while it sprang from the past, conflicted with the spirit and methods of the past.

Fortunately for them, there were still countries in Europe where the upsetting ideas of France had not penetrated. There was Russia, for instance, a land wholly untouched by the Revolution. There concessions and operations on the classical lines were still possible; there the name and prestige of the House of Rothschild shone with its old glamour; and there, above all, the second generation need feel no compunction about walking in the footsteps of the founders. Twice within five years Alphonse and his brothers planted their flags in the vast empire. In 1883 the Tsar, embarrassed financially by the consequences of an expensive war and unable to raise funds in the regular way, was persuaded to grant the French House of Rothschild a concession in the Baku petroleum region so comprehensive as to make that firm the chief competitor of the Rockefeller interests. Oil, to be sure, was in those primitive days, not the stake of empire which it has since become; its sole use was as a substitute for candles; but as gas-lighting was still in its infancy in most places, and the incandescent lamp hardly more than a scientific toy at Menlo Park, the profits of the new Bnito Petroleum Company were not to be despised. As for Russia, the concession yielded only temporary relief, and in 1887 she addressed herself again to the capital markets of Europe for a loan. It was the period when statesmanship was busy projecting the *Drei-Kaiser-Bund*—the "natural" alliance of the three imperial powers of Austria, Germany and Russia against the democratic forces further West. But Bismarck had other plans, and he forbade the Reichsbank to give any financial support to the Tsar. The result was that Russia was obliged to turn to France, the loans were floated by the Paris Rothschilds, and the Oriental autocracy became the "cordial" ally of the Republic.

But this ability of James's heirs to keep going on their momentum was a thorn in the flesh of their rivals. Despite the failure of the Péreire challenge, joint-stock banking corporations continued to arise and to flourish, and ever-new combinations went on forming to break the power of Rothschild's. In 1876, the picturesque French financier, Bontoux, conceived the idea of enlisting religious and racial sentiment in the service of business. His *Union Générale*, founded that year, was designed primarily to deliver France and the world from the Semitic exploitation and incidentally to divert the proceeds into the pockets of deserving Catholics. The fact that the Holy See itself was a client of the unbelievers, did not disturb the logical Frenchman. His scheme was hailed with enthusiasm by the clerical, royalist, reactionary elements. All the aristocratic families that still had money to invest brought him their nest-eggs and the concern was floated with an initial capital of four million francs. The experiment might have succeeded had not Bontoux been too ambitious. Unwarned by the fate of Péreire, he yielded to the temptation of making a clean sweep by spreading his net to Vienna also. He was, in consequence, caught between the upper and nether millstones, and the *Union Générale*, which had begun under such hopeful auspices, came to a disastrous end after a brief career lasting barely six years. Hundreds of noble French families were reduced to beggary by the crash; while Bontoux, finding himself equipped with both leisure and emotion, took to the pen and in a pamphlet entitled "Le Krach de l'Union Générale; la finance juive et les francs-maçons" enlightened the world about the methods whereby the allied monsters of Judaism and Free-Masonry despoil honest but rather futile Catholics of their wealth.

It is difficult to tell how much the bitterness caused by the Rothschild-Bontoux struggle and its dire consequences contributed to the growth of anti-Semitism in France. Certain it is that the legacy of hatred and mistrust survived the episode for many years and affected people who had never so much as seen a stock-certificate. When one considers the line-up of the contestants in the violent Dreyfus battle a dozen years later, it appears not unlikely that the dynamite for that extraordinary explosion was planted on the bourses of Paris and Vienna on Black Sunday, 1882. In any event, it was while Dreyfusards and anti-Dreyfusards assaulted each other on the boulevards that the French House of Rothschild went through its stormiest period. The very name of the bankers became a sort of symbol in the fierce controversy; and although the dominance of the House was by that time hardly more than a memory, the mass of literature in French dealing with the antecedents of the family and the origins of its fortune dates from that period. Nor did their enemies stop at verbal weapons. The property and the very lives of the descendants of James were in constant peril during the years 1896–1903; and Edouard, the only son of Alphonse, was actually forced to resort to a duel in defense of his life.

The long-drawn out struggle had just come to an end when Alphonse died at the age of 76. Though his two brothers Gustave and Edmond, who had all along been associated with him in the firm, survived, they were too old to take over the direction of its affairs; and the succession fell to their sons—Robert Philippe (Gustave) and

James and Maurice (Edmond). Their administration has been notable for a progressive contraction of the family's interests. In 1911 they took a spectacular step in the liquidation process by selling the Bnito Petroleum Company to the Royal Dutch-Shell combine. While in London St. Swithin's Lane is to this day an institution, the French House is nothing more than an office through which the various members handle their investments and their charitable endeavors.

CHAPTER XVIII

TWILIGHT

GENTZ, racked with maladies, disappeared; Prince Metternich saw his laborious system crash to earth, and fled, a terrified mummy in his night-clothes, with the howling mob clamoring for his head; the emperor of Austria laid down his crown and put it on again; but all the while Salomon carried on, watchful but unperturbed. All the props and buttresses of his House trembled and gave way, but its foundations held firm. The death of Gentz, indeed, removed an associate whose services he only now fully appreciated. "He was a friend," he wrote regretfully to James, "whose like I shall not surely ever meet again. He cost me something frightful; you have no idea. He would just simply write down on a scrap of paper what he required, and the amount would be handed to him without further ado. Yet now he is gone I can see how valuable he was to us. Gladly would I give three times as much if I could but have him back." He did not get him back, alas! and so Salomon was obliged to collaborate with other men who, if they were neither as discreet nor as useful, were less expensive.

Times changed, and he adapted himself to them with astonishing ease. State financing struck out into unwonted paths; competitors of a new and formidable species arose; railroads came, and industrial expansion, and mining; he made the best of a difficult period. His zest for toil continued unabated, and so did his appetite for distinctions.

Already away back in 1831 he had begun to see the new drift. Therefore when that year the Austrian government was once again struggling with its budget, he proposed that in lieu of a loan it might obtain somewhat more enduring relief by leasing to him for a term of years the state domain of Idria with its mercury deposits. He knew nothing of the mines and metals; it was enough that mercury had a field to itself in certain manufactures and in pharmacopœia, and that the trade was ill-organized so that the mineral was commanding a low price. Idria alone, however, would not enable its possessor to control the market. As it happened, the other great deposit was in Spain, and Nathan being at the moment in touch with the authorities of that country, Salomon urged him to secure the concession on Almaden as well. And thus the House of Rothschild established one of the first great monopolies of modern times. Mirror-makers, physicians and philanthropists protested loudly; the hostile press charged that the sick and dying were deprived of necessary medicines while an international band devoid of human feelings was getting rich; but Salomon, known throughout the empire as a generous giver to charities and as the protector of the poor, need only reply by pointing to his record; and mercury went on rising in price.

As in France, Austria began with a policy of state railroad construction. The difficulty was to finance the undertakings. When the plans for the *Nordbahn* came up for consideration, it was found that, the best resolutions notwithstanding, the bankers would have to be appealed to. The political pattern of the empire (and, individuals apart, the moral tone, too) was very different from that in Louis

Philippe's France, and there is no indication that the grant to Rothschild was accompanied with the methods employed by James. On the other hand, the flotation of the stock on the bourses was reminiscent of the days of the lottery loan. Now it was that Salomon felt the absence of Gentz most keenly. Still, the *Augsburger Allgemeine Zeitung* and the late Baron Meseritz' syndicate did their best. The shares were offered to the public before so much as a spade of ground was turned; and although the project was new and risky, the propaganda was so skilfully handled that within a short time the entire issue of twelve million florins was absorbed and quotations soared to fifteen points above par. Afterwards, to be sure, the operating company had all it could do to stay out of bankruptcy, dividends were passed year after year, and the security was a drug on the market. But long before that time Salomon had disposed of his holdings. He is to this day remembered in Austria as the "builder" of the Kaiser-Ferdinand-Nordbahn, but in reality he had neither part nor concern in the actual construction. The heirs of James remain in control of the *Chemin de Fer du Nord,* but their Viennese cousins are in no sense rail magnates.

On the other hand, what is still left of the Rothschild power and prestige in present-day Austria consists in the main of the *Oesterreichische Kredit-Anstalt,* an institution founded by Salomon in the 'forties of last century. The success of the joint-stock banks abroad, and especially of the *Crédit Mobilier* in Paris, gave the Austrian authorities the idea of organizing the capital forces of their own dominions in like manner and thus weaken the stranglehold of the House of Rothschild upon the national finances and the economic life of the country. In this latter hope, as the event showed, they were to be disappointed, for a time at least; but the new type of bank did arise in Austria. Bruck, the finance minister, first entered into negotiations with the young Franco-Jewish wizards, the Péreire brothers, and he did his utmost to turn the concession their way. It was they who had begun the movement in France and had made themselves the most powerful rivals the Rothschilds had over there. Nevertheless he did not dare run the risk of antagonizing Salomon, and Salomon was pulling wires in high quarters to secure the charter for himself. It then occurred to Bruck to try a compromise. He called in the two principal bidders, and suggested that they compose their differences and found the institution jointly. Neither side welcomed the proposal; but Salomon, knowing perfectly well that his competitor could not accept unconditionally, made a show of agreeing. Péreire said that he would be willing to enter the combine, providing the Rothschilds would cease their hostilities against the *Crédit Mobilier*. This was dragging in foreign and irrelevant matters, as Salomon was quick to point out and as Bruck was obliged to concede. Péreire was thus outmanœuvred, and the charter was awarded to Rothschild.

All in all, then, Salomon was getting on well enough, in spite of his great age (he was over seventy), the changed times and even the loss of Gentz. And yet he was discontented. His brothers, or their heirs, were citizens of the places in which they lived, and great landed proprietors. He was neither. All his power and influence had not sufficed to remove the disabilities of the Jews in Austria. He himself was a foreigner in the country, and only his status as a citizen of Frankfort made it possible for him to enjoy such civil liberties as he had. Indigenous Jews were still restricted in their movements and occupations. Even he was obliged to reside in a hotel, and the only way he could live comfortably was by renting all the rooms. But he did not own even that improvised home; Jews were not permitted to buy property. If he or his family wanted to spend a week or a summer in the country, they must go to a public inn—he, the most powerful private man in the empire—while the most poverty-stricken and improvident of his debtors, by the mere accident of the "noble" and Christian birth, spread themselves out on their sumptuous, if mortgaged, estates. It irritated and embittered him. He hinted to Metternich, he exerted pressure on the imperial finances, he relapsed into ominous silences, he begged and protested openly. His efforts seemed to go for naught. He gave munificently to the poor and to public institutions, until his benevolences became the talk and admiration of the community, and his fellow-philanthropists were moved to appeal to the authorities, pointing out the absurdity and injustice of so generous a public benefactor being treated as a pariah. This, at last, had the desired effect, and the City of Vienna made Salomon in 1843 an honorary citizen. Some time later, Salomon having endowed a hospital for the insane in Brünn, the Emperor by a special dispensation permitted him to acquire the castle and park of Schillersdorf in Silesia.

II

But the great disappointment of his life was Anselm, his only son and the heir of his firm and fortune. The boy did not seem to be a Rothschild at all. He was extravagant, a high liver, fond of show, he got into scrapes, he was wild, he had not the smallest inclination to toil and save,—a typical scion of a great house. At least that was how he appeared by the parental criteria. Salomon did everything he could to lead him into the path of righteousness. He sent him to be educated at the University of Berlin. He cut down his allowance; whereupon the young man made debts. To check his flightiness he married him off at twenty-three to Nathan's oldest daughter, hoping that responsibility and the soberer ways of the London cousins would have a good influence upon him. Before that, when Anselm had had an escapade at college, his father had called him home, and after a review of his misdeeds and dark prognostications of what future delinquencies might have in store, he apprenticed him to his uncle James in Paris. That move proving ineffectual,—Paris being scarcely the place to tame young prodigals—Anselm was exiled to Copenhagen and Berlin and put under strangers. But he was incorrigible and Salomon was in despair about what to do next. The great foreign capitals seemed to be demoralizing the young scamp, and to bring him home was out of the question, the tension between father and son being what it was. It therefore occurred to him to get Anselm a berth in the ancestral House at Frankfort. Old Amschel was lonely, having lately lost his wife, and his simple, austere, and very pious example should, if anything could, bring his too spirited nephew to a conviction of sin. Anselm remained in Frankfort for seven years. He was still there on January 27, 1855, when Salomon, on a visit to his daughter Betty, died in Paris, and Anselm came into his inheritance.

But really Salomon might have spared himself many a gray hair and many a sleepless night; for, after all, his successor proved himself worthy of the traditions of the family. He was fifty-two, to be sure, at his accession, and doubtless the long wait for his patrimony and the varied training he had received from his uncles had served to sober him; but he seems to have had the makings of a Rothschild from the start. The very year after his father's death he paralleled Salomon's railroad coup by taking over from the state the "construction" of the *Südbahn,* and made a better thing of it than his father had made of the *Nordbahn.* So successful, indeed, was this venture that presently he became a specialist in this type of financing, and engaged in extensive railroad operations in Italy. His very prodigality was an asset. Known from boyhood as a blood and a spendthrift, he easily gained entry to social circles in which his predecessor had been barely tolerated. While Salomon had been obliged to manœuvre endlessly for a mere honorary citizenship, Anselm the gay and irresponsible lightly stepped into the Imperial House of Lords, an unprecedented distinction for a man whose coreligionists had not the right to marry or to change their address without the special consent of the police.

Yet it is not to be supposed that Anselm had it easy. For all that he was standing, as it were, on his parent's shoulders, getting on in the 1860's and '70's was very markedly a more arduous business than it had been in the '20's and up to the middle of the century. It was not so much that an inherited fortune and a university training tended to paralyze initiative—Anselm was not suffering from those advantages as much as his cousin Lionel—nor was he irked by Victorian scruples. It was that times were not the same. The sheer glamour of the Rothschilds had produced a crop of determined aspirants for a like destiny. Thus, for instance, there arose a veritable plague of joint-stock banks in imitation of Salomon's *Kredit-Anstalt.* In their wake followed an immense wild-cat speculation not unlike that of the early 'twenties. The new financial institutions were incredibly successful, and for a time it looked as if they would attain their avowed goal—to break the Rothschild supremacy. Anselm watched the movement with apprehension. It was small comfort that most of the multifarious industrial enterprises underwritten by his rivals were unsound. Every sane man on the bourse knew that, and his rivals were manifestly in the secret; for they were disposing of their holdings in the classic Rothschild style. At first Anselm played with the idea of gaining control of his competitors. He ordered his brokers to buy for him every loose share of stock they could get their hands on. But no sooner did he have the inside grip on the situation than he changed his mind. What did he want with a brace of new banks? It was so much simpler to destroy them. He struck swiftly and hard. At the height of the boom his agents all at once began unloading. Men on the bourse could hardly believe that it was Rothschild who was bearing the market. They decided they had better find out. When Anselm's representative appeared on the exchange a broker went up and asked him whether he would be interested in half a million florins' worth of bank securities. "Half a million!" exclaimed the Rothschild man loudly. "Why! all the banks put together are not worth half a million." The echoes of that statement reverberated on every bourse in Europe, and the terrible panic of 1873 was its consequence.

It was not the last time that the heirs of Salomon were to play the part of destiny. Henceforth, however, they are fighting a defensive battle. Anselm died the next year, and his youngest son Albert reigned in his stead. Nathan, his first-born, had long ago wandered from the ancestral path, devoting himself to sports, travel and authorship. No more was Ferdinand, his next of age, a true Rothschild. Having married Evelina, a daughter of Lionel, and lost her soon after, he settled in England, where he occupied himself with politics (when Lord Nathan went to the House of Lords, Ferdinand inherited his seat in the House of Commons), with the management of the Evelina Hospital which he had founded in his wife's memory, and with the writing of a book on "Personal Characteristics from French History." Albert was not the absolute monarch his predecessors had been. He went on losing ground in Austria, and he tried with a good deal of spirit to compensate himself by annexing the finances of Hungary. One final flicker of the old Rothschild fire he did manifest in 1881–82. When Bontoux, the moving genius of the *Union Générale,* shifted his line of attack from Paris to Vienna and organized a coalition there around the Austrian *Laenderbank,* Albert, reinforced by his father-in-law Alphonse, made a vigorous assault first on the *Union* itself and then on one of its allies, the *Banque de Lyon et de la Loire,* which was only too successful; for the crash brought on still another European panic, and Albert was obliged to come to the aid of his enemies lest he and the entire financial structure of the Continent be dragged down to ruin with them. For his unselfishness he was rewarded with the honor which his father and his grandfather had coveted in vain—he was invited to court functions.

Thereafter the Vienna House relapsed into the splendid innocuousness which had come over London, and after Albert's death in 1911 even the fortune of his descendants underwent a painful contraction. This and the suicide of one of Albert's sons and the diminished vitality of the present generation as a whole has caused eugenical people to speak of degeneration and to lay the cause of it to inbreeding. Be the biological case what it might, the fact is indisputable that of the three remaining branches of the family the Austrian is the feeblest. Its preponderance vanished decades ago, and—as is credibly reported—its losses during the late war have been so immense as to destroy its significance even in the capital market.

III

For only three of the establishments erected by the sons of Meyer are still standing. Naples and Frankfort barely survived their heads of the first generation.

The last to open, Naples was also the first to close. So long as Karl was alive and Italy remained an agglomeration of petty states and foreign dependencies, affairs went along satisfactorily enough. The glamour of London, Paris and Vienna never came to it. It shone chiefly in reflected glory. Yet Karl lived and died a happier man than any of his brothers. Gentler than they, mediocre, simple-minded, he did not fall a prey to that consuming ambition which gnawed at the vitals of Nathan and James. With his clever and beautiful wife by his side, he was furthermore spared the snubs which made all their success turn to gall. Adelaide was from the start a brilliant success in Naples society. For Italy knew nothing of anti-Semitism.

The progress of the Naples House was, by comparison with that of its fellows in the North, singularly undramatic. Karl ended as he began—a runner-up for his more brilliant and more ambitious brothers. The fierce upheaval which was so soon to rock the Peninsula from end to end and bring about the birth of a united Italy, was reserved for his successor. The dark year 1855 came and removed Karl along with two of his brothers from the scene. Of his sons the eldest and the third had for some time past been associated with their uncle Amschel in the old home office at Frankfort; the succession, therefore, fell to his second-born, Adolph. He was not destined to enjoy it for long. Five years after Karl's death Garibaldi and his Red Shirts entered Naples, the Bourbon dynasty was abolished, and the ancient and inglorious Kingdom of the Two Sicilies soon afterwards became part of a new nation. Young Adolph—gently nurtured, easy-going, timorous—lacked the energy, the self-assurance and the political detachment which had enabled his uncle James to work and feel at home with such a variety of personages as Villèle and Polignac, Louis Philippe and Louis Napoleon. The departure of his father's old friends from power made him feel lonely and uncomfortable. He decided he would go with them. Why should he stay on and expose himself to all the risks and worries attendant upon revolution? He was enormously rich, he bore a great and distinguished name, a welcome awaited him in any one of three or four stable countries, and anyhow he loved books and flowers and art a great deal more than finance. And so, in 1861, the Naples House of Rothschild, after a quiet existence lasting forty years, was liquidated and closed.

IV

Exactly forty years more elapsed before the parent-House at Frankfort, too, disappeared. It has been moribund, however, for a long time, and its final liquidation was scarcely more than an official act. Amschel, like Karl, was (in Gentz's phrase) one of the weaker Rothschilds. Had it not been for his brothers in London, Paris and Vienna, the firm which he conducted would surely not have achieved anything more than a local importance. Even as it was, its affairs were curiously limited. In his capacity as the head of his own concern, Amschel occupied himself for the most part with money-lending to petty German principalities and impoverished nobles. The great and spectacular operations with which the name of his family became synonymous were neither conceived nor executed in Frankfort. Even in Germany itself, ranking states like Prussia addressed themselves directly to London when they needed loans, and when Nathan died the leadership reverted not to the oldest but to the youngest of his brothers.

Yet so long as Amschel lived the rôle of the paternal house, while subordinate, was far from insignificant. A plain, unassuming, mediocre man, quite devoid of the extraordinary gifts of Nathan and James, Amschel none the less had qualities that fitted him to fill a useful place in the family organization. His very simplicity was an asset; he did not chafe at the contradiction of being nominally the head of the House and in practice the agent of his younger and more brilliant brothers. Geographically his position was strategic: Frankfort not only lay on the trade route between Paris and Vienna, it was the leading security market in the Northern sector of the Continent and thus the natural distributing point for Germany West of the Danube and the small countries contiguous to it. Every great operation originating in London, Paris, Vienna, reached the investors in those markets through Amschel's hands; and the Frankfort bourse, as the outlet of the Rothschild world consortium, attained an importance it had never had before.

Thus Frankfort, though the mother of all the other Houses, was greatly overshadowed by its sturdy offspring. It was the dependency, the branch; they the central offices, the main trunks. But, thanks to its location, it was a branch through which the whole system must communicate. Unlike Karl's far-away outpost, Amschel's was a point of convergence. In his own territory, at any rate, his lustre was unrivaled. He was the first-born son and the testamentary heir of old Meyer, the creditor of countless states and nobles, and the potentate of the homeland from which all the powerful Rothschild colonies had issued forth. To the business world in Germany and to the official world as well, he was still the head of the family and the representative of its might and glory. Save for a finance minister here and there in some major capital, few people were aware of the actual distribution of power within the family council; and Amschel enjoyed a prestige fantastically out of proportion to his personal importance. Thus, for instance, the North German Confederation—the parent of the modern German empire—kept its funds on deposit with him; and when it needed a loan to lay the foundations of that imperial navy which was one day destined to be one of the main causes of the Great War, the Federal Council, sitting in Frankfort, almost inevitably turned again to him.

It was this contact of Amschel with the Frankfort Diet which led to his acquaintance with Bismarck, then merely Prussia's delegate to the Confederation. Characteristically, their first meeting was a clash. Amschel proposed that the naval loan be guaranteed by the Federal's bank deposits in his keeping. Prussia, supported by several of the smaller states, protested strenuously. Speaking in the Diet, Bismarck declared it was an insult to ask for guarantees at all, that the Rothschild plan would in effect oblige the Confederation to pay interest on its own money, and that unless a more equitable offer were made Prussia would move for the withdrawal of the funds altogether. Upon this Amschel stepped down; and once their differences were composed, the future Chancellor showed that he could be generous as well as pugnacious. At his instance the king of Prussia conferred upon Amschel the title of Royal Court Banker. Personally, it would seem, the hard, unyielding Junker was much attracted to the aged and somewhat pathetic son of the Ghetto; or perhaps he was sorry for him.

"A man of small stature," he wrote later, "slight, silver-haired, the oldest of his generation; but a poor man in his palace. Childless, a widower, robbed by his subordinates, badly treated by his Frenchified and Anglicized nephews and nieces, who inherit his treasures and return him neither thanks nor affection."

Toward the family generally Bismarck was less sympathetic. "I have known many members of this House," he said. "The most striking thing about them is their chasing after gold. This is due to the fact that they all want to leave to each of their children as much as they have themselves inherited; which is, of course, absurd."

Amschel was the third Rothschild to die in the fateful year 1855; and just as Garibaldi and Cavour had through their work in Italy undermined the Naples branch, so Bismarck's labors for the unification of Germany eventually did for the House in Frankfort. Karl's two sons, Meyer Karl and Wilhelm, inherited their uncle's business and fortune; and though the elder of them was a very able man, he was too deeply interested in the political movement which all through the 'fifties and 'sixties so agitated the country, to devote himself wholly to his private affairs. Elected to the assembly of the North German Confederation, he left the conduct of the firm more and more to his morose and slightly eccentric brother. Then, as the last stage in unification was being accomplished through the war with France, Prussia appointed him a member of her House of Lords and he virtually transferred his residence to Berlin. With the proclamation of the new German empire Frankfort began gradually losing its commercial importance, and the capital of the united nation supplanted it as the center of banking and finance. In the heyday of the firm the situation would have been readily met by following the flag. But Meyer Karl was otherwise occupied, "Baron Willy" was moping over the cruel fate which had sent him six daughters and not a single son, and both were men past middle age.

So the antiquated House dragged out its last days amid the lengthening shadows of a city which, like itself, had outlived its glory. Meyer Karl died in 1887. For fourteen years more his brother kept up appearances, but there was no vitality left in the ancient shell. The Houses in Vienna, Paris, London, no longer sent daily couriers to Frankfort. It was not so much that the stream of affairs had cut a new channel; decline had set in all along the route. Upon "Baron Willy's" death in 1901 the family council resolved to lop off the decayed branch. Fifty years earlier such a step would have shaken the foundations of the city's commerce, and might even have wakened echoes on the bourses of Europe; now it was hardly remarked. The only person to whom the decision came as a sad blow was the Baroness Mathilde, Wilhelm's widow. She appealed to her brother Albert, the head of the Vienna office, pleading in the name of their great-grandfather Meyer and dwelling on the sentimental bonds with the past. But what could he or anyone else do? The Rothschilds of the fourth generation were preoccupied with their yachts, their racing stables, their social obligations, or else with art, philanthropy and politics. Few of them had either the inclination or the training for business, and those who had could hardly be blamed for preferring livelier capitals than Frankfort. Frankfort, where old Amschel had after the passing of his mother Guetele turned the House with the Green Sign into a center of Rothschild charities—Frankfort was a precious family shrine teeming with glorious memories, and the younger folk were willing to come there on occasional pilgrimages. They could not see themselves rooted there again. One might as well ask them to return to Palestine, even though many of them were Zionists. And no more was it possible to allow strangers to govern in the old place; the entire policy and tradition of the family made against that. There was no choice but to put a lock on the door.*

* Of late years a son-in-law of the Baroness Mathilde, Herr Maximilian Goldschmidt, better known as Max Goldschmidt-Rothschild, piously turned the clock back by reviving the Frankfort House as a branch of his Berlin banking firm. Since his death both places have been under the direction of a Madame Frahnburger, his niece.

CHAPTER XIX

RETROSPECT

WE do not know—no one will probably ever know—all the factors that went into the making of the House of Rothschild. This much only may be said with certainty: its founders, or at least three of them, were extraordinary men who happened along at a period in the world's history which was peculiarly susceptible to their endeavors. They themselves had not the remotest inkling of the broader causes of their success, as Nathan's naive gropings on the subject make sufficiently plain. Originally small merchants, then blockade runners and general war speculators, they had gained a fortune and much valuable experience during the years of their apprenticeship. Then, with the close of the Napoleonic era, came their great opportunity and their epic rise. For that struggle had been something more than a series of wars; it had been, in effect, a European Revolution. When it began Europe, and especially the Continent [illegible]st of the Rhine, was still living under a patriarchal [illegible]ne. By 1815, when it was [illegible] as the head of a family runs his household. If he was virtuous, provident and thrifty, he paid his way as he went along, spending no more than he took in, and laying by a little for a rainy day. If, however, he was extravagant or when, despite his best efforts, extraordinary expenses came up, he borrowed quietly—just as any reputable citizen would—from some private capitalist like the Elector of Hesse, and usually paid fancy rates of interest. The idea of extorting loans from their own people occurred only to the most despotic monarchs; and even they resorted to it only under the severest pressure. The consequence of all this was—notably in the German lands—an arrested development of the economic and financial mechanism of the state. The Continental bourses were, by comparison with the London Royal Exchange, quite rudimentary; capital was unconcentrated, mistrustful, and prone to emigrate; credit was unorganized, haphazard and expensive; and the banks were primitive and lacked effective connections abroad. When, therefore, the long and bitter struggle with France came at the turn of the century, the German states were caught almost helpless. Forced into a stupendous modern enterprise, in which their existence was at stake, they must fight, economically speaking, with rusty and antiquated weapons. Inevitably they were beaten; fearfully overburdened, their credit collapsed, and they went into bankruptcy; England at last came to the rescue, but they had not the machinery even to obtain the proffered subsidies safely, cheaply and expeditiously. The money, handled by their own inadequate banks, reached them in dribbles, at incredible cost and only with the greatest risks.

It was at this stage that the Rothschilds first lent an

efficient hand. Fresh from their hard training in Wellington's campaigns on the Peninsula and in France, keen, energetic and supremely self-confident, they had besides, the unique advantage of their numbers and their geographical distribution. With Nathan in London and the rest of them mobilized for service wherever the contingencies demanded, they functioned like a kind of natural syndicate. Without ever having heard the word, they had by pure accident set up the first clearing house. Their long and varied experience in trade, in contraband, in bullion shipping, and their complex interests on both sides of the Channel, had led them to stumble on what may appear to us as the obvious enough idea of remitting funds from one country to another without the actual movement of coin. It was at the time a revolutionary innovation; and coupled with Nathan's influence in London, it enabled them to perform services for the Continental Allies which no one else could perform, and in the process to make contacts for times to come.

But it was in the period next ensuing that their spectacular spurt forward came. The fighting over, Europe must set her house in order. Politically, to be sure, what with Metternich and his cronies in the saddle, the new order was roundly snubbed. The Bourbons were restored, the Revolution was declared a mistake, and East of the Rhine monarchs whom Napoleon had sent packing returned home from exile to rule virtuously or extravagantly, as their temperaments dictated and as if nothing had happened. But the economic hard facts could not be cold-shouldered so cavalierly. Not only must the damage of the quarter-century junket be repaired; the future must be faced; and to do either or both of these things, money, unheard-of quantities of money, were needed. Economically it mattered little whether one faced backward and harped on legitimacy, or forward and acknowledged that the patriarchal régime had been hopelessly superseded by the nation. The days of subsidies were gone; the era of peace-time national armies had arrived. To pay for this expensive establishment necessitated a complete reorientation in ways and means. And all the while there was the heritage of the past to liquidate. The veterans must be paid off and seen to their homes. Hosts of widows and orphans must be provided for. Devastated regions, ruined industries, disrupted trade, must be rehabilitated. And before anything else could be done, it was imperative that the mass of unsecured paper currency be withdrawn from circulation and the vast accumulation of floating debts be funded. The whole complex of problems, that is to say, when closely examined, reduced itself to one basic problem: how to reorganize the national economy in such a way as to uplift the credit of the state and obtain the required wherewithal.

In finding a solution the Rothschilds were aided as all along, by circumstances. For it so happened that England, the world's leading capital market, had emerged from the war with her prestige enormously enhanced. Throughout the preceding quarter of a century, Consols, depressed and fluctuating, had been a favorite security of speculators both native and foreign. With the return of peace they had become stabilized and unprofitable; and the consequence was that the Continental investor turned his attention to fields nearer home, where he was presently joined by his British colleague. Nathan and his brothers were the first to perceive this drift, and they did everything they could to speed it up and to exploit it. Until their time Continental government bonds were virtually unknown on the London exchange. By persuading the borrowers to accept a low flotation figure and pay a temptingly high rate of interest and redeem coupons in sterling, they made Prussian, Austrian, Neapolitan and even Papal issues nearly as popular in England as the British "Stocks" themselves.

Undoubtedly the posture of events played it into their hands. But the same can be said of Napoleon and of every other significant figure in history. Genius, after all, is the capacity to make the most of opportunity. At least, that is true of genius in affairs. Other men of their time—Baring in England, Ouvrard in France, and David Parish in Austria—came before them and enjoyed opportunities that were closed to them. As individuals it may even be doubted whether the Rothschilds were a match for those three. It was as a group that they were unexcelled and unbeatable. Their pooled resources had, as early as the Congress of Aix in 1818, made them, according to Gentz, the wealthiest concern in the world. Working harmoniously together, letting no stranger gain a foothold of responsibility in their oganization, their respective abilities dovetailing like the organs of some super-body, they formed a unique corporation.

Their very limitations served to advance them. They were foreigners in all but one of the lands in which they resided, and in none did they ever acquire so much as a respectable command of the language, let alone a citizen's feeling for the traditions and aspirations of the country. But it was precisely that detachment, that aloofness from temporary and partisan concerns, that very colorlessness, which gave them the international character they needed, enabled them to work with successive governments and even (as in France) with constantly changing régimes, and to put their resources at the disposal of a Continent made up of mutually warring states. And wherever they were and whoever was in power, it was rarely they were at a loss as to who was the man or the group likely to be useful. Considering their lowly origin, their uncouthness, their ignorance, surely the most remarkable of their faculties was their uncanny knowledge of men. From Buderus to Metternich, from the Manchester weavers to Herries, from the police prefect at Dunkirk to Villèle and Louis Philippe, they almost always knew who was who and how to make him their own.

Coarse-grained, unscrupulous, determined to win at all costs, they resorted freely to corruption. Utterly innocent of the processes that work in history, even in so far as they concerned their own amazing success, they were keenly alive to the significance of individuals in the inner councils of government; and appreciating the value of direct and reliable information, they bought men as they bought stocks. But in justice to them it should be borne in mind that they did not invent bribery. They invented nothing and they created nothing, not even corruption. In this as in everything else they were content to work with the instruments which they found ready to their hand. After more than a century of dazzling eminence, the House of Rothschild has, excepting only the Northern Railway of France, left not a single industry, not a single significant or original landmark which identifies their name with the great period in which they flourished.

II

They bequeathed their fortunes and the luster of their names to their heirs. But as might have been expected they could not hand on to them their singular gifts, and still less the exceptional times and the curious combination of accidents by which they had become great. The Rothschild family has, therefore, for many years past, been going the way of all human institutions.

The causes of the decline are as varied and complex as were those of the rise. In Italy and in Germany they have been political; elsewhere they have been economic and social; but all along the line the essential factor has been a change in the mental bent, the outlook and the interests of the succeeding generations. With the disappearance of Naples and Frankfort as capitals the five original Houses were reduced to three; the improvement of the methods of state financing in Europe after the Revolution of 1848 and the introduction of joint-stock banking a little later seriously weakened the power of the rest; but in the long run it is the human element far more than external circumstance that is making for disintegration.

The incentives of the fathers do not spur the descendants. Inherited wealth, education, refinement, a secure social position, are softening influences. They breed scruples, morbid ideas of responsibility, squeamishness about methods, over-sensitiveness toward public opinion. Still more destructive of the will are roots in the soil; and the later Rothschilds let patriotic and party considerations interfere with business interests. Their international outlook becomes clouded, and their very relations to their cousins beyond the frontiers are, in times of stress, troubled with doubts and questionings. All the sturdy directnesses of the founders are turned into hampering "advantages" with the heirs. And that leading principle, the unity and exclusive control of the family, becomes a dynastic superstition infinitely more rigid than it is with royal houses; since monarchs, limited by constitutions, are at least obliged to admit new blood to the state and yield their powers and privileges to ministers and generals.

So the luster of the House of Rothschild is sadly dimmed, and but for the survival of its fortune the latter-day banking corporations would hardly think it worth consulting. But, speaking humanly, can there really be any rational talk of a decline? Suppose Nathan and his brothers had been soldiers or poets or statesmen. Would anyone consider that there had been degeneration because their descendants had taken to painting or exploration? The parallel is exact. There is not the slightest sign that the sturdy Rothschild stock is dying out, or that healthy-minded and even highly talented men are lacking in the family. Only the talents and the tastes are of a different kind from what they used to be. An astonishing quota of Rothschilds in this and the preceding generation are to be found in the ranks of science (insects, snakes), sport, philanthropy, art, book, snuff-box, even flea-collecting, and in other fields of human endeavor. Who is there so wise as to say that such interests do not require as high an order of physical stamina, intelligence and moral character as that necessary for floating international bond-issue?

www.ingramcontent.com/pod-product-compliance
Lightning Source LLC
Chambersburg PA
CBHW071422230926
51846CB00001B/107
9782925611295